# ZACHOR:
## NOT ONLY
## TO REMEMBER

# ZACHOR:
## NOT ONLY
## TO REMEMBER

The Holocaust Memorial and Tolerance Center
of Nassau County . . . Its First Twenty Years

# Marcia W. Posner

**To order additional copies of this book, contact:**
Xlibris LLC
1-888-795-4274
www.Xlibris.com
Orders@Xlibris.com
539455

# Contents

### PART I: *Holocaust Memorial & Education Center: Opening Ceremony*

# DEDICATED TO BORIS CHARTAN

Founder

Chairman Emeritus

# FOUNDER AND CHAIRMEN

BORIS CHARTAN
1992-2002

HOWARD MAIER
2003-2012

## STEVEN MARKOWITZ
Chairman
2013-

# RABBI MYRON FENSTER

**1**937–DURING THE SHOAH
I was 11 years old and we were living in Brooklyn. Like Rip Van Winkle, we slept through the Holocaust.

The perversity of it still haunts me. The enormous monstrosity of what people are capable of still makes me shudder. Apparently, it is possible for some to shut off all compassion and emotion when it comes to other human beings. They are completely unaffected. I still don't get it. (p.42)*

1943–I felt keenly, even though I was still a teenager, the pain and powerlessness of my family and my people. I began to have nightmares about the Shoah, the Holocaust, as it is called. I couldn't understand then, nor do I understand today, how the world and even the Jewish people sat there and allowed their young and old to be burned up alive while Roosevelt was smiling with his pince-nez and cigarette holder and Churchill was chomping on his cigar, taking baths and drinking whiskey. Both were excellent statesmen and eloquent orators. Why not put those talents in the service of my people?–Why didn't one million Jews from New York and all over, go to Washington, sit down in front of the White House, and refuse to move until something was done? Almost a half-million people were arriving at Birkenau-Auschwitz from Hungary; most of them, killed upon arrival. And during that time I was enjoying the sun and the lake, eating substantial meals and having a good social time. (pp.34-35)*

**\* From the rabbi's book: UP FROM THE STRAITS**

# IT TAKES A VILLAGE

## Stanley and Phyllis Sanders and Alan Mindel

IT TAKES A village and two decades to develop the techniques and exhibits that we employ today to teach the Holocaust and its lessons. Thanks to visionary leaders, compelling testifiers, dedicated volunteers and teachers, generous donors who share our vision and an active dedicated Board, we have attained where we are today.

## Second Generation Stanley Sanders explains:

"Why have I devoted over 20 years of my life and donated generous sums of money to the Center? Why is a piece of my soul inside the bricks of this building? Simply put, my mother's family came from Poland. Her oldest sister and entire family were swallowed up in the Warsaw Ghetto and then the Auschwitz death camp. My mother, of blessed memory, was never able to talk about the Holocaust but it was obvious that losing her sister and family broke her heart. I promised her that I would never forget the 6 million Jews who died in the Holocaust and that their memories would never die. That is why I have worked so hard to make the Center successful. Part of my family's story is in our Holocaust Center exhibits.

## Alan Mindel:

My parents, Sam Mindel and Mary Mandelbaum tolerated the antisemitic hate they faced in their native Poland. Although they survived the efforts of the Nazis to eliminate the Jewish people, they never forgot their

family members who were lost. That is why I do all that I can to support the Center and its activities, hosting guest speakers and Center events in the family's hotels.

# FOREWORD

## by Marcia W. Posner

Z ACHOR: NOT ONLY TO REMEMBER describes the inspiration and striving of people who dreamed of and brought to reality the Holocaust Memorial and Tolerance Center. It is also a compendium of the Holocaust experiences of our survivors and liberators and the lessons learned from their tragic experience, that no one can afford to be a "bystander." There are as many ways to tell a story as there are people who want to be part of the telling. The author of our first two chapters is Irving Roth. He describes what the Council and more specifically, what Boris Chartan, Thomas Gulotta, Simon Zareh, Ike Blachor, and he contributed to the founding and directing of the Center in its first years. I recall how I fulfilled Irving's Roth's request for a library. Jolanta Zamecka relives how she perfected Irving Roth's dream of a garden dedicated to the souls of martyred children. Many other people have contributed to the growth of the Center and to this book. Most of their names are indicated at the end of the book and in the ensuing narratives.

I remember one afternoon in the beginning, after I had been working with Irv, his wife Addie, Donna Rosenblum, Vincent Marmorale and others for about 6 months to set up the exhibits, library and programs, when I was suddenly overcome by a feeling of joy, quickly followed by guilt. "Irv," I asked. "Is it wrong to feel happiness while working on such a tragic task?" "No," he replied. "We suffered enough years when we were powerless. Now we can rejoice in the achievement of what we promised to each other that we would do if and when we survived." Further progress of our Center is owed to Boris, Neil, Eileen and especially to Howard Maier and his powerful board, who, by the end of the Center's second decade, had brought us to our current level.

# PREFACE

## by Steven Markowitz, Chairman

I AM GRATEFUL AND proud to be the current president of the Holocaust Memorial and Tolerance Center of Nassau County. Unlike others in this volume who arrived earlier on the scene and who still play important roles in the Center's development and growth, I am not a survivor of the Holocaust nor a child of survivors. Among my earliest memories however, are the neighbors in Crown Heights, Brooklyn who had funny accents and numbers tattooed on their arms. It was only as I got older that I began to understand the horror they and their families had been through.

Learning about the Holocaust became a passion. I am a voracious reader and student of the Holocaust, visiting concentration camps, museums and memorials all over the country and world. Regardless of whether one has family relationships to victims or survivors of the Holocaust, every Jew is a descendent of the worst genocide in history. Every Jew has a responsibility, just as we are required to remember and teach the story of the Exodus, to commemorate the victims of the Holocaust, to honor its survivors and to do whatever we can to ensure that similar events never happen again. Truthfully, the responsibility to remember and teach about the Holocaust should fall upon every human being regardless of background or religion. Although Jews were the Nazis' primary targets, this was a crime against humanity . . . and all of humanity must learn and remember.

My first involvement in Holocaust related activities came in the early 1990s when I organized and chaired the *Shoah* (Holocaust) Committee at Temple Israel of Great Neck for five years. We developed widely emulated *Kristallnacht* and *Yom HaShoah* programs and published annual *Zachor* (Remembrance) books in which congregants could memorialize family members lost in the Holocaust. We also identified and honored survivors in the community, many for the first time.

The Holocaust Memorial and Tolerance Center is dedicated to teaching about the Holocaust, memorializing its victims and honoring its survivors. The Center's initial mantra: "From Prejudice to Genocide" directs us to defeat acts and expressions of prejudice and intimidation through teaching about the Holocaust. This is so essential now that the United States is experiencing a rapid change in its racial and ethnic population. Diversity brings with it tensions, misunderstandings and intolerance. Who better to understand and deal with these than we? Our new Claire Friedlander Education Institute affords us an added facility in which to teach the acceptance of differences and denial of all forms of intimidation.

The Center began in 1993. Since then, many thousands of students, educators, employers and law enforcement personnel have participated in the Holocaust Memorial and Tolerance Center's education programs. Every time I walk through the front door of the Center and see the many volunteers and visitors, sit in a class at which one of our survivors is giving testimony, view a video-conference viewed by a group of young people in some remote part of the country or world, and spend time with our talented and dedicated staff, I realize just how privileged I am to be associated with the Center.

# PROLOGUE

## by Boris Chartan

WHEN I WAS a young boy I lived in Poland with my family. We were terrorized to see Nazis marching into our town. We tried mightily to avoid being found by them and to protect one another. Like countless others, my family made a pledge not to give in, to resist as best we could by planning and daring. Despite our efforts, many were caught and many were killed. My father and I were sent to a labor camp. Eventually we managed to escape and to join some partisans in the forest. During those fearful days of hiding in bunkers and forests, we never lost faith. Later, as we wove our way through the forest to join some family members who were being hidden by Polish friends, we promised each other that should we survive, we would teach the world what had been done to the Jews of Europe during that time we know now as the Holocaust.

Eventually, my family emigrated to the United States. I married, started a family and built a business, but I never forgot my vow to bring the story of the Holocaust to light, to speak and educate as many people as I could about the terrible tragedy that had befallen the Jewish people. I talked in synagogues, temples and schools whenever I could. Once a year we survivors stood on the courthouse steps to recite the names and camps in which they perished, but just to remember was not enough. I wanted to teach a new generation about what happened in the Holocaust, and after them another and another ad infinitum. I had to make sure that the world would never forget. There were others who felt as I did, both survivors and non-survivors. After I was appointed to serve as the Commissioner of Services for Nassau County, I went to the County Executive, Thomas Gulotta, and suggested that we form a Commission which would explore the feasibility of establishing a Holocaust educational center for Nassau County to commemorate the millions of innocent victims, Jews and Gentiles alike, and to help fight ignorance, racism and antisemitism. Those of us who survived had an obligation to teach future generations that there is no place in this world for prejudice. We have to respect another's right to live in peace and security.

*Boris Chartan and Thomas Gulotta*

In 1988 a Commission was formed with Roman Catholic Bishop John McGann and Rabbi Myron Fenster as co-chairmen. There were 35 members of the commission, including Jack Stein and myself. Once the Center was officially opened in 1994, essentially 4 people ran it: Irving Roth, Eileen Tannor, Neil Tannor and myself. In this book you will read how we grew as an organization and a cause. It recaptures the long journey that finally led to the establishment in 1994, of the Holocaust Memorial and

Education Center of Nassau County where I served as President for a decade. We have been fortunate in the people who joined us in our mission: Eileen and Neil Tannor, Irving Roth, Regina White, Marcia and Lou Posner, Gloria Jackel, and Jolanta Zamecka were among the many who joined us at the beginning and enthusiastically did whatever needed to be done.

As you read through this double decade journey, you will witness the name change, many of the Center's events and plans, and the sense of ownership we all had and have invested in it. I am grateful for the inspired leadership of those who, following me, have assumed responsibility for our Center and fulfilled its promise.

Boris Chartan, Founder
Chairman Emeritus

*Eileen and Neil Tannor*
*2013*

# PART I

## HOLOCAUST MEMORIAL & EDUCATION CENTER: OPENING CEREMONY

*County Executive Thomas Gulotta, Isaac Blachor, Irving Roth,*
*Bruce and Roselee Morrell, Eileen Tannor, Simon Zareh and*
*Boris Chartan*

Irving Roth, who writes our first two chapters, is a founding member of the committee that worked with Boris Chartan to establish this Center. Irving became our first Director in charge of Education and formulated many of the educational practices upon which we have built over the years.

Irving was born on Sept. 2, 1929, in *Kosice*, Czechoslovakia. His family enjoyed a harmonious existence there until one day when he was told that he couldn't play soccer with his friends. "There was a time when the world stood by and did nothing," Roth said, describing the years when millions of people throughout Europe were murdered because of their religious beliefs. "I remember that world." Irving survived Auschwitz, the largest Nazi  death camp, as well as a death march to the Buchenwald concentration camp, but his brother, Bondi, did not. Irving's autobiography, *Bondi's Brother*, describes their ordeal.

*Irving Roth is the Director of the Holocaust Resource Center at Temple Judea of Manhasset, N.Y.*

# CHAPTER 1

## THE BIRTH OF THE CENTER

**By Irving Roth**

THE CREATION AND development of the Holocaust Memorial and Educational Center of Nassau County did not take place in a vacuum. To fully understand its history we must consider the state of Holocaust conversation and education since the end of WWII.

The horror of the Holocaust, while portrayed in newsreels immediately at the end of the war, existed primarily in the recesses of the minds of those who lived it and the soldiers who were witness to appalling scenes in the concentration and death camps. The trauma was too severe, the images too distinct for the survivors and GI's to communicate it to others. How could anyone who did not witness it fathom a government such as the Nazi regime, organized to murder millions of children and civilians? For a long time, survivors spoke of these horrors mainly among themselves. It was not until the 1960s, upon the capture and subsequent trial of Adolf Eichmann in Jerusalem that the Holocaust was brought into focus to the American public. This was followed by the Hollywood miniseries "Holocaust" on TV. It spurred the media and schools to look at the Holocaust as a historical event. School history textbooks began to include a few pages on the Holocaust, going from a footnote to actual text. By the late 1970s, survivors began to speak about their experiences and to feel secure enough to tell their children's generation about their experiences. The idea of building monuments, museums and educational institutions specifically devoted to the Holocaust was on the rise. On Long Island, Holocaust survivors built and dedicated memorials with the help of community groups. A monument was erected and dedicated in Long Beach. The Shelter Rock Jewish Center (SRJC) created a Holocaust Garden and Learning Center in the spring of 1981.

In Nassau County an informal group of survivors and like-minded others met with a desire to bring a Holocaust Education Center to Long Island. Fortuitously, Boris Chartan, a survivor and participant, was the Commissioner of Services for Nassau County. He began to explore the possibility of forming a county-sponsored Holocaust Commission and getting county land or a building where a Center could be located. Even before the Nassau County Holocaust Commission was officially formed, the group of survivors decided to sponsor a bi-county *Yom Hashoah* (the Hebrew name for the Holocaust) event. The venue that became available was the gymnasium of Nassau Community College. Posters for the event were created and distributed by Boris Chartan and Irving Roth. They contacted Jewish and secular schools, synagogues, political figures and the Long Island Board of Rabbis. The program participants included County officials, singer Theodor Bikel, the *Parparim* Dance ensemble, and a violin quartet. Rabbi Herschel Schacter delivered the keynote address. Over 2,000 people were in attendance. Soon after the *Yom Hashoah* program, the Nassau County Holocaust Commission was formed.

In 1945, during World War II, Rabbi Schacter was a chaplain in the Third Army's VIII Corps and the first US Army Chaplain to enter and participate in the liberation of the *Buchenwald* concentration camp. He had cried out in Yiddish to the Jews of *Buchenwald*: "You Are Free!" As the rabbi passed a mound of corpses, he spied a flicker of movement. Drawing closer, he saw a small boy, Prisoner 17030, hiding in terror behind the mound. Unfamiliar with the uniform, the child thought that the rabbi's uniform belonged to a new kind of enemy. With tears streaming down his face, Rabbi Schacter picked up the child and speaking to him in Yiddish, asked what was his name. "Lulek" was the answer.

In his autobiography *Out of the Depths: The Story of a Child of Buchenwald Who Returned Home At Last,* Rabbi Israel Meir Lau tells his version of Rabbi Schacter's role in liberating him at Buchenwald:

"I remember the looks of horror on the faces of the American soldiers when they came in and stared around them. I was afraid when I saw them. I crept behind a pile of dead bodies and hid there, watching them warily . . . Rabbi Herschel Schacter was the Jewish chaplain of the division. I saw him get out of a jeep and stand there, staring at the corpses. He thought he saw a pair of living eyes looking out from among the dead. It made his hair stand on end, but slowly and cautiously he made his way around the pile, and then, he came face-to-face with me, an eight-year-old boy, wide-eyed with terror.

I remember how in heavily accented American Yiddish and with tears in his eyes, Rabbi Schacter asked me,

'How old are you, *mein kind?*

'What difference does it make?'

I answered. 'I'm older than you, anyway.'

He smiled through his tears and said,

'Why do you think you're older than me?'

And I answered,

'Because you cry and laugh like a child. I haven't laughed in a long time, and I don't even cry anymore. So which one of us is older?'

Rabbi Lau is the former Ashkenazi Chief Rabbi of Israel and current Chief Rabbi of Tel Aviv, who was called "Lulek" as a child.

~ ~ ~ ~ ~ ~ ~ ~ ~ ~

After 5 years of hard work the Commission organized a non-profit entity to be called "The Holocaust Memorial and Educational Center of Nassau County" and began to discuss what they hoped the Holocaust Center would accomplish. The Commission's two challenges in this period were: (1) to look for a site for the future Nassau County Holocaust Center and (2) to define its mission. One Commission member observed, "Let's just have a memorial museum. It's better than standing on the courthouse steps reciting names of the victims. With a museum, we can show visitors what it was like." But they soon realized that while it would serve their emotional needs, it would not help to educate future generations. The Commission believed that all people must learn to respect each other's right to live in freedom and security. The Center would not only be for Jews, it would be for everyone, every religion, every color. Upon serious deliberation, the mission statement of the Holocaust Memorial and Educational Center of Nassau County was created and accepted by the newly elected board.

# THE HOLOCAUST MEMORIAL AND EDUCATIONAL CENTER OF NASSAU COUNTY, DEFINITION of TERMS

## Genocide:

"Genocide," a word coined by jurist Ralph Lemkin in 1944, is defined as "The systematic killing of a whole national, religious or ethnic group." While acts of genocide have taken place throughout history, the effort of

Nazi Germany against subject people represents the most unspeakable example of barbarism in the human experience.

## Holocaust:

At the Wannsee Conference in 1942, the German Nazi government formulated plans to implement Adolf Hitler's desire to eradicate the Jewish people. Stemming from an antisemitism that had became all too deeply rooted in Europe, the National Socialist policy vowed to kill every Jew (defined as anyone with at least three Jewish grandparents) and to destroy Jewish learning and culture, this to insure that no rebirth of Jewry would ever be possible. Every Jew, regardless of Jewish belief (including conversion to Christianity), political affiliation, economic status, profession or previous service to the nation, was slated for slaughter. Out of the estimated 8.3 million Jews living in German occupied Europe after 1939, approximately 6 million were killed, of which 1.5 million were children. The intent was the extinction of an entire people, an entire religion. Every Jew, no matter how tiny a child, was marked for slaughter. Thus the Holocaust was a Jewish event in particular. While not all victims were Jews all Jews were victims.

As if excited by their blood thirst for the Jews, the Nazis began to look at other subject peoples and cultures for extermination. *Roma* (Gypsies) and the mentally retarded were marked for slaughter. *Jehovah's Witnesses* were rounded up and sent to concentration camps. The Slavic people, considered subhuman, were to be enslaved and their culture destroyed. Early in 1940, for example, the clergy and the intelligentsia of Poland were targeted as the beginning of an attempt to wipe out Polish nationhood. In all, 11 million people were victims of the tidal wave of hatred that began with the Jews.

~ ~ ~ ~ ~ ~ ~ ~ ~

## How the Holocaust Was To Be Accomplished:

The final solution was achieved in steps. First, Jews were separated from the rest of the population and identified by a yellow star. Next, their economic existence was destroyed as businesses and property were taken away and their ability to practice their professions and crafts limited. Eventually, Jews were assigned to live in designated areas (ghettos). Finally, they were sent to death camps where crude and newly engineered techniques were utilized to murder and dispose of the bodies. Prejudice had turned into genocide. Building on the longstanding European antisemitism, the Nazis were able to enlist the support of tens of thousands of people from the lands they conquered. This is one of the great tragedies of the Holocaust; some of the subject people who were also victims of the Nazi racial hatred, became abettors of the genocide of the Jews. The oppressed had become the oppressors.

## There Was Scant Chance of Escape from Europe:

During the period when it was still possible to leave Europe, the gates of the democracies were closed to Jewish refugees. America had a quota system to insure very limited influx of immigrants. Breckinridge Long, an assistant secretary in charge of the Visa Division, was extremely paranoid and prejudiced. He believed that he was constantly under attack from "the communists, radicals, Jewish professional agitators and refugee enthusiasts," and managed to reverse a 1938 Roosevelt initiative that eased extremely restrictive immigration requirements. He cut immigration numbers again and again so that no Jews could enter the United States. As a result of his policies, 90% of the quota places available to immigrants from countries under German and Italian control were never filled. Long also obstructed rescue efforts in the House of Representatives and pushed for FDR to dismiss Secretary of Labor Frances Perkins (1933-1945), who was trying to achieve reform of immigration quota policies. After President Roosevelt established the War Refugee Board that relieved the State Department of responsibility for rescue efforts, as many as 200,000 lives were saved.

Palestine was also unavailable to Jewish refugees, closed by Britain so as not to anger the Arabs. Canada, with its large area and small population, was not a willing host, and even a place as far away as Australia was not willing to accept large numbers of Jews. As late as 1942, when the atrocities were documented, conferences that were scheduled to discuss the matter publicly were deliberately sabotaged to ensure that no major influx of Jewish refugees would take place. Sadly, the extermination of Jews was not deemed a high priority by the world's democracies. Even during the last months of the war when allied bombers were within easy reach of the death factories, military action was not directed at facilities to slow down the progress of annihilation in Auschwitz and other extermination camps.

## Did Anyone Care?

There were individuals and some groups who saw the evil. In a variety of ways they helped Jews and others escape and hide under the noses of the Nazis. These righteous people risked their lives and on occasion paid with their own lives in order to protect the persecuted from certain death. Clergy who preached openly against the killings were themselves executed. Pope Pius XI's campaign to stop Hitler, might have attributed to this Jesuit pope's demise *(The Pope's Last Crusade by Peter Eisner)*.

Those who hid Jews or aided in their escape often gave their lives. These rescuers came from all walks of life, from the richest to the poorest, from the most educated to those who could hardly read. These righteous people are heroes of the Holocaust. They must be honored and their work memorialized for the future. Regrettably, the number of the "righteous" is small in comparison to the population of Europe. Nonetheless, their heroic example still challenges us today.

~ ~ ~ ~ ~ ~ ~ ~ ~ ~ ~ ~ ~

## The Original Mission Statement Is Reproduced Below.

## MISSION STATEMENT

The Holocaust Memorial and Education Center of Nassau County was established by an Interfaith Commission. It was called together by County Executive Thomas Gulotta, and chaired by Bishop John R. McGann and Rabbi Myron M. Fenster.

The aim of the Center is to educate young and old on the horrors of antisemitism and hatred and to show clearly that prejudice against any human being because of race, color, religion, national origin, sex or physical attributes can bring about the destruction of anyone within society.

The Center will develop a curriculum for Holocaust Studies to be utilized by public, private and religious schools as a supplement to their social studies programs. It administered teacher-training programs including, but not limited to, educating junior and senior high school students in prejudice reduction through training at the Center; and utilizing scholarships for schooling at Yad Vashem in Israel.

In addition to its formal curriculum and training for teachers and students, the Center will be a complete educational facility for the public providing a library, media center, speaker's bureau and world wide data access through computer interface with other like facilities. In an age when ethnic and racial animosity are still rampant, the Center seeks to teach the tragic lessons of Nazi Germany's attempt to wipe out every

Jew in Europe and to destroy millions of others because of their race, nationality, religious or sexual identity, or physical disabilities. Its board and staff are committed to the building of a society for this generation and succeeding ones where all people can live in harmony and without fear of extinction.

## A Building for the Center:

In 1989 County Executive Thomas Gulotta announced plans for a permanent Holocaust Memorial and Educational Center to be located at Eisenhower Park in East Meadow. Those plans called for a 20,000 square foot one-story structure with a courtyard and reflecting pools on a four-acre parcel just south of Stewart Avenue. The plan was rejected when veterans of World War II, for whom the park was originally named "Veterans Memorial Park," heard about the proposal and wanted their own memorial. A second location was proposed at Nassau Community College but the board of the college rejected that saying the campus had limited unused land that should be kept open for college purposes.

In early 1992 the Harold and Harriet Pratt mansion that had been used by the Nassau County Sheriff's Department, was about to become available. It was by then in terrible disrepair. Besides the ravages of time and nature, it had been a training site for police cadets for ten years, closed to the public. Now, Commissioner Gulotta was offering the mansion to the Holocaust Memorial and Education Center. It wasn't until February 1993, however, that the New York Times reported that the 96 year-old Pratt mansion built in the Georgian style, once the scene of lavish parties and banquets attended by the Prince of Wales, Chiang Kai-shek, Henry Luce, the Morgans and the Astors, was to become a Holocaust educational site. That September 1993, the Nassau Board of Supervisors voted a resolution authorizing the County to issue a "use and occupation" permit to the Holocaust Commission. The Commission first had to obtain approval from the County Legislature to obtain a 99-year lease on the property in order for it to begin renovations. The money for the operation of the Center would come solely from donations to the Holocaust Memorial and Educational Center of Nassau County.

In June, 1993, County Executive, Thomas S. Gulotta, sent out a remarkable letter to the citizens of Nassau County. It included this paragraph:

> *"The Holocaust's uniquely Jewish roots, supplemented by other materials, teach us that any form of discrimination is in fact each individual's "Holocaust." Bigotry and intolerance can mean the death of us all. Ignoring what is done to some, will eventually hurt us all."*

~ ~ ~ ~ ~ ~ ~ ~ ~ ~ ~ ~ ~ ~

At the founding dinner on December 1993, Boris M. Chartan, President, paid a tribute to those who helped make the new Holocaust Memorial and Educational Center a reality. He listed in order: The Honorable Thomas S. Gulotta, Nassau County Executive; Most Reverend John R. McGann, Bishop, Diocese of Rockville Center; Rabbi Myron Fenster of the Shelter Rock Jewish Center; Sam Mandelker, Former Executive Vice President and Partner Kimco Development Corporation; Jerry Lazarus, Lazarus, Burman Associates; Naomi and Jerry Lippman, Publisher and Editor of the *L.I. Jewish World.*

*MSG. Donald Beckman*

# CHAPTER 2

## FIRST STEPS: SETTING THE PATTERN
by Irving Roth

THE DEED WAS accomplished. The old Pratt mansion became the home of the Holocaust Memorial and Education Center of Nassau County. The decrepit old building had to be gotten into usable shape, educational concepts formulated, exhibit material obtained and displayed, speakers organized and visitors invited.

Before any attempt at renovation began, which required financial support, the board decided to hold its next meeting at the "new" Center. Fortunately, one of the 16 bathrooms was actually operational. Boris Chartan, president, and two members of the board, Simon Zareh and Irving Roth, spent many hours clearing the debris from the first floor of the building, swept the floors and obtained chairs. Finally, the board met in the Center's new home. At that meeting concrete plans and schedules were presented. Everything from initial renovations, education plans, exhibits and inviting visitors to the opening was discussed. To begin with, some money had to be raised for even minor renovations. Boris Chartan undertook the task of raising funds and supervising the building repairs. The most pressing building issues, making the first floor ready for exhibits and renovating the second floor for offices were undertaken first. Under the guidance of Boris and Simon Zareh, an early benefactor, the task was accomplished and the building made ready for occupancy. Irving Roth volunteered to be the Educational Director and to run the Center.

From the outset, it was established that the Holocaust educational program must be placed in a historical context, consist of survivor testimony, have exhibits depicting various aspects of the Holocaust and video presentations geared to the age group of the visitors. The exhibits had to demonstrate that the destruction of European Jews was a step-by-step process that began with the formation of the Nazi Party in the early 1920s. Its intentions with respect to the Jews were clear from its very platform: the disenfranchisement of the Jewish population and eventually making Germany *Judenrein*, (free of all Jews) by whatever means were necessary.

The Center featured many well-documented exhibits of this step-by-step process. Using historical material from *Yad Vashem* in Jerusalem and the *Ghetto Fighters Museum* in Naharia, Israel, an 8 poster display was created that used text and graphics to show the legal steps taken by the Nazis to rid Germany and the world of its Jews. It began with separating the Jews from German society and ended with the utilization of gas chambers and crematoria to rid Germany and eventually all of Europe of its Jewish population. An exhibit that showed the transformation of Jews from citizens to ashes, formed the introduction that visitors saw upon entering the Center.

As our Center became known on Long Island, we received photographs from a number of American liberators. The first of these was a photographic record of the liberation of *Ohrdruf* Concentration Camp as seen by a US army sergeant on the day of liberation and ended with the inspection of the camp by Generals Eisenhower, Bradley and Patton.

The second exhibit was based on photographs and text from letters of a GI (James Van Realte) as he described what he and his company saw and felt as they entered Buchenwald. The third exhibit was obtained directly from Lt. Colonel William Denson, chief prosecutor in the war crimes trials of Hitler's operatives, the men and women who ran concentration camps: *Dachau, Mauthausen, Flossenburg* and *Buchenwald* in what became the American zone of liberation.

## Survivor Testifiers

The gathering of survivors to give presentations was a rather easy task. After a long period of keeping silent, many were ready to tell their story. To ensure that they would present their experiences in ways the students could comprehend yet not become traumatized, we met in seminars and discussed the content and technique to be used until it was agreed upon by the survivors. It was also essential that the survivors tell their story with accuracy, but without inadvertently speaking about events not corroborated by historical evidence. This factor was critical due to the increasing numbers of groups formed by Holocaust revisionists and deniers.

With the Center ready and survivors and historians anxious to begin speaking, we needed visitors. The community had to be made more aware of the new facility and a library had to be established. So many decisions had to be made and then the reversals of the decisions . . . now the alternatives and the compromises. Eventually, classes were given; volunteers who streamed in were successfully educated and managed; survivors found and their stories streamlined and later recorded. Since our finances did not allow placing ads in daily newspapers, we decided to invite principals and superintendents of Long Island public and secular schools to the Center. This showcased our facility and also our educational programs that would enrich the Holocaust education some schools had begun to teach. With the help of principals and teachers, in the first 6 months of operation we exceeded 2,000 students. Four years later in 1998, over 12,000 students visited our Center with their teachers.

During these visits we observed that many of the teachers had very limited knowledge of the Holocaust and did not possess a methodology

to present this material to their students. To alleviate this condition we embarked on organizing a teacher's seminar, including a session on teaching techniques.

Donna Rosenblum, a history teacher from the Glen Cove School district who had been a participant in the "Teacher Training Program at Yad Vashem brought us their well-tested concepts in teaching the Holocaust. The seminar, taught by Donna, included the history of anti-Semitism from antiquity through the Holocaust and how it applies to the racism of today.

An outline on how to best present the material in a classroom setting was given by Vincent Marmorale, a teacher from the Sachem School District who had developed a curriculum on the Holocaust for their district and who had won the New York State Louis

E. Yavner Citizen Award given to a citizen who has made an outstanding contribution for teaching the Holocaust. The seminar also included instructional strategies and classroom techniques on the teaching of the Holocaust so that teachers could exit from their workshops and walk into any classroom prepared to teach its history and ramifications. Each teacher received a bound document that contained material to aid the teacher with the historical events, a time line and survivor testimony to help in presenting the material to students. Many of our future educators and docents came from this group of people. Multiple copies of books were selected and purchased to prepare teachers to teach about the Holocaust.

Shortly after, Vince met survivor Walter Wolff who confided in him how he, his brother and his mother fled Nazi Germany into the welcoming arms of Italian villagers. Vince and Walter became a pair who spoke in numerous venues and were slated to go to Rome to visit the Pope, except that Walter became too ill to join them.

*Walter Wolff*

Programs were created for docents to provide the history of the catastrophe followed by survivor testimony. The survivors all had their own stories to tell. That is the pattern still followed today.

By March 1995 the first seminar, "Teaching the Holocaust" was attended by principals and social studies chairpersons from 36 local school districts.

Our school visitors were primarily history and language arts teachers who brought their students to the Center. In our desire to broaden the disciplines represented, we invited art teachers from all over L.I. Island. What started as a meeting with high school art teachers blossomed into our yearly art and essay competitions. Students, individually and in groups, created artwork that was exhibited in our Center and on exhibits at other venues, such as conferences and institutions. The most difficult part was choosing the winners and finding wall and floor space to ensure that the artwork was displayed properly.

# Judging the Art Competition

*Gloria Jackel, Marcia Posner, Boris Chartan, Eileen Tannor*
*Regina White, Janice Pullin, Richard Weilheimer*

We eventually purchased artists display screens that could be configured in various ways. In addition to the pride that these art students took in their creations, it remained as part of their portfolio as well part of their educational experience that remained with them into their college and adult life.

The Essay Contest was most exciting. Hundreds of students participated. We awarded prizes for the best essays and we published them in our newly started bulletin. Students, teachers, parents and administrators attended the award ceremony. The Essay and Art Contests had the additional benefit of introducing many adults to the Holocaust Memorial and Educational Center of Nassau County through the participating students.

*Donna Rosenblum and Irving Roth*

The Holocaust Memorial and Educational Center partnered with two prestigious educational organizations, "Facing History and Ourselves" and "The World of Difference." Both of these organizations are involved in teacher training. This partnership brought educational topics on racism and prejudice to the Center and the Center provided survivor testimony to their seminars as well insight into the political structure of Europe that made the Holocaust possible.

By the third year of our operation, our reputation had gained some prominence in the local school system. We were approached by the North Shore H.S. of Glen Cove Senior Class Advisor to provide a "Senior Project" for a number of graduating students. The students were brought to the Center once a week where they would spend a few hours in discussion with Irving Roth on wide ranging topics. They were also utilizing the newly established library. The Senior Project (SP) students suggested that it would be instructive if the whole graduating class would tour the Center. During the visit of the seniors to the Center the SP students acted as guides during their visit. It was a particularly poignant moment when one of the participating students, who was an exchange student from Germany, gave a talk on the step-by-step process of the Holocaust from *Kristallnacht* to the gassing in Auschwitz.

In the spring of 1996, "The Million Pennies Project" was conceived by Irving Roth. The monies were to be used to create a Holocaust Children's Garden. The Project was an alliance between the Holocaust Memorial and Educational Center of Nassau County and school children from Nassau, Suffolk, Queens and Brooklyn. Matching one million pennies to the 1½ million young Jewish victims of the Holocaust, by the year 2000 the Center had collected over $10,000 in pennies.

At a Tribute Dinner of the Holocaust Memorial and Education Center of Nassau County, Director Irving Roth, summarized the feeling that was within each member:

"Reflecting on the last two years at the Holocaust Memorial and Educational Center helped me to validate my feelings, corroborate and document my knowledge of Shoah history, challenge revisionism and witness the birth of a new educational model on Long Island. I am extremely fortunate to have found kindred spirits: Joan Mandel and Bonnie Garelick who continue to inspire students with essay and art contests, Dr. Marcia Posner and Gloria Jackel who took a pile of books and transformed them into a 3,000 volume computerized library after only two years; Jay Feldman, who coordinates our survivor speakers of the "Speakers Bureau" and creates order out of havoc, and our wonderful educators: Tina Tito, Donna Rosenblum, Marcia Posner, Vincent Marmorale and myself.

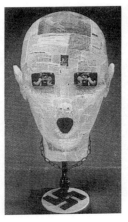

*Skinhead*

Our team of educators and Holocaust historians accomplishes the workshops, seminars and in-service courses that we present to teachers and docents. We could not have made such strides without the cooperation of Msgr. Donald Beckman who has been my partner and active participant in the development of the Center since its inception. Boris Chartan, our President and his administrator, Eileen Tannor, foster an environment that allows for free expression of the creative talent."

~ ~ ~ ~ ~ ~ ~ ~ ~

Many New York area Holocaust artists contacted the Center.

Harold Lewis, who was what is now called an "outsider artist," donated his marvelous sculptures and assemblages to the Holocaust Center. We displayed them for many years until time and temperature took their toll.

Other notable artworks by students include, beginning at the left, a life-size model made of papier maiché that depicts child prisoners of an age approximate to their creators. At the upper right is an iconic work commenting on the past Vietnam war—the difference between war and peace. Below it, there is a photograph of a bench supported by two giraffes on either end. This is in honor of the Resistance, "Those who stuck their necks out."

One of the most brilliant exhibits was the chess game played for the lives of prisoners, by the forces of good, the Red Cross and the forces of evil, the Nazis. The game was played on an ordinary gray enamel painted table with two matching chairs.

~ ~ ~ ~ ~ ~ ~ ~ ~ ~ ~ ~ ~ ~ ~

Barbara Green, a master artist whose pastels looked like oils, staged several art exhibits at the Center. The most exciting was the exhibit: The Holocaust: Through the Eyes of Artists. (See p. 45)

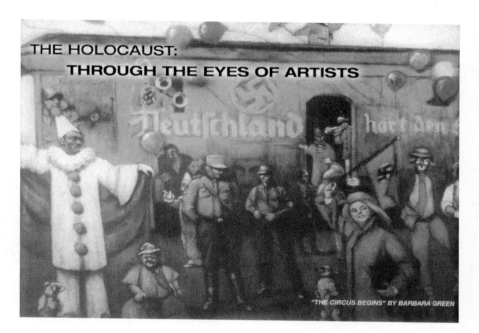

THE HOLOCAUST: THROUGH THE EYES OF ARTISTS

*"THE CIRCUS BEGINS" BY BARBARA GREEN*

*These artistic depictions of the Holocaust augmented the Center's graphical and textual exhibits.*

~ ~ ~ ~ ~ ~ ~ ~ ~ ~ ~ ~

Joshua M. Greene, a filmmaker and author, used the Center as home base for a while. His wife's cousin, Isadore Mayrock, was a Center board member and Josh was doing research connected with his 2000 award-wining PBS Television broadcast "Witness: Voices from the Holocaust," based on interviews garnered from his wife's family's Fortunoff Video Archive for Holocaust Testimonies at Yale University; we were very proud to have him in residence. The program was viewed widely and had earned a number of awards. But something else occurred while Josh was at the Center that excited him even more. It was when the Holocaust Memorial and Educational Center became involved in helping him to memorialize Col. William Denson.

Josh recalls that right after the PBS broadcast, the phone rang in his office and a voice sounding eerily like an aged Katherine Hepburn said:

"Are you the fellow who made that documentary?"

'Yes.'

'Well, I'd like to meet you."

*Col. Denson and Mrs. Denson*

As Josh describes it: "A few days later, I showed up in Lawrence at the home of Huschie Denson, widow of Col. William D. Denson who had passed away a couple of years before. Huschie took me down to her basement. There were filing cabinets overflowing with trial transcripts, boxes of microfilm, stacks of photographs and other evidence from the trials. For years before his death, Bill Denson had been compiling material in hope of getting the story of the Dachau trials published. After looking into it, I realized this was an amazing story, one that had never been told. Everyone knew about Nuremberg. The Dachau trials were ten-times bigger: the biggest, yet least-known series of war crimes trials in history.

I needed a space in which to study all the files and plan the script. When Boris Chartan, Regina White and Marcia Posner learned of the Denson project, they offered my crew and I a room in which to conduct our research. What emerged from those many months was a book titled *Justice at Dachau: The Trials of an American Prosecutor*, published by a division of Random House. The book has gone into multiple printings and several foreign-language editions and it is one of the few books to remain in hardcover print after more than 11 years. A short-form documentary adaptation is available from Discovery Education. Lectures about the

Dachau trials and the precedents they established for proceedings today at the International Criminal Court in The Hague have been given at schools and colleges nationwide. Looking back, it is clear that what drew us together was more than that available space. From its inception, the Center has been a vibrant collaborative of educators and visionaries seeking to create a place of learning on Long Island with a particular focus on students and young people.

Coincidentally, the Center would soon be loaned a life-size carved wooden sculpture of the Nazi perpetrators at the Nuremburg war trials, sitting in the jury box awaiting their verdicts.

# CHAPTER 3

## THE CENTER MATURES

THE SECOND FLOOR was semi-occupied by offices for Eileen Tannor and Boris Chartan who had not yet retired from his County work and could only be at the Center on weekends. Irving Roth ran the Center as well as serving as Director of Education. His office was on the second floor as was his secretary Sandy Lipton's, whom Irving Roth had brought along from UNISYS. Sandy typed Irv's letters, later copied and used for mass mailings that were sent out with the help of volunteers. These were mailed to schools, synagogues and churches in the area informing them of our existence and programs. There were still many problems to solve, mainly, transportation to bring the students to the Center. Neil Tannor was able to acquire a grant from the Camber Foundation that paid for buses. Although Sandy Lipton was the only paid employee, money had to be raised to accomplish all of the above and more. Boris was an experienced fundraiser and worked ceaselessly on finding the funds to support the Center and its activities.

The annual dinner, its journal ads and good-will inscriptions subscribed to by local businesses, friends, family and well-wishers, supplied the funds for the Center's expenses for a year, but the budget had to be kept tight. Boris, of course, was always fundraising and with the help of some key financial people was able to meet all of the Center's financial needs at that time.

*Woodbury Jewish Center,*
*3rd Annual Dinner*

By 1995, Boris and Eileen were planning their third annual fundraising dinner. All of the *Holocaust Memorial and Educational Center* Tribute Dinners were totally organized and designed by Eileen Tannor, including its journal, food, music, flowers and so on. The Dinner journal was the Center's main fundraiser.

*(Photo from left to right: Neil and Eileen Tannor, Boris Chartan, Ike and Evelyn Blachor, and Jacob and Jean Stein.)*

Journal ads paid tribute to the Honorees and those who helped to run the Center including: Educational Director, Irving Roth; Executive Administrator, Eileen M. Tannor; Marcia Posner for the library and the various volunteers who handled the leadership of committees, but primarily to Boris Chartan and his Board of Directors. Neil Tannor did all the bookkeeping and banking. Another member of the team was legal Counsel, Isaac Blachor.

*Picture: Irving and Addie Roth with Tom Gulotta*

Irving Roth wielded the telephone like an artist handles his brushes. His calls to the newspapers were very productive; the Center received ample publicity. He also knew how to attract the public by having a monthly art show. Irving continued to invite artists from Long Island who depicted the Holocaust either literally or symbolically, to participate. By holding exhibitions of their work in the mansion's former ballroom, he made many valuable contacts not only with the press whom he had invited to review the art, but also with worldly, bright survivors and their children, the "Second Generation," who came to view the art but not yet take on their parents roles as testifiers and docents. That would come in the future.

The 3-day seminars for teachers continued. Roth was an exciting speaker. He described his and his brother's Holocaust experiences with such emotion that once having heard him, teachers and children were changed. They had felt the strain, fear and darkness that lay before the Jewish people and emotionally transmogrified into their roles. In later years, Roth actually asked each of his pupils to "become a survivor," to become the survivor whose story they had heard and to transmit the story to the next person and the next. Before long there was a waiting list for visits to the Center. Irving also had the Center produce a 45-minute video that documented our exhibits and featured his lecture to an eighth grade class from the Herricks school district.

The literary competition produced some wonderful writing such as "The Weeds Sing" by Alexandra Moss. It is a poem about a ghetto, possibly Terezin.

## The Weeds Sing

### Alexandra Moss

The emerald plots have been trampled.
The landscape has been vandalized.
The neat bundles of humanity are
disheveled from
the beatings.

Battered hearts thump along with the
goose-stepping monsters.
The lawns are barren; buildings–
bombed-out shells;
bodies–hollow cavities.

In the ghetto, the weeds sing.
They cry out for help, in exasperation,
but also with lust for life,
in jubilation.

The tulips have been plucked and dried.
The roses all have withered.
Those are the beautiful ones–
the quintessential weaklings.

The only ones left are the unwanted ones.
They are the ones who rise up resiliently
where their presence is most feared and hated.

In violent times, the weeds keep quiet,
one hardly knows they are there.
But when the world is silent,
after the passing of a storm,

The weeds puncture the solid earth,
throw back their heads
and let out a mighty roar
that makes the strewn dirt
tremble.

In the ghetto, the weeds sing.
They cry out in determination.
They shout in defiance.

By the end of the 1997-98 school year, the Center was fully established and on a solid educational and financial footing. All the programs were running smoothly and efficiently. Sandy left to work at a job closer to her home and Irving Roth retired to write his reflections on the Holocaust that was eventually published as a memoir titled "Bondi's Brother." Later, he would establish another Holocaust Center at Temple Judea in Roslyn, New York.

Upon reflection, we may have not yet been "state of the art" in those early years, but even before our world-class exhibits were installed, we were doing wonderful things at the Center. It was always a stimulating, exciting place to be, and very successful at communicating its message. Because we helped to create it, there was an extremely deep family connection between the Holocaust Memorial and Educational Center and its volunteers—a camaraderie stemming from building something together that was very satisfying.

# CHAPTER 4

## CARRYING THE TORCH: CAROL RAGIONE AND DR. REGINA WHITE

W E HAD GROWN into a much more complicated organization. Boris Chartan had retired by now and was able to be at the Center full time, but we still needed a new secretary and a new Educational Director.

### Carol Ragione

Carol Ragione came to be interviewed for the secretarial position. She seemed personable and efficient. We wanted to hire her but she took several days to decide whether or not to accept the job. Finally, she did. Sometimes you just get lucky. Carol not only became our Office

Manager, she became destiny's gift to the Center, a dynamo who was also a philosopher. An able juggler of duties as well as a volunteer of kindly deeds, she welcomes the newcomer, tunes into our joys and sorrows and brings safely to harbor the myriad tasks needed to keep us functioning and succeeding. We are devoted to her.

## Dr. Regina White

We found a Director of Education in Dr. Regina White. Through Regina, we gained entrance to the realm of the Long Island and New York Social Studies environment. Dr. White's background was in Social Studies, not in Holocaust studies, but she had read widely on the Holocaust. She would continue to do so as well as to attend meetings related to that subject. Regina had been the head of the Social Studies departments of several schools on Long Island and in upstate New York. She had returned to Long Island to be closer to her grandchildren. Because she was so much a part of this teachers' world, she was privy to all the initiatives in which they were engaged. She not only brought her knowledge and expertise to our Center, but also the Long Island educational network. Boris Chartan and I used to say: "Regina White put us on the map." She knew almost every educator in every Long Island School and was forever going to his or her meetings.

Tom Aird and Abbie Lasky were two teachers from Herricks Junior

High School who not only brought their students to the Center for research assignments, but also held well-attended seminars where they taught teachers how to incorporate the Holocaust into their classes. Students often interviewed survivors in the library as this child is doing with Inge Gurevich.

We practically became part of the Long Island school system, participating in the latest programs being

*Student interviews Inge Gurevich*

developed by the Long Island Social Studies Department. We were invited to join two of the most important program advancements: "Video-conferencing" and the "Tolerance Workshops,"

## VIDEO CONFERENCING

Video-conferencing is a wonderful way to relate to students. It enables our survivors to describe their experiences and engage in conversations with children in distant places. The format for the Center's video-conferencing sessions includes a brief historical overview that provides a context for survivor testimony, followed by an opportunity for questions and answers. These are broadcast from the Center and are available to locations as far away as Australia. The *Holocaust*

*Memorial and Tolerance Center* (HMTC) was awarded the "Pinnacle Award" by the *Center for Interactive Learning and Collaboration* (CLIC) in 2011-2012, for its outstanding video conferencing program.

## THE TOLERANCE WORKSHOPS

The Tolerance Workshops use the lessons of the Holocaust to teach understanding and inclusion. They are vastly popular. These workshops led to the annual Middle-School Tolerance Conference. The conferences, which now include "Anti-Bullying," bring together hundreds of students from Nassau, Suffolk, and Queens Counties. Our facilitators are often deeply affected by student reactions.

Lois Lutwin, a Tolerance facilitator, described an experience she had many years ago with a small breakout group of high school students when they were at the point in the discussion when emphasis is put on the conditions and situations that the students see each day in their own schools and daily lives, regarding bullying, teasing, exclusion, etc.

"I remarked that in almost every school, there are at least one or more students who are very much isolated. They are ignored by all and hate going to school. They especially try to avoid the cafeteria. School is such a lonely and unhappy place for them. I often wish that other students would just smile, say 'Hi' or 'How are you doing?' Just this little bit of effort would make that person's day so much better.

The students were listening quietly and then, a smallish size boy spoke up and said: 'I am that kid!' You could hear a pin drop. All eyes turned towards the speaker. I, too, was taken aback by his remark and what it took for him to speak up like that. I said to him: 'You are the bravest person in this room!' There was no time for further discussion. I walked down the steps with him and we talked a bit, but I cannot remember what was said. I do remember having really been shaken by his statement and also feeling proud that I had made the group experience sufficiently comfortable for him to speak up like that. I should have tried to follow it up more, although I alerted the other teachers to advise the guidance counselor to possibly make an appointment with him. I always think about that boy and wonder how he is doing. By now, he may be finished with college and gained more confidence by having been able to speak up that day in our program. I think of him so many times and wonder if I had done enough."

~ ~ ~ ~ ~ ~ ~ ~ ~

Linda Finn, a teacher, tells another fascinating story. It is about "Tod" and survivor David Gewirtzman. Linda was teaching history at Huntington High School and saw a flyer that had been sent to the school describing the new Center and its mission, and decided to take her classes there. She writes:

"It was a profound experience for me and my 11th grade students. My belief has always been that to understand the experiences of others, you not only have to be able to step into their shoes but to feel their pain as well. I wanted my students to get a knot in their stomachs, to have a physical and emotional reaction that would result in sowing the seeds that would promote tolerance and build bridges. The impact of seeing and hearing a survivor, of their realization that this person was just like their grandfather, their aunt, created a tableau like no other. I was amazed at the kids' reactions, the discussions we had and the growth and empathy that resulted. Most were able to apply what they heard and saw to school and neighborhood situations, as well as in a global way, except for Tod. Tod might whisper to a friend on the way out: 'I know for a fact that it is all a lie. It never happened!' In disheveled attire, half-laced sneakers and a shaven head, Tod would sit sideways in a front row, deliberately avoiding eye contact with the speaker and distracting the students around him with mimics and gestures. But this time, at the end of the speech, Tod approached the speaker, David Gewirtzman, with a bent head. Still not looking him in the eye, Tod handed him a black marble, mumbling: 'Here! I want you to have this. It brought me luck. I want it to bring you luck too.'

The black marble was put in David's night-table drawer and forgotten.

Todd R. J. Wright returned from the Holocaust Center a changed boy. In the following year, his senior year, Todd took 2 courses on the Holocaust. One was an intensive course in the literature of the Holocaust taught in his English class, and the other, the history of the rise and fall of the Nazis in his Social Studies class. The image of emaciated bodies, especially the skeletal hands of the victims was burned in Tod's mind forever.

He felt a need to create. He felt the need to heal. He approached his shop teacher for help, declaring: 'I know it is too late for me to become a

Memorialize The Past
Honor The Present
Dedicate
The Future

real student but I have always been good with my hands and you see, there was this man at the Holocaust Center . . . Then, Todd told the teacher about David Gewirtzman: "He told us that when he was a kid all the odds were stacked against him. Everyone around him tried to kill him, but he managed to study and work and never gave up. And when he came to the United States he learned English and went to college and became a pharmacist, and had a really good life. And he said that he doesn't hate anybody. And here I am; school is almost over and I have wasted all of my time.'

At the end of the following school year, David received an urgent telephone call from the Center. It was a request for his presence at Huntington High School. Some sort of an event was to take place involving the presence of the school's board of directors, the teachers and parents. There was a gift to be given to our Holocaust Center that only David could accept. At the entrance to the school a handsome young man in a white shirt extended a hand in greeting and identified himself, not as 'Todd,' but as Scott Wright.

David went to accept the gift. Upon closer scrutiny, Scott turned out to be the donor of the black marble. 'Come with me,' he said to David, leading the way, 'I have something for you.' On an easel at the front of the room stood a beautifully framed stained glass picture. It portrayed an arm that bore a tattooed number reaching up from the ground towards a rescuing hand of an American soldier. 'My grandfather fought in World War ll.' Scott explained, 'I made this for you!'

Todd had worked on the project five days a week from afternoon until evening when the school closed down, weekends whenever possible–just to complete this picture. Todd explained: "I was particularly moved by the hands. Victims that once stood at 160 pounds were starved and tortured to 80 pounds and that is the reason for the difference in the size of the hands in the work." He learned many skills in designing and producing it. At the end of high school he was accepted to an upstate arts college. As for the stained glass window, a beautiful piece of art, it was gratefully accepted and hung at our Center." *(Adapted from Lillian Gewirtzman's article.)*

~ ~ ~ ~ ~ ~ ~ ~ ~ ~

Linda, who has since moved to Cape Cod, Massachusetts, writes: "The Tolerance Programs in which I took part enabled the students to spend a day involved in group activities that were unique, thought-provoking and had a huge impact on them. When I gave programs to individual classes in schools and provided exercises that were challenging, I felt wonderful. I saw them beginning to understand situations from different viewpoints. As a teacher, I was thrilled with their responses and reactions. My relationships with the Center and the survivors were gifts that have enriched me in ways I never imagined. I am involved in programs now that are extensions of the Center: building bridges, caring, promoting tolerance, and stopping bullying. I like to think that many of my former students are doing the same."

~ ~ ~ ~ ~ ~ ~ ~ ~

# THE LEAS PROGRAM

The first LEAS classes were conducted at our Holocaust Center in 2007. Howard Maier had visited the USHMM (United States Holocaust Memorial Museum), and was impressed with the LEAS program. Soon, the Center was invited to join it. Our volunteers, Lois Lutwin, Lynda Weinstein and Honey Kern were among those who attended training workshops at the USHMM to prepare future facilitators to run the LEAS program for cadets of the Nassau County Police Department. Jim Garside, retired Deputy Chief of the Nassau County Police Department, became one of two Anti-Defamation League facilitators who provided the ADL's portion of the program. The other facilitator was Nancy Kaplan, PhD from St. John's

*Lois Lutwin and the Police Cadets*

University. Lois describes an experience she had as a docent participating in one of the programs, after she had been at the Center for about 12 years and had countless numbers of very emotional and memorable experiences.

"Years ago, when Lynda Weinstein and I helped to create the LEAS (Law Enforcement and Society) program, it was quite different from what it is today. We selected scenes from hundreds of photos depicting horror and brutality that we posted in the room where the program was being presented. A museum tour and the film Survivor Reflections followed, after which we gave the police cadets and officers a chance to process what they had seen and heard and to comment on what was most meaningful to them. At each program I was struck by how sensitive, bright and insightful so many of these young men and women proved to be. They were very different from the stereotypical image that I had of the police and I was so proud to see who was going into this profession today.

During one of our sessions I noticed that one of the police cadets had walked over to the window and appeared to be looking out. The blinds were closed and he was just staring at the blocked view. When I went over to speak with him, I realized that he was trying to hold back tears. He was a handsome 6 foot 2 *macho* fellow who had been so moved by what he was seeing and hearing, but didn't want to cry in front of the others. We chatted a bit and I told him that even after working here for so long, I still can get very teary and that so many others feel the same way. That helped to validate his feelings and gave him a chance to get collected and return to the group. I don't know if anyone else had noticed him. I will always remember that time. It helped me to realize two things: my own stereotyping of police cadets and also how well our message was getting through. During our lunch breaks there were many conversations. The students' evaluations held very heartfelt comments, and we hoped that they would reinforce what these officers were taking away with them.

The Nassau County Police Department made the training mandatory for incoming police officers. The Suffolk County Police Department made the same commitment starting in 2009. LEAS has primarily been directed at newly hired police officers undergoing initial job training. Police Officers need to remember that they have unique access into the recesses of people's minds and lives and that their actions have a significant  effect on those they serve. Both Nassau and Suffolk have also assigned high ranking executive level officers, including Division Chiefs and Unit Commanders, to participate.

The LEAS program asks them:

"What guarantees that you won't abuse your power?

"What are the safeguards, the safety nets, the checks and balances regarding policing in the United States that prevent the type of systemic and systematic abuse witnessed in the Nazi era?

## DR. REGINA WHITE AND INTERFAITH ACTIVITIES

In addition to the activities noted above, in 2006 the Center hosted several interfaith activities that were very well received by everyone involved. First, there was a series of programs sponsored by the Louis Posner Memorial Library.

In October, the program topic was a symposium on "When and How to Forgive, "based on Simon Wiesenthal's book: *The Sunflower.* Representatives from various religious denominations will give their opinions and the audience was invited to give theirs.

In November, the library showed a film about Sophie Scholl, a Christian German girl who dared to defy Hitler and paid for it with her life.

In December, Scott Cairns, President of a Masonic lodge, gave a lecture whose topic was: "The Persecution of Freemasonry in the Third Reich."

In March and April, Dr. Regina White and Sister Millie of the St. Patrick's Roman Catholic Church in Glen Cove arranged for a "Confirmation Retreat at the Center." There were 90 children attending the awe-inspiring "Retreat for Preparation to Receive the Sacrament of Confirmation." In order to accommodate all the children, half attended one day, and half, the following day. Each day Sister Millie explained the meaning of the Confirmation retreat to the children, followed by an overview of the day.

After an introduction to the history of the Holocaust, they went on a tour of the Center's exhibits, heard survivor testimony from Eddie Weinstein on one day and from Charlotte Gillman, on the second. Following lunch, the children were taken on a tour of the Children's Memorial Garden and then to the Center's special exhibit: "The Fabric of Our Lives," which are hand-made quilt squares and wall hangings, many depicting rescue experiences by Christians who saved Jews.

**EXHIBIT: The Fabric of Their Lives: The December Exhibit** *Marcia Posner*

An earlier demonstration of expressive needlework was the wall hanging entered in the Center's Art competition. Its 16 squares depicted elements of the Nazis' harassment, torture and murder of their Jewish citizens.

In April, Dr. White was invited by Katie Leo, a student at Holy Trinity High School in Hicksville to talk to students after classes ended in the afternoon and to bring a survivor of Holocaust with her. Julius Eisenstein went with her.

Before introducing Dr. White, Katie started the program by explaining that those who had not received black circles earlier in the day, which they were now wearing, were to stand. They were few. In a somber voice, Katie then explained that only those standing would have lived. Then Regina spoke to them about the Center, followed by Julius who received a standing ovation when he described their liberation by American soldiers. The program lasted 1 and ½ hours, when Regina finally ended it. The whole school heard about it and everyone wrote Julius Eisenstein letters of appreciation. Only 100 had been invited, but 800 had attended. Katie won her "Gold Badge," the Girl Scout equivalent of the Boy Scout's "Eagle Badge."

# CHAPTER 5

## VOLUNTEERS: LIVES FULFILLED

### WILMA DIAMOND, QUEEN OF VOLUNTEERS

FROM THE CENTER'S earliest days, it was understood that the heart of its operation would be volunteers. Letters inviting survivors to volunteer at the Center were sent to synagogues and temples, printed in local newspapers and highlighted in our CENTERNEWS that was mailed to all the names on our mailing list. Everyone knew someone who would want to volunteer because it was an opportunity to pay respects to those who perished and to teach the lessons of the Holocaust to young people. For 12 years, before we had a "staff," we had volunteers. After Jay Feldman, Wilma

Diamond volunteered to become the "coordinator of volunteers." She sent the volunteers on their assignments to schools and within the Center to speak to groups. Wilma also helped the non-survivor volunteer to find the right place for him or her, such as the library, clerical, hospitality and other positions. She was a practiced "booker" from years of having booked patient appointments for her physician husband. She was never without her little book of volunteers and their phone numbers. Regardless of where she happened to be—at lunch, food shopping, at the ballet—Wilma's office was never closed.

Recruiting volunteers had not proven to be difficult, especially with populations who were no longer engaged in their professional careers. When professionals retire and want something interesting and stimulating to do, it is not unusual for them to turn to museums for challenging activity and the company of bright people of varied experiences and interests. Even people with busy lives and those who are still working, make time to volunteer at the Center. Many continue to practice their former professions as volunteers. Wilma used the CENTERNEWS to communicate with volunteers. Here is a column she once wrote (with a few updates by the editor).

"This year our educational activities have increased greatly, thus challenging our staff and all of our volunteers—including those who man the reception desk, act as docents, answer the phones, work in the library, the office, video-conferencing, and do all the mailings and other administrative tasks and hospitality. Volunteers provide the extra dimension that results in meaningful encounters between the public and us. It is easy to become a volunteer. Lately, we have been getting a new crop of volunteers, both "Second Gens" and "Civilians" as I like to call those of us without Holocaust antecedents.

Carolyn Dinofsky became a volunteer docent in June 1999. Newly retired from her career as a Special Education teacher, Carolyn had visited the Center before retirement, listened to survivor testimony and spent time in the galleries. She writes: "While I always took the Holocaust seriously, it was not the same as taking an action—an action I have never regretted. It brought me to extensive research and intensive training under the most competent and highly trained leadership and I have met incredibly committed colleagues that have led to lifelong friendships. My interaction with the Holocaust survivors—many who had to overcome the most heinous and inhumane crimes—changed my life. Their battle could not have been fought on the battlefield where possibly they could have defended themselves; but their resiliency, their tenacity and their capacity to breathe in life again and live it to the fullest is their victory. Inspired by them, I set my compass toward reaching thousands of diverse students throughout the school year by capturing and awakening their sensitivities. Having moved to Chicago to be closer to my children, I am again searching for the right place to volunteer.

## Debbie Cohen, a "2G" writes:

My mother, Ilse Morgenstern Loeb, helped to create an exhibit entitled "Hidden Children: The Youngest Survivors of the Holocaust," and in 2001 it was housed at the Holocaust Memorial and Education Center of Nassau County. While the exhibit was in Glen Cove, I decided to help tell her story of being hidden in Holland during the Holocaust. My mother does not live locally and I knew that the students coming to the Center would find much more meaning in the exhibit if they heard the story of one of the survivors profiled in the exhibit, told by one of their children. That was the beginning of my relationship with HMTC. It is now very dear to my heart. My parents both were experienced in telling their stories of survival to many different groups, but I had never realized that I could do the same. Although a member of the Second Generation, I had never done this kind of work before. Once I started to relay my mother's story of survival, however, and I saw how the students responded, it was very gratifying. They have written me many letters of thanks, just like the survivors have received. Students have said that despite reading books and seeing movies on the Holocaust, it wasn't until they heard an actual survivor's story that it really made an impact on them. The Holocaust Memorial and Tolerance Center has evolved through the years, but the message has always been the same: Please do not be a bystander in the face of evil. Be an "Upstander" when you see that someone needs help and provide it. I have given many tours through the new multi-media exhibits in the museum. It lends itself so well to educating future generations about the horrors of the Holocaust and other genocides. We also explain to the students how relevant these lessons are in relation to bullying and cyber-bullying through our Tolerance and Holocaust programs. I am so glad that I have been a part of this Center. It has been an extremely rewarding experience to watch the students respond, to see them understand how people can overcome such cruelties and how they themselves can become better people and treat each other with respect and dignity. (See also: Debbie Cohen, Chapter 11, Second Generation.)

Renee Katz, a jazz enthusiast, has been a docent at the Center for 11 years with her buddy Sheila Rind. Renee is a former teacher and excels at leading both children and adults around the exhibits. Both Renee and

Sheila have all sorts of ideas and stories to further enhance their work because being a docent fills one's life and psyche with possibilities and excitement.

If you want to become a docent, simply call 516-571-8040 and leave a message asking for a

volunteer interview so that we can work together to find a job that we need filled and which you will enjoy. Working at the Center does as much for the volunteer as the volunteer does for the Center. To show our appreciation of how much we value your generous sharing of time, each year the Center has a Thank You Dinner for at least 122 volunteers and their significant others, including family or friends, so, as Julie Andrews sings in Sound of Music, "We must be doing something right!" We are not only volunteers; we are a family!

*At the Volunteer Dinner*
*L to R: front row: Lois Lutwin, Sheila Rind;*
*second row: Renee Katz, Sarah Cushman;*
*background are: Gloria Glantz and Giselle Warshaw*

When Robert Friedman. a member of the Second Generation, came on board, his company, *RF Creative Graphics*, was a wonderful gift to the

Center. The CENTERNEWS made it possible for us to communicate with a much larger portion of the Long Island population. It reported on everything that was happening at the Center and helped us to build an audience. On its pages we publicized what was currently happening, future events and discussion of relevant topics. We celebrated good news and mourned the bad. It helped us to publicize our monthly events that were posted on the margins of its pages, and find volunteers and testifiers. Archived copies of the paper are helping me to write this book. And as writer and editor, I loved the fan mail.

We never even thought to give Bob a reward. We just took his service for granted. I thought that he was paid for his services, but he was not. Yet, Robert Friedman performed the most professional of services for us and never stopped. Eventually, we stopped publishing the CENTERNEWS because it became too costly to print and mail. We now have a computer blog that reports on current and forthcoming events but has few discussions or stories. When I asked Bob to contribute something to this book, he wrote:

"When the initial idea to create a newsletter for the Center was suggested, I was more than pleased to undertake the design. At the time, I had been working as a graphic designer for more than 20 years and I saw this as an opportunity to not only develop a "design look" from scratch, but also as a way to contribute to advancing a cause I believed in. Over the years the layout was updated, more and better photos were used, we added a second color, went from 4 pages to 8 and occasionally to 12. Poignant editorials and focused articles on social, political and general interest topics enhanced the quality of content, and ultimately our focus shifted from what the Center hoped to accomplish to what we were doing. My involvement over a 15-year period also included designing some brochures, and developing some ads, yet it is the newsletter that remained my main focus and what gave me the opportunity to connect with a period in time that still forms much of my life's perspective."

Volunteers come to us in different ways: some come through referrals or ads, and some through serendipity. Following are two stories about chance encounters from survivors Ethel (Etunia) Katz and Anita Weisbord.

*Ethel Katz and Ariella M.*

Ethel Katz–At our recent annual Volunteers Dinner (June 9, 2013) Ethel recalled for the audience how she had come to HMTC. One day, while riding on a bus, Ethel's daughter Ruth happened to sit next to a young man who was reading *Alicia, My Story* by Alicia Appleman Jurman. Ruth mentioned to him that her father was the author's cousin; then she added that her mother, Ethel Katz, was also writing a book about her Holocaust experience. The man was a voracious reader of Holocaust material and begged to read the manuscript and to meet Ethel. Soon after, he brought her to our Center. They walked in on one of Irving Roth's lectures. Ethel says: "That was my initial contact with the Center. I began attending meetings and lectures. I got involved with the Center's work. I was impressed that they wanted to remember the Holocaust by eliminating hatred between peoples, which was of imperative interest to me." Ethel recalls the moment when commemoration became her task. She and her family had had many close encounters with the Gestapo. She escaped, but her father had gasped in a feeble voice–"Who will tell the world of our torment?" After the war, Ethel swore that she would, and so she does and will continue to do so. Ethel has profoundly touched the lives of hundreds of young people and adults across Long Island with her message of love and tolerance and has defused the hatred of non-believers in the classes to whom she speaks.

Anita Weisbord–signed up at the Center as a simple volunteer but was informed by Jay Feldman (who was then the Volunteer Coordinator), that she was a "survivor-testifier–volunteer." At one time, those who escaped Europe on the Kindertransport were not considered to be survivors by those who suffered the ghettos and camps. Kindertransport children, torn from their homes and families are definitely survivors. What a  shock they suffered, brought to a strange country in which they did not speak the language and were uncertain of the housing and housemates who they might find there. Sometimes it was a beneficent surrounding, but other times, it was not. Plus, they suffered the bombings. Are they survivors? They most certainly are.

Our Center has started something new. We no longer have a 12-14 page newsletter, we have a frequent one page "Blog," There is a "Volunteer of the Month" in each blog. Eventually, everyone has been or will be a "Volunteer of the Month" because we have so many volunteers and they are all happy workers. Just as I queried Irving Roth so many years ago, if it was unseemly to feel happy in a place like this, the truth is that when you are doing something worthwhile with your time, when you are making a difference, when you have a sense of camaraderie with like-minded people, you are happy.

Werner Reich wrote that when he retired some 18 years ago, for the first time in his life he had the time to do things he had never done

before. "One day I saw a newspaper article that wrote about a Holocaust course given to students at my local high school. Although I did not speak about my experiences for close to 50 years, I offered my services. I had been a prisoner at Mauthausen. A couple of years later, my grandson was born and shortly afterwards, on an impulse, I visited the Glen Cove Center. Again, I offered my services to speak and haven't stopped since. Nowadays, I speak close to 100 times per year.

The original presentations were strictly about my experiences, but I soon realized that students knew very little about the Holocaust. And so, with the aid of a 14-year-old student, I created a PowerPoint presentation that included some thoughts about the Nazis ideology and various persecutions of other minorities. I also compared the bullies of the Holocaust with the bullies in our schools. And then I added the dangers of being a bystander. Suddenly, my presentation made sense: it is not so much about the Holocaust but more about the need for ethical behavior. While at the start, my story occupied 100% of the time, today it is reduced to about 40%. Frankly speaking, I could speak to students about the Holocaust without even mentioning my story. As part of my involvement, I donated to the Center my wife's document created by Nicholas Winton, the document that saved her life, allowing her to go on the Kindertransport. I also donated my Mauthausen release document. And finally I loaned The Center my Mauthausen number wristband, a band that a prisoner made for me in exchange for a small piece of bread."

# CHAPTER 6

## THE CHILDREN'S MEMORIAL GARDEN AT WELWYN: BUTTERFLIES LIVE HERE
by Jolanta Zamecka

THE CHILDREN'S MEMORIAL Garden is the only garden of its kind in New York State. It was at first conceived by Irving Roth as a living memorial to 1.5 million Jewish children who perished in the Holocaust and was later expanded to honor the memory of all children who died during World War II. This garden is a reminder of how many innocent young children were the victims of this tragic period of history. Named "The Million Pennies Project" in the spring of 1996 by its originator, Irving Roth, the Project was an alliance between the Holocaust Memorial and Educational Center of Nassau County (the Center's name at that time) and school children from Nassau, Suffolk, Queens and Brooklyn. Matching 1 million pennies to the 1½ million young Jewish victims of the Holocaust, by the year 2000 the Center had collected a little over $10,000 in pennies.

Irving showed me his plans for the garden first; then he showed me a room next to the library where water jugs filled with pennies were stacked from floor to ceiling! These pennies would provide the seed money for the future Children's Memorial Garden. The Board of the Holocaust Center had wanted to create a small tribute garden in the back of the Center, but Irving and I spoke about creating a much larger garden on the west side of the building. His idea was that the garden be a tribute to Dr. Janusz Korczak who sheltered the children of the Warsaw Ghetto and who later escorted them on their final train ride to Auschwitz, refusing offers to save himself. But it morphed into a related theme, a garden dedicated to the lives and spirits of all children who perished in World War II.

As noted previously, the Welwyn Preserve was once the estate of Harriet and Harold Pratt. Harriet Pratt had hired the famous Olmsted Brothers to design the grounds around the estate. This was the same firm that had designed Central Park in Manhattan and Prospect Park in Brooklyn. In their usual way, Olmstead created a dense wood of native trees, bordered by hundreds of rhododendron bushes. A road piercing the wood eventually opened to reveal a meadow. At its apex stood the magnificent manor house surrounded at that time by many lovely garden areas. Harriet Pratt was such an ardent garden enthusiast that she had the Welwyn gardens dug up and transplanted in 1938 to replace the gardens at the New York World's Fair that had been devastated by the largest hurricane the east coast of New York had ever experienced (similar to the 2013 Super Storm Sandy). Naturally, Harriet Pratt's army of gardeners soon replaced the flora she had so gallantly donated, but for the past many years her gardens had been neglected, indeed they had disappeared from sight and all that was left were brambles and weeds.

Thanks to Gloria Jackel, a longtime resident of Glen Cove and the history department of the Glen Cove Public Library, I learned that this overgrown mess on the west side of the building had once been a beautiful garden. Gloria showed me pictures of the garden at its most magnificent. Knowing that there was a central fountain in the foreground and a dolphin fountain under an arbor in the back, a friend and I started to hack away with a machete to see if anything was still there. This was a true treasure hunt, but Gloria kept assuring me that it was still there. After hours of cutting a small path through scrub brush, barberry bushes and ivy, we arrived at the arbor in the back.

The dolphin fountain was intact, perhaps protected from vandals by the overgrowth. This was truly a secret garden. At that moment I knew in my heart that the Children's Memorial Garden must be located in this wreck of a formal sculpture garden.

The next day, Irving and I met with Boris Chartan, President of the Board. We had a new proposal. We wanted to create the Children's Memorial Garden on a much grander scale and to locate it on the west side of the mansion, the site of Harriet Pratt's beloved garden. Boris took my enthusiasm with a bit of humor but since I had worked on the garden committee to restore the Marian Cruger Coffin Garden at the Nassau County Museum of Art in Roslyn, perhaps he also took me seriously. Irving graciously accepted my proposal that the Garden should be a setting for reflection and contemplation and not a physical depiction of the Holocaust, therefore there would be no statuary representing various death camps.

From the beginning, I had a vision of what I would like to see in the Garden. Moved by 17–year–old Pavel Friedman's poem "The Butterfly" written while he was a prisoner in the Terezin ghetto, an excerpt of which read:

". . . *Only I never saw another butterfly. That butterfly was the last one. Butterflies don't live in here, in the ghetto . . ."*

I wanted to bring the butterflies back to the children; the plants in the garden were to be a natural habitat for butterflies. Butterflies have become an international symbol representing the souls of the children who perished during the Holocaust.

I met with the Board to present my idea. With their approval, I felt empowered to start fundraising immediately. The first person I called was my friend Suzie Kadish who was most supportive. The second person I called was Peter Tilles. Peter and I both served on the garden committee at the Roslyn museum. I wanted him to see the site as I always valued his opinion. By this time it was late fall; most of the leaves were gone and the vegetation was dying down. Now, you could see the hardscapes (paved areas) more clearly. Peter started laughing on the phone and said "Jolanta, I've seen that overgrown mess; what you need are people with heavy duty equipment to clear it." Two weeks later John Geral, the owner of Geral Associates called to tell me that Peter Tilles told him that I needed help.

I had met John Geral and Tim Conway, his landscape designer, earlier at the Nassau County Museum of Art. Geral's crew worked on clearing the future garden site for eight days. Tim and I went around seeing what could be saved, unfortunately very little. Most of the trees were invasive scrub trees and the shrubs were choked out by ivy or knotweed. Tim and I spent days discussing the Garden. I shared my vision with him. I told him that I wanted the Garden to be a natural habitat for butterflies, to be alive twelve months a year. Remembering that the disabled were the first to be murdered by the Nazis who believed they were unworthy of life, I particularly wanted the Garden to be accessible to physically challenged people. This immediately presented a problem as the Olmsted Brothers' design had included stairs, walls, fountains and an arbor but no walkways, only grass.

Tim said that he would be honored to design a plan for the Garden. This would be his donation. He would also help obtain the plants and supervise the planting. A few weeks later Tim showed me his design. It was more beautiful than I had ever imagined.

To make this plan a reality I had to start fundraising. I must admit that I was very naïve. I had worked on various fundraising committees, but this was very different. This was a larger project and one that was very personal to me. My reasoning was that if over $10,000 could be raised by school children, we adults should be able to raise $100,000 with no problem. Our first donation was $1,000 from David Spodak. He not only donated money from his Bar Mitzvah, but he and his parents, Bonnie and Jason and his grandparents, Florence (Cookie) and Murray Slimowitz volunteered to help work in the garden. David, and later his younger brother Chad, his parents and grandparents, organized garden clean-ups with their school friends. My gratitude to them is heartfelt; they have set a wonderful example for others.

After David's generous donation, very little came in. I shared my frustration with my friend Suzie Kadish. An hour later I received a call from her husband Lawrence, Lory. He had heard that my fundraising was not going well. I told him that was an understatement; it seemed as if my big plans had fizzled. Lory said that he wanted to see the design for the garden and depending on the presentation, he would give me $5,000 or $50,000. I told him "Lory I will give you the $50,000 presentation!" Two days later I met him at his office and although I knew him well, I was quite nervous. I showed him the design as well as photos of the existing hardscapes designed by the Olmsted Brothers. Lory's knowledge of architecture and design was remarkable. As we made plans for him and Suzie to come out to the Center, he gave me a check (filled out before I had even arrived) for $50,000. With this money plus the money we had collected earlier, including the pennies from the Million Pennies Project, the Garden was becoming a reality. Once we had a major donor, others came forward. Now the checks were no longer $50 or $100, but $1,000 to $10,000.

As with any project in which I was involved, my biggest supporters were my husband Jack and my two daughters, Karolina and Monika. Originally the Garden was dedicated to the 1.5 million Jewish Children who perished in the Holocaust. During the planning of the Garden, however, my daughter was reading *The Rape of Nanking* by Iris Chang, about the atrocities of the Japanese soldiers on the Chinese civilians of Nanking. One evening Karolina came to me with tears in her eyes and asked:

"Why can't the Children's Memorial Garden be dedicated to all the children who were murdered during World War II?" Why not, indeed? The next day I spoke to Boris and Irving and they both agreed that the garden should be dedicated to all the children who perished during WWII. At the next Board meeting I presented the idea of the new dedication. After much deliberation it was decided that the Children's Memorial Garden would be dedicated to the 1.5 million Jewish children who perished during the Holocaust and to all the other children who died during WWII.

At the ground breaking ceremony, Lory and Suzie pulled me to the side to tell me that they were not giving me $50,000 for the Garden, they were giving me $100,000! During my presentation, I proudly announced that Mr. Lawrence and Mrs. Susie Kadish had donated $100,000 to the Children's Memorial Garden. Boris whispered, "$50,000" and I smiled and said, "$100,000, and here is the check!" This was one of my happiest moments! New York State Parks Commissioner Bernadette Castro stated that this was first garden of its type on public grounds in New York State, and the third in the Nation. We had made history!

In accordance with Irving's original plan to honor Janusz Korczak and the children of the Warsaw Ghetto, I wanted the first tree planted to be dedicated to Dr. Korczak and the children, and for it to be a symbol of defiance in the face of adversity, I chose a tall and proud redwood not native to Poland but native to this country.

Janusz Korczak, a children's author, humanitarian, pediatrician and pedagogue had moved his Jewish children's orphanage into the Warsaw Ghetto in 1940. In August of 1942, German soldiers came to collect the orphans and staff to transport them to the Treblinka extermination camp. Korczak had been offered sanctuary by *Zegota*, a Polish underground resistance and rescue group, but repeatedly refused, saying he would never abandon his children. On August 5th, he told his children that they were going on a long journey; they would go where the air is clean, meadows were filled with flowers and they would never have to suffer again. The children dressed in their best clothes, each carrying a knapsack and a book or favorite toy and marched two by two to Umschlagplatz, the deportation station. At the station, an SS officer recognizing Korczak as the author of one of his favorite children's books, offered him freedom. Korczak refused. He boarded the train with the children and staff. They were all killed in a gas chamber upon arrival at Treblinka.

Attending the groundbreaking ceremony was my husband's friend, Peter Hagedorn and his wife Miriam. After the ceremony Peter said he would like to restore the arbor in the back of the Garden in memory of his Jewish grandmother Blanche Hagedorn, at a cost of $27,000. He also added that he would donate all the Miracle Grow we would need. Peter

and Tim Conway secured many plant donations from various growers on Long Island. Another family who had been very generous to the Garden is the Keil family, nursery owners.

We wanted to put the Children's Memorial Garden on the map for Long Island's East End residents and visitors. Paul became a strong supporter of the Garden. On July 5th 2002, a multi-day silent auction was held in Vered Gallery in East Hampton with a party at the Slimowitz's home in Sagaponack. I had known Ruth Vered and her partner Janet Lehr for years. Paul Rothman, a friend of

Cookie and Murray Slimowitz, generously donated works of fine art to the auction. Thanks to the financial success of the auction, the garden had an irrigation system.

The Center revealed the results of our 7 year effort on *Yom Hashoah*, Holocaust Remembrance Day, April 29, 2003, with the dedication of the Children's Memorial Garden. Hundreds of students and adults including many dignitaries were present. The dedication included the presentation of "Wings of Witness," a 150' wide by 70' deep butterfly made from more than 9 million soda can tabs. Each tab represented an innocent life destroyed during the Holocaust. The project was conducted and conceived by artist Jeffrey Schrier with more than 33,000 individuals. Most were students from 23 states including 4,000 from Long Island. The tabs were converted into feathers, the feathers into a giant butterfly.

By April of 2003, all the existing structures had been repaired, brick and bluestone walks laid down, three bluestone patios and two handicapped ramps installed. All the plants from Tim Conway's design were thriving thanks to our new irrigation system. With the Children's Memorial Garden now a reality, everyone could enjoy its beauty and contemplate how the world would be so  much more beautiful if each of us tried to be a little more tolerant and appreciative of the diversity of people with whom we share our planet. The essay that follows describes this so beautifully.

~ ~ ~ ~ ~ ~ ~ ~ ~ ~ ~ ~ ~ ~ ~ ~ ~ ~ ~ ~

Teacher Dr. Elaine Weiss describes the importance of the garden to her special needs students.

Building our Children's Memorial Garden was one of the most rewarding experiences of my teaching career. In 1995, I became

responsible for Holocaust education at Great Neck North High School. I was certainly well qualified. I have a PhD in European History and had been on a study tour to Poland and Israel led by Ben and Vladka Meed in 1990. Vladka Meed had been a leader in the Jewish Resistance of the Warsaw Ghetto. She spoke flawless Polish and smuggled in arms for the Warsaw Ghetto Revolt. But teaching the lessons of the Holocaust to all students was my challenge. The Holocaust elective at Great Neck North included many students who were grandchildren of survivors and the required assignment was an intergenerational history project.

We were among the many schools on Long Island that participated in the Million Pennies project to restore the garden of the Holocaust Memorial and Educational Center. The students in the elective seminar wanted to expand the fundraiser to the entire student body. I decided to implement this by assigning a special group of 10th grade global history students to be responsible. One of my 10th grade classes was a special needs inclusion class. Despite extensive support from the school and their parents, most of these students struggled every day to stay in a comprehensive public high school. The Million Pennies Project was to be their global studies human rights project. They worked with their personal aides, with the lunchroom aides, and the school security aides to try to get every student not just to give a penny but all the change from their lunch and snack money.

They spoke about how this would be a memorial to murdered children. One of the special needs students was a grandchild of a survivor who had lost her entire family. Motivation became passion. Confidence grew. They were leaders of a school-wide project! Pennies, nickels, dimes, quarters came in every day. We sorted them and took the two-block walk to the bank where our school extra curricular accounts were held. We filled out deposit slips and gave them to the administrator in charge of overseeing the accounts. We withdrew money to send to the Center. This went on for almost a year. Some of the students went to the official opening of the Garden. They had learned through testimony and experience. They had earned the respect of their peers. They felt the self-confidence that achievement brings. How better to demonstrate that our garden is a living memorial to the handicapped children murdered by the Nazis who believed that they were unworthy of life.

The Children's Memorial Garden has assumed another function as well. It has had an important role in comforting survivor, Ethel Katz. Ethel's family was slain by the Nazis in the snows of Poland, buried by a Polish classmate without Jewish rites. Ethel held a funeral service for them in the Garden. She had a rabbi and cantor officiating at the ceremony, her family giving their eulogies, and a congregation of HMTC volunteers. Although there is no headstone at a burial plot, there is a bronze memorial plaque marking this event on the brick wall near the entrance to the garden. Ethel, the only survivor, now in her 90s has found some peace. Since then, others have placed bronze memorial markers for their departed loved ones in the same area.

# CHAPTER 7

## THE LOUIS POSNER MEMORIAL LIBRARY
## Marcia W. Posner

IN 1994, IRVING Roth invited me to establish a library at the new Holocaust Center. Irving and I were friends from the Shelter Rock Jewish Center where I had originated a library with a special alcove for books on the Holocaust. At the new Holocaust Memorial and Educational Center, I would be challenged to fill an entire room with books on that subject. Although I was anxious to begin, I needed a year to find my replacements at UJA-Federation and the Jewish Book Council. Exactly one year later, I received a phone call. "So," said Irving, "What time are you coming?"

At first, I thought that the Library of Congress scheme should be used for this single subject library but soon realized that the "Holocaust" was not a single subject. I allowed the books to lead me. I would allow them freedom to broadcast that there was no part of Jewish life in Europe, no subject, no area that was not touched by the Holocaust. The Holocaust dealt with every part of Jewish and world life. It impacted upon every aspect of life: ethics, psychology, religion, science, ethnic studies, medicine, animals, literature, and of course history, geography, marriage, family, and sociology. Nowhere is this demonstrated more clearly than in a library of Holocaust literature.

After greeting me at the mansion, Irv pointed to a room. "In there." he said pointing to a room full of moldy boxes and books. Had they been sitting there for a year? I started to empty them. The smell of mildew prevailed. These and yellowed paperbacks had to go out immediately as mildew spreads quickly to uninfected books. Few of the books were about the Holocaust.

Gloria Jackel and Helen Manassee came into the room out of curiosity and Gloria became my right hand associate and close friend. We discarded the books for which we had no use. One or two books about Germany in the early 30s were gems. There might also have been some author-signed copies, too. I especially remember Dorothy Thompson's fiercely negative appraisal of Hitler. A prominent journalist, she had him sized up correctly as she described what was going on in Germany in the 1930s. I immediately selected the book as the first to be kept in an archive reserved for rare or special books. Gloria, who became a talented researcher and head of technical services, received her first lesson that day. We sorted the selected books into 10 Dewey Decimal classes indicated with cardboard signs. Now we had to locate the room that was to be or library.

Since I am a devotee of British literature, the Pratt mansion intrigued me. It was a typical Georgian manor house on the English style. I searched for a grand library like the one I had seen on the "Upstairs, Downstairs" TV series imported from England. Was there a serious library in the mansion, we hadn't spotted it yet. There was an impressive, even grand room, but that turned out to be the former dining room, seating 40. Both family and famous personalities had once been served there. Now however, it served as our auditorium.

Refusing to desert the British mansion image, I recalled another: two adjoining rooms, one where genteel women sipped their sweet after-dinner libations, while in the adjoining room gentlemen would smoke their after-dinner cigars, have their whiskies and possibly play a game of billiards. Usually, the women's sitting room would also be a "library light" containing an alcove for books. We began to realize that we were already in it! Didn't the room we were in have two sets of shelves, one on either side of its cold fireplace? But where was that male adjoining room? Then, Gloria detected a closed interior door upon which still adhered a thin veneer of leather imprinted with shelves of books that led to it. Best of all, the adjacent room indeed bore the markings of a former men's billiard's room and drinks facility. The two of us were as excited as two girls reading a mystery novel.

Boris Chartan furnished the library with a collection of discarded shelving units of various sizes collected from county buildings and had them sprayed black. I thought they looked interesting, all different heights and widths. When my husband Lou, saw them, he volunteered to pay for a properly furnished library. I find great satisfaction in remembering that he was so much an enthusiastic part of our library, now named: "The Louis Posner Memorial Library."

At the library's grand opening and dedication, author David Shavit discussed his book: *Hunger for the Printed Word: Books and Libraries in the Jewish Ghettos in Nazi Occupied Europe*. Most ghetto residents read fiction. Novels were their escape from the world in which they were forced to live. My friend, Dina Abramowitz, of blessed memory, was a librarian in the Vilna ghetto. She hid books under her floorboards. Dina escaped the Vilna Ghetto by dressing nicely and boarding a streetcar with Nazi officers on it. Here, in Manhattan, Dina became the head of the YIVO library.

During the Holocaust, despite the best efforts of Jewish librarians and scholars to hide their most important books from Nazi thieves, the Nazis absconded with an enormous amount. In a book called: *As If It Were Life: A WWII Diary from the Theresienstadt Ghetto*, Philip Manes explains how the ghetto came to have such a huge library stocked with about 49,000 volumes. These books were works of Jewish literature that had been stolen by the Nazis from prestigious collections in the finest Jewish libraries. They were intended for use in a future Nazi library to be named: The Institute for the Scientific Study of Judaism. Its purpose would be to teach German citizens about what the Nazis assumed would be an extinct race, the Jews.

After the war, Colonel Seymour Pomerenz of the Allies "Monuments Men," not only recovered looted artworks, but also looted literature. (Most of the retrieved books were eventually sent to YIVO to Dina Abramowitz's welcoming arms.) Until then, the books were housed in two rooms of a former barracks building in the ghetto of Terezin or Theresienstadt, in German. Lack of space made it impossible to allow all the ghetto inmates to come and borrow books at one time, so every house received a box of books to lend out internally and at the end of the month, these books would be exchanged for another box.

Manes writes:
"Some found favorites, books that they had owned.
Then they would gently stroke them, feeling the joy of being reunited."

Now that we had the shelves, we needed to build the collection. Added to the selected donated books were about 100 books that I had brought with me. Soon, we were gifted with additional handsome collections from various donors, especially Rhoda Morgenstern. Rhoda's husband helped her to collect books about the Holocaust. She was so worried that no one would believe the Holocaust had really happened, she wanted to have books proving that it had. Upon her husband's death, she gave all these precious books that they had collected together, to our library. For several years her children continued to give us one or two books annually in honor of their mother's birthday or their father's. I hung a small plaque in his memory. People who were downsizing began to donate books that they could no longer accommodate, and also the books of parents who were moving to smaller quarters or who had passed away. Some gifted books to the library in memory of a departed family member. A dear friend, Marilyn Moscowitz, and her cousins, the Gildens, memorialized Marilyn's deceased husband, Edward, with a set of 20 *Yad Vashem* Proceedings. Others memorialized or honored their loved ones with a book donation.

Arnold Bassuk honored his parents, Jacob and Mary Bassuk and his beloved wife, Gloria with a gift to the library of $25,000. A memorial plaque is prominently placed in the new Louis Posner Memorial Library.

*Sarah Cushman, Arnold Bassuk, and Marcia Posner*

The library has also served to memorialize Henry Kauders and his grandfather. Henry Kauder's grandfather had built a large a large elegant synagogue in Vienna, an etching of which, accompanied by his grandfather's picture was hung in the small room that was now part of the tour. The synagogue was destroyed during *Kristallnacht*. We rehung both pictures and also a photograph of Henry Kauders, who had recently passed away, on the library's window wall between the two windows. Then, we invited his wife Anne, family and close friends to the library and held a service for Henry Kauders. We reviewed the history of his grandfather and the synagogue. I recalled how Henry always mailed me articles of interest about the Holocaust and how much I appreciated his interest. After that, we invited each one sitting around the reference table in our library to say good things about Henry, any stories that they wished to relate. It was a most wonderful and satisfying service and helped fill the emptiness in the hearts of his widow, Anne and his son.

I built the collection by requesting Holocaust books to review from the Jewish Book Council where I was a reviewer and board member. We also buy books from catalogues, inherit books from public libraries doing their annual weeding and libraries that are closing. We distribute 3rd copies of books to other libraries. Right now we are sending books to a new Holocaust library in Hong Kong and to a university in New Jersey.

Each book is a surprise. One never knows what information is contained therein, nor what forces of mental telepathy will be called into play. Sometimes, in addition to the main subject, there will be a kernel of ancillary information that stored away in the librarian's unconscious is matched in the future by another bit of information in a different book. It is like embroidering bit by bit until suddenly, there is a pattern. Among a group of books being discarded or "weeded" (in library jargon) by the Shelter Rock Public Library and gifted to us, was a book that dealt with stolen art being hidden in Italy during World War II. Our library "actors" had just finished presenting a "Readers Theater" play entitled "Smoke and Mirrors: Delusion and Despair" that took place in Terezin. It had furnished part of the public libraries programming related to the book selected as winner of the annual "All Long Island Reads" event. That year, the winning book, *The Lost Wife* written by Alyson Richman, was set mainly in Terezin. Why did I think that Alyson would need one of the discarded books presented to us by the Shelter Rock Public Library, I can't figure out. But she did! On some impulse, I called and asked if she could use a book about stolen art secreted in Italy. She had already been searching out books on the topic for her next book. Such mental telepathy among bookish people!

Over the past 20 years we have built a handsome and impressive library of about 8,000 books, art and photos, recordings and films. Oddly enough, the vertical file of pamphlets, line drawings, maps, photographs and clippings, that might be considered to be outmoded, continues to be maintained and to grow, despite the ease of "Googling' for information. Sometimes, we too Google and then file the information where it belongs topically. There, it joins clippings, etc. that when housed in adjacent folders arranged chronologically, present a story spanning many years. Some of the older information and articles filed there have become archival and fill in information that may no longer be available anywhere else but on archival film. Recently, a newspaper article from 1980 supplied from our vertical file was given to ORT for their recent exhibit. It was available on Google, but not in its original form. In writing this Center history, I sometimes go to the "Vertical" to introduce a certain subject.

We love it when authors use us as their primary source. Scholar-author, Emily Taitz was directed to us by Rabbi Myron Fenster. When she was hired by Greenwood Press to research and write a 2-volume set: *"Holocaust*

*Survivors: A Biographical Dictionary"* he sent her right to us. She includes the library in her "Acknowledgements" printed below.

"Of course, I would have been lost without the facilities of some excellent libraries and the librarians who helped me. Among them, most honorable mention must go to Dr. Marcia W. Posner and Gloria Jackel of the Louis Posner Memorial Library located in the Holocaust Memorial and Tolerance Center of Nassau County. The advice and counsel of Dr. Marcia Posner, director of the Center library, proved invaluable. Her help and encouragement was unequaled in my early background research. She recommended books; then she and Gloria Jackel took charge of my reading list of survivor memoirs, searched for those I wanted and made sure that I saw all the new material that came in. This book would not have happened without their help and encouragement."

The playwright, Kenneth Lin also wrote to thank the library:

June 18, 2010

Dear Marcia,

I wanted to take a moment to thank you for all the help you and the Nassau County Holocaust Memorial and Tolerance Center gave me in writing the play: "Intelligence-Slave." The library was particularly helpful to me and became increasingly important to me the deeper I delved into this subject matter. Books are so important in their ability to expand one's knowledge. Often I use the Internet to fill in the gaps of my knowledge, but books expand the horizon and make me see the spaces that I never knew existed. I am profoundly changed by my experience at the Center. Please thank everyone for me for helping me and for continuing to do this important work.

Love,

Kenneth Lin

We were about to enter Part II of the Center story. Our dynamic chairman, Howard Maier, who had been working on the concept of a state-of-the-art exhibit for many years and had been devoting himself totally to it, was at last ready to begin Stage II of our Holocaust Center. It became clear to us that the library's location would have to be changed. We were in the path of the new tour.

Our nostalgic lobby bookstore had to move also, but to oblivion, I am afraid. The entire building and lobby was being upgraded. The charming little bookstore that Irving Roth had helped us to establish in the corner of the lobby was removed.

We librarians approved of all the modern improvements, but we found it difficult to bid adieu to our little bookstore. A relic even when new, constructed from counters given to us by Fortunoff's, a famous store that is now closed, we will never forget it. I wrote the following about the store in its "heyday."

"On the way out to the school bus the children pass the store. This time they pause. They need to hold on to the experience–a talisman, perhaps–some book of fiction or memoir, even a pencil with the name of the Holocaust Center on it, something. There is pushing, jostling. Each child vies for attention. Erika Novick, our store proprietor calls out for backups. Finally, all are satisfied and the teacher has placed an order for books needed to continue the study of the Holocaust in the classroom. The docent is thanked. The survivor-testifier is thanked again. And the Holocaust Center staff feels assured that the message of tolerance, respect for differences and remembering the victims and survivors has been accomplished again."

Erika Novick recalls:

"It was my privilege to participate in establishing our own little bookstore in the lobby of the museum. After the children had finished their docent led program and survivor testimony, many children, as well as their parents, purchased books that told stories about boys' and girls' lives during the Holocaust. Some teachers also purchased and ordered books from us. Aside from books, copying the practice of famous museums, we sold small souvenirs of their visit with the Center's name on them. It wasn't otherwise related to the Holocaust, but charming and very popular."

~ ~ ~ ~ ~ ~ ~ ~ ~ ~

The library had to move, but to where, remained a mystery for a while. Here is a lesson on how you can fit a library into any space, even a former kitchen, a servants' dining room and thanks to the Claire Friedlander Foundation, an office in the formerly unheated servants' sun porch. And—what do you know! It worked out very well.

Mansion kitchens of that era were at least three times the size of modern day kitchens. The Pratt mansion at Welwyn had the usual two adjacent kitchens. Prior to their being dismantled and shipped out for use in other Long Island mansion museums, we enjoyed looking at these rooms from another era. The gorgeous tall windowed cabinets, the Delft tiled cooking wall fronted by an enormous iron stove and the banks of servants' bells, etc.—all were removed.

Our library would occupy the first kitchen, the cooking kitchen. The adjacent kitchen would be absorbed into the new tour. The future library room was totally redone with new walls, new smaller horizontal windows set closer to the ceiling to accommodate the 5'6" high shelving; new electrical wiring, paint and moldings, etc. We began to design the library on graph paper, figuring out the heights, widths, and the configuration of the rooms, the books and files we owned and the furnishings needed to accommodate them. After carefully measuring the rooms, we contracted with a company that made library shelving and furniture to order. We figured out how much shelving we needed to allow room for our current collection to grow, measured everything, ordered the furniture and prayed that it would all work out. It did.

Adult fiction and non-fiction books circulate. The art book collection is housed on deeper and wider shelves. Recently, a graduate student preparing a paper on the art of this period was delighted to use it. A bank of free standing shelving units, graduated in size, comprise the Children to Young Adult sections. The collection contains books of both *HOLOCAUST SURVIVORS: A BIOGRAPHICAL DICTIONARY (Volumes 1 & 2)* and "Tolerance," arranged by age levels. We even have hand puppets and a storytelling "magic carpet" available to whisk our younger readers away to other times and other climes.

The former servants dining room now hosts the Adult Reference collection. It has a wall of tall bookcases, three computer carrels, a copy machine and files of clippings and photographs. A table and 8 chairs center the room. The refurbished and newly equipped former servants sun-porch is our office. One thing remains the same, the name: *The Louis Posner Memorial Library.*

The library serves a variety of clients: the staff, students, authors and researchers of a particular topic. People come in seeking information on towns, families, and genealogical research. Nothing surpasses the joy and sometimes tears, we see on the faces of those who come into the library looking for information on lost relatives and find it in our reference books. Just to see their name in print, proof as once having existed, is sad but also satisfying to them.

We are getting more serious students from high school and college who want to delve deeply into a subject. After they have received a high mark, we get a thank you letter as well. Here is one example:

Dear Dr. Posner,

Thank you for spending time with me and recommending the 2 books that I am returning. My mother and I were both excited to learn about some of our family history. I purchased Richard Weilheimer's book: *Be Happy, Be Free, Dance: A Grandfather's Book for His Grandchildren* for my own library.

I'll return to the library again, looking for other interesting books.

Thanks again, Debbie Smith

We also usually have an author or scholar with us who essentially move in for months and work with books dealing with their topic from several aspects. Authors and scholars have learned that we collect books in depth, that is—a range of books on a particular country or aspect of the Holocaust. Our reputation is growing as a scholarly library for that reason.

*Linda Burghardt, and Elizabeth Young*

Linda F. Burghardt, Ph.D., is the third author to use the library's collection of books when writing a work of her own. She is researching Viennese Jews during the Austrian Anschluss, Hitler's annexation of Austria, and is the Center's first Scholar-in-Residence. Dr. Burghardt wrote her Ph.D. dissertation on the survival of the Viennese Jews in the Holocaust. Our library has enabled her to expand and deepen her research and to develop it into a series of useful lectures, articles and presentations. She has lectured at the Center, contributed articles to academic publications and the mainstream press, spoken to Second Generation groups and synagogues and presented papers at academic conferences, both regional and international. Because she is the child of

Holocaust survivors, she says that to work at the Center holds a special passion for her. She writes:

"When I came to work here I was very impressed at both the depth and breadth of the library's holdings. I rely very heavily on them," she said. "There are over 7,000 volumes here, covering virtually every major topic in the Holocaust and genocide studies and extending to a wide range of anti-bias materials. I have a deep commitment to the HMTC and its core mission; and a strong belief in the value of continuing research on the Holocaust and the dissemination of major findings regarding the topic. Without the outstanding resources of the Center library, it would be so much more difficult to continue that work. It has been a treasure trove for me. Materials I found there have supported just about every major breakthrough in my research, and the two librarians, Marcia Posner and Gloria Jackel, have been my steady guides throughout the process. Through the HMTC, I have been able to extend and offer my research to the broader academic community and thus enhance the Center's already fine reputation as an organization that promotes education and scholarship," she said. Her hope is to continue to mine the resources of the library and work closely with the HMTC staff and board of trustees to create and implement an agenda that will establish the Center as a top-level research institution within the Holocaust community."

Among the letters we have received are:

December 19, 1997

Dr. Marcia Posner
Holocaust Memorial & Educational Center
of Nassau County
100 Crescent Beach Road
Glen Cove, NY 11542

Dear Dr. Posner:

I would like to express my sincere appreciation for the assistance you recently provided to me. It was my first experience doing research for a pathfinder for my Library Science graduate class. As my topic was "Holocaust Resources for the Secondary School Educator," I found your library to be an invaluable source of information. With your knowledge and guidance I was able to focus in on my particular needs and work in an effective manner.

Sincerely,
Stephanie Benson

October 10th, 2013

To the Polite and Kind Ladies of the Holocaust Memorial and Tolerance Center of the Nassau County Library, 100 Crescent Beach Road, Glen Cove, New York 11542

Dear Ms. & Ms.?

Thank you so very much for the loan of the enclosed 2 books!! Very sad reading-but necessary! And, thank you for giving me extra time to return them. I spent much time cross-checking the reference. Unfortunately, I was not able to find anything regarding my father, Marcel Cadet, who was interned in Buchenwald.

With much sincerity,
André Cadet

# Library Staff

*Top row from L to R: Bernice Danis, Linda Burgardt, Liz Young,*
*Marcia Posner*
*Center: Judy Eisenman, Gloria Jackel*
*Bottom row: Barbara Murray, Eleanore Blackman*

At our 20th Annual Dinner, my nephew, Ed Koch, noted that the library was listed prominently in the brochure among the main attractions of the Center. I summed it up in a poem, as usual.

## The Louis Posner Memorial Library– Who Resides Here?

*Here, on the shelves of our library are the memoirs*
*of disparate groups:*
*Jews from Persia and Paris argue with the Jews of Palestine,*
*Jews of Lebanon with the Jews of Western Europe*
*marking time in Shanghai,*
*waiting for someday to*
*embark to South and Central America,*
*but mostly to the United States.*

*The heroes who saved us, compete with villains*
*who enslaved us.*
*A world and eons of history reside quietly*
*in our library*
*until the reader enters their realm,*
*brings them to life and decodes*
*the victor and the vanquished.*
*All are here. Just pick them up and they spring to life.*

When Dr. Ruth Gruber sat in our previous library while waiting to appear as an honored speaker, even she could not find enough words to express her delight and wonder. She said: "This library is a gold mine! Imagine being in a library and surrounded by books on the Holocaust. It is so wonderful!"

Dr. Linda F. Burghardt's book will be titled: *Night Falls on Vienna: Escape and Survival at the Dawn of the Holocaust.*

~ ~ ~ ~ ~ ~ ~ ~ ~ ~ ~ ~ ~ ~ ~ ~

Thanks to our wonderful staff: Gloria Jackel, co-director, Liz Young and Eleanor Blackman who are professional librarians, Barbara Murray and Judy Eisenman who complete the physical processing of the books, the library works efficiently and enjoyably and we have a wonderful camaraderie."

# CHAPTER 8

## REACHING OUT TO THE PUBLIC: EXHIBITS, FILM, PROGRAMS AND THEATER

F^OR MANY YEARS, the library planned and organized monthly Sunday programs. These included films, book talks, dramatic readings of chapters from books and "Readers' Theater" in which the text is dramatized and read aloud by several actors. Other well-attended Sunday programs sponsored by the library have included the *Dora Teitelboim Foundation's* presentation of *The Last Lullaby: Poetry and Music of Eastern Europe,*" programs about World War II and Liberation; and lectures about celebrities who found out in middle age that they were Jewish as described in Madeline Albright's *Madame Secretary: A Memoir* (Miramax) among others.

One year, we tried something new, a program series that would appeal to both children and adults. We will never forget the first and most wonderful program of the series. On a Sunday afternoon in January, the Canadian composer and violinist, *Ruth Fazel,* brought her musical work, the *Oratorio Terezin,* to the Center. She was to perform it at the Tilles Center the following evening. It is based on stories and poems from the Terezin ghetto written by children who were incarcerated there. The Oratorio weaves her music with these writings. At some point, a film of children singing the Oratorio in various countries was shown in the background while Fazel played

*Werner Reich and Ruth Fazel*

heavenly music on her violin. Werner Reich, one our most powerful speakers who had been incarcerated at Terezin, a holding camp for Auschwitz, toned down his usually highly dramatic testimony for this younger audience. Then the talented young vocalist, Michelle Raitzen sang the moving "Light a Candle" for the children who had perished. The following evening, many people associated with the Center attended Fazel's memorable performance of this oratorio at the Tilles Center of C.W. Post.

Some programs were based on books. *The Secret of the Priest's Grotto* is a photo picture book for all ages that describes how Jews, hiding from the Nazis, managed to survive in an underground grotto in the caves of the western Ukraine. The author showed slides of the grotto while he told the story to a spellbound audience. Two other book-based programs in this series, shown on succeeding months, were *Life in a Jar* and *6 Million Paper Clips.* The first was a program about Irena Sendler, heroine of the Polish rescue organization *Zegota* and the play: *"Life in a Jar."* Sendler smuggled sedated Jewish children, one by one, out of the Warsaw Ghetto to live with Polish Christian families. Their true names and families were deposited in one jar and their assumed names in another. Both jars were hidden deep in the dirt under a tree in her friend's backyard.

A program about the book *6 Million Paper Clips* by Peter and Dagmar Schroeder was presented on the following month. German journalists, they wrote about a Southern teacher in the United States, who wanted to teach the Holocaust to his students who had never heard about it. To dramatize the number of Jews who perished, a student decided that they might collect one paper clip to represent each Jew who perished and house the clips in jars. According to *Wikipedia*, "Paperclips were chosen because it was said that some Norwegians wore them on their lapels as a symbol of resistance against the Nazi occupation during World War II. Paper clips were sent to the project from people all over the world. Letters came from 20 different countries. Celebrities as George W. Bush, Bill Clinton, Steven Spielberg, Tom Bosley and Tom Hanks were among those mailing in the clips. As of the summer of 2004, the school had collected about 24 million paper clips. As of 2005, more were still coming in."

But where would they store the jars? The students wished to house them in a German cattle car as a museum of the Holocaust. Enter the Schroeders, German natives who were reporters and writers. They not only wrote about the story but also managed to procure a German cattle car for the project! We got to know the authors better when the two, Dagmar and Peter, who were not due at their next assignment for another day, became the guests of board member Alan Mindel at his Great Neck hotel. Dagmar Schroeder and I got to have lunch at Cold Spring Harbor and Peter Schroeder got to write his column.

*Mitsue Salador* held the audience enthralled as she described and showed a film about *Chiune Sugihara*, the Japanese Counsel to Lithuania. Sugihara destroyed his own career and put himself and his family in grave danger when from July through August of 1940, he disobeyed his country's orders and issued more than 2,000 transit visas to Jewish refugees that enabled them to escape to Shanghai via Russia. *Mitsue* had her own story. Her family was forced to spend World War II as internees in an internment camp for American Japanese from the West Coast. Our library has an excellent novel, *Hotel on the Corner of Bitter and Sweet* by Jamie Ford partially based on a similar situation where the Chinese-American boy's Japanese-American sweetheart is deported with her family to an interment camp.

One of the most exciting and well-attended programs we ever had was when the then 95 year-young Dr. Ruth Gruber, famous journalist and photographer, discussed her book: *Haven*. Gruber is a journalist, writer, photographer and the youngest person ever to receive a doctorate from a German university facilitating her being a witness to the early rise of Adolf Hitler. She is also the woman who shepherded 1,000 Jews to safety in Oswego, New York, told in her book: *Haven*. Although the U.S. Congress refused to lift the quota on Jewish immigration to the United States from Europe, probably due to Eleanor Roosevelt's pleading with her husband, President Franklin Delano Roosevelt, they were allowed to enter the United States and were kept in this emergency shelter in Oswego, New York until the end of the war, when they were, at last, able to apply for American residency.

**Chairs as Canvas** was one of our most exhilarating projects. It gained us publicity and earned the Center a nice sum of money. Instead of sending the donated plastic stacking shell chairs formerly used in our auditorium, to the town dump because more slender donated chairs were replacing them, we invited Long Island artists to paint a chair or two that would then be sold to benefit the Center. The project served to publicize the library's collection of art books, got us publicity in the local newspapers and produced chair-art. Beverly Nassau helped with that project. The shell-shaped plastic chairs were repainted and decorated by Long Island's artists in a cheerful vein that envisioned recovery and starting a new life. Ellyn Sheidlower, a quilter and artist, painted a chair with a country quilt-like theme that I immediately purchased.

**The Fabric of Their Lives** was another museum-worthy project conceived by our members and held at the Center. We asked our survivors to tell their stories of rescue to fabric artists. Margaret Goldberger, a Kinder (as those who had been in the *Kindertransport* were called), brought in 3 quilts made by members of their organization, the KTA (Kinder Transport Association). Annie Bleiberg, Wilma Diamond, Inge Gurevitch and I, embarked on the project, creating six fabric art scenes. Ellyn Sheidlower, a member of the *Long Island Study Group* of the *Pomegranate Guild*, arranged for her group to gather their own survivor testimony through interviews and books. They created 7 more wall hangings. All were exhibited at the Center during the month of December in 2008 and were given ample press PR, most notably in Newsday. Ray of RTS, (printers), donated the descriptive signage (as it has donated the cover to this book).

Other innovative programs and art exhibits throughout the years contributed to our attracting more press and visitors to the Center, but none more than the three years when our Center joined with the other historic home/museums on Long Island in presenting *Living History*. These were re-enactments of the lives of the families who had lived in the mansions in the early 1900s. We did 6 performances of *"Becoming the Pratts"* for 3 successive years. Each year we dramatized a different time period.

### *The Pratts of Glen Cove in World War I and the Roaring 20s; The Pratts of Glen Cove in the Great Depression of the 30s; and The Pratts of Glen Cove During World War II.*

A setting at the far end of the "art exhibits room" (which is now the "classroom,") was assembled to represent the era and focus of each play. We wore clothing appropriate for the period. In fact, the audience who sat on folding chairs in concentric rows often got confused between then and now; everything was so realistic. The configuration of the rooms resembled the original more than now. A docent who was "Mrs. Pratt's secretary" would show visitors to their seats.

*Marcia Posner, Jolanta Zamecka, Gloria Jackel, Karl Heiman,*
*Jay Feldman and Anrold Sheidlower*

Meanwhile, we intelligent, but middle-aged plus professionals, had no trouble in absorbing the history that I had researched and presented to them, but none of us could memorize the dialogue of the script. So we just did "Improv." We were so realistic that the audience was completely captured and paid attention to every word of the play. Arnold Sheidlower was always "Mr. Pratt" and Jolanta Zamecka, Mrs. Pratt. (Arnold was our "book-lecturer" as well as a docent and actor. He was beloved by all and is missed very much.)

The ringing of the phone by an "urgent" phone call interrupted the play at a most dramatic moment, startling the audience. This was accomplished by an actor's surreptitious pressing the tail of a brass turtle while another actor picked up the earpiece of a fancy period phone to answer it and looking worried. At this surprise ending of the play, the docent would return and "tactfully" lead the audience on a tour through the mansion ending at our Holocaust exhibits. These presentations were exceedingly successful; audiences paid to attend each performance. Each year we had 2 performances a day for 3 days. Children went free.

At the third and final play dramatizing World War II, another startling effect was achieved when the anti-Semitic harangue of the despicable

Jew-hater Father Coughlin could be heard coming from a period looking oak radio, interrupting the Pratts and their friends' serious conversation. A facsimile of an old radio with a slit in its side that accommodated CDs accomplished this. I had inserted a CD of the notorious Father Coughlin. What a shock it was when Coughlin's screaming voice with its anti-Semitic rant interrupted the family's discussion of the war and boys whom they knew who were fighting in it. Tickets were only $5.00 each; children went free. Once gain, we appeared in all the local newspapers. Too bad it wasn't televised.

## A Visit From the Pratts

We once hosted the Pratt Family descendants who, that year, included our Holocaust Center on their annual cemetery and remaining Pratt homes tour. At first, we wanted to prepare chicken salad sandwiches for them but

when we called the agency handling the day's arrangements, they said not to. There would be 50 people coming and besides "they were going to have lunch in their mausoleum!" It was a hot day, so we prepared pitchers of refreshing lemonade and ice tea and had cookies set out on our long glass table for their refreshment, of which they most enthusiastically partook.

This was the time of the previous exhibit, of course, not the one we have now. Gloria Jackel and I straightened every photo, dusted their frames and the chair rails, the fireplaces and swept the floors. We also took them on a tour of the Center that still resembled the former mansion and explained the story of the Holocaust to them along the way. One of our visitors was Harriet Pratt's granddaughter. She leaned over to us and said that her grandmother would have been so pleased at the present use of her home. Harriet Pratt was a high-minded woman with empathy for civic affairs, history and the disadvantaged, and so were their immediate ancestors beginning with Charles Pratt, the founder of the family fortune, and certainly by Harold, his son and former owner of our home. Sometimes, I feel that we were directed to their home by some mysterious force to use it for good the way we do.

## Readers Theater Presentations

2002 was also the year that the books in the library came alive through Readers Theater presentations. We dramatized the story: *The Golem of Auschwitz* from the book *Black Grass* by Dr. Bernard Otterman. It was wonderful. The author and his wife were in the audience. Afterwards, Mrs. Otterman told me that tears were rolling down her husband's cheeks.

With a little encouragement and rehearsal, the members of the board of the *Council for Social Justice of The Sons of Italy*, performed an original play, *It Happened in Italy*, adapted for them from the book: *It Happened in Italy* by Betty Bettina, which is in our library. The play starred Vincent Marmorale as the grandfather, our student-intern, Hannah Skopicki as his querulous grandchild, and the CSJ board. This non-fiction book describes how Italian villagers and a priest helped Jews who although interned in their mountain village were never confined. After checking in daily with the mayor in the morning and evening, they were free to roam the town often mixing with its citizens or getting into a card game.

Bettina's book was inspired by her grandmother's stories and by our former survivor-testifier, the charming Walter Wolff, plus Bettina's own investigation. Walter was a German Jew, who with his mother and brother, fled Germany and found shelter in Italy during the war. Additional books found in the library and by computer research on the topic, further enhanced the stories. Many of the citizens of Southern Italy are probably descended from Jews who fled Spain and never admitted that they were Jews, yet have a feeling about Jews that they can't explain. Other Italians may have had less benevolent attitudes towards the Jews, but none in the little villages of which we have read.

*Gloria Jackel, Marcia Posner, Emily Berkowitz, Gail Kastenholz,*
*Charlene Noll (Director of the Hillside Public Library),*
*Beverly Nassau, Anita Weisbord, and Robert Samson*
*posing after the performance of "Smoke and Mirrors."*

Our most ambitious Readers' Theater production was *Smoke and Mirrors: Delusion and Despair: The Story of Terezin.* Long Island libraries have an annual event called: "All Long Island Reads." The committee selects one book. In 2002, the selected book was *The Lost Wife* by Alyson Richman. It takes place in Terezin, the ghetto waiting room to Auschwitz in which were interned some of the brightest and most talented Jews of Europe. The Long Island libraries called me at our Holocaust Center library to ask for survivors to testify regarding Terezin. I told them that at present we had no one currently available, but would call them the following week. Then I remembered that in our catalogue, we have listed many memoirs written by Terezin survivors. From these, using the exact words of the memoirs, my colleagues and I fashioned a play that we performed on site in 15 public libraries. I used some of those books for the narration and others for the dialogue. This demonstrates that libraries are living places whose citizens, the books residing on the shelves, are granted eternal life.

As the actors, including myself, became too tired to continue daily performances, our friends, Camilla and Enrico Annichiarico and Margery Moschella from the *Sons of Italy: Council for Social Justice*, came to our aid and performed the parts of Jews living on borrowed time. Robert Samson, a Jew from B'nai B'rith, played the part of a Nazi, and Shelley Friedman, drafted from B'nai B'rith, also stepped in to relieve us from our strenuous daily performance schedule. In the Spring of 2014, we will perform the same play: *Smoke and Mirrors: Delusion and Despair: The Story of Terezin* at the Shelter Rock Jewish Center in observance of *Yom Hashoah, (Day of the Holocaust)*. We read from scripts dramatically. We do not charge for admittance, but it gains us publicity and usually a substantial donation. We have not yet performed at our Center, but perhaps, someday we shall.

# Exhibits

# Displaced Persons Camps: Rebuilding Culture and Community in the Aftermath of World War II

When Lillian Gewirtzman displayed and discussed her stunning exhibit on the *Displaced Persons Camp* in Ulm, Germany where she and her family had lived from 1945 to 1948, programs describing the Displaced Persons Camp were held on Sundays during the whole month. Owing to the intervention of General Eisenhower and President Truman who saved Jewish survivors from having to share the Displaced Persons Camps with survivors who were anti-Semites, the Jews had an opportunity to heal and recover some semblance of themselves. Religious services began to be held and representatives from the Jewish Joint Distribution Committee, commonly known as "the Joint" were on hand to help. Representatives of Zionist Organizations came to enrich their lives, teach them Hebrew and encourage them to emigrate to the Israeli Yishuv and the agricultural training camps.

There were also theater and other entertainments, mainly Zionist in flavor. ORT (the Organization for Rehabilitation through Training) trained the residents in skills that would be useful in the countries to which they hoped to emigrate. Lillian taught younger children in the school within the camp. Anxious to obtain more education, she actually attended a German high school outside the camp when she barely was able to speak the language. Many years later, Lillian resumed her friendships with two friends from the camp: Ada Gracin, one of our survivors who testifies, and another, Miriam Hoffman, an actress and professor who is now Lillian's neighbor and close friend in Riverdale, New York.

In one of our CENTERNEWS issues, Lillian wrote these words:

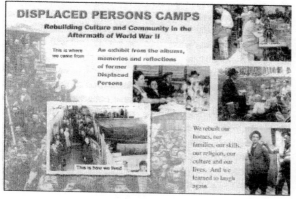

"On September 8, 1951, when I boarded the converted military vessel SS General Stuart for the United States, I left my Displaced Persons Camp in Feldafing and my high school in Munich, vowing never to return to that cursed land. Yet, on May 18, 2004, I stood on the podium of the Jewish Community Center in Munich as a guest of the Bavarian State Archives, addressing an audience of German educators, state officials, museum curators and former Jews who have made Germany their permanent home. Along the walls of the hall stood an elbow formation of tables set for a lavish reception featuring hot and cold canapés, fruit and wine; downstairs on the walls of a small Jewish museum hung the 20 panel photo documentary–the DP Camp exhibit which I had put together for our Center in 2003."

Lillian spoke in German to her audience, some of them titled. She did not expect to return to Germany again, but then the Mayor of Ulm in Germany desperately wanted Lillian to come to Ulm with her exhibit for the town's special anniversary, and finally, she agreed. Her return to Ulm Germany, with her husband David, as guests of its current mayor was described in our CENTERNEWS.

"On January 24th, 2008, during a paralyzing snow storm, David and I arrived in Ulm; this time at the behest of the Oberburgermeister–the mayor, Ivo Goenner, who made it his mission to ensure that the city would never forget their past history. During the 5 years that the city of Ulm hosted 5 D.P. camps, my family and I had spent 2 years in one of them, "Sedan Kaserne." The day after we arrived, we found my exhibit prominently displayed on the walls of the Town Hall. That night, speaking in German, I addressed a large audience. The tourist office told us that the exhibit was attracting a large audience. 4,500 people had viewed it in the past 4 weeks. The respect with which the town of Ulm treated the exhibit was unprecedented. Stenciled on a wall in huge letters was a German translation of the summary paragraph from the last panel of the exhibit: "We Are No Longer Displaced."

A brochure bearing a full translation of the narrative was made available to the public and a film documentary was running continually on the screen of a small TV. Numerous brochures of town events featured the exhibit, giving full credit to our Holocaust Center. People were curious about it. David and Lillian became the guides for the exhibit and participated in an interactive event with members of the audience who asked challenging questions and contributed their own thoughts. 7000 Jewish Displaced Persons, "DPs," had once lived in Ulm, yet most of its citizens were hearing about it for the first time. Some Germans, perhaps trying to atone for their country's past crimes, had spent summers in Israel, learned Hebrew and a few were making attempts at Yiddish. Lillian said:" For the first time, I was able to see the damage that Hitler has done to his own people." The DP exhibit toured many locations in the United States.

## 2002, THE 10th ANNIVERARY OF THE HOLOCAUST MEMORIAL AND EDUCATION CENTER OF NASSAU COUNTY–

The "Boris Chartan Decade" was ending and we who were with him from the start had mixed feelings over the inevitable. We were happy with what we had. Would we be happy with the changes? Time would tell. Chairman Boris Chartan was preparing to hand over the mantle of leadership to Howard Maier, the following year. County Executive and Glen Cove neighbor Thomas R. Suozzi greeted us at the 10th Anniversary of the Holocaust Memorial and Education Center of Nassau County. Honorees included: Cookie and Murray Slimowitz, Jolanta and Edward Zamecki, in regard for their being in the vanguard of the Children's Memorial Garden. Susie and Lawrence Kadish would be equally honored another year. In addition, my library colleague, Gloria Jackel was the recipient of the Bruce Morrell Educational Award.

Meanwhile, congratulatory letters were coming in. The letter from the Bishop of Rockville Centre says it all.

DIOCESE OF ROCKVILLE CENTRE
OFFICE OF THE BISHOP

Mr. Boris Chartan, President
The Holocaust Memorial and Educational
Welwyn Preserve
100 Crescent Beach Road
Glen Cove, NY 11542

Dear Mr. Chartan:

The ten years since the Center's founding have sadly shown how important is your work. The world has seen no diminishment of hatred based on religion, race and culture. The evils of religious bigotry have grown into ever new examples of violence. We here in the United States have seen all too clearly that are not immune to the effects of this hatred.

In the face of this reality, your Center stands as a bright beacon of hope. The thousands of students who visit you each year, the deep dedication of your staff, the great generosity of your supporters, such as those we honor tonight, all testify to the impact for good you have accomplished on Long Island and beyond.

We remember those whose vision has made this good work possible. Rabbi Fenster and Bishop McGann, working with County Executive Gulotta, embraced a vision of respect, tolerance and understanding that survivors such as yourself presented to the people of our communities. You must surely take well deserved satisfaction on this anniversary. I pray that the work of the Center will continue to prosper. May it continue to be a source of deeper understanding and respect for all our neighbors.

With my prayers and best wishes, I am

Sincerely yours
William F. Murphy
Bishop of Rockville Centre

November 18, 2002

Dear Friends,

I am pleased to greet all of you who have gathered to celebrate the 10th Anniversary of The Holocaust Memorial and Educational Center of Nassau County. This year's event gives us the opportunity to recognize the contributions of five outstanding people: Cookie & Murray Slimowitz, Jolanta and

Edward Zamecki, and Gloria Jackel. These honorees are being honored for their dedication to the successful fruition of a Children's Memorial Garden. The Center is to be commended for providing the means through which selfless acts of public service can be demonstrated. I would like to thank all of you who work toward forwarding the goals of the Holocaust Memorial Center throughout the year as they establish the importance of faith, family and continuity in our neighborhoods. It is with your help and example that we will make Nassau the "Best County in the Country."

Sincerely,

Thomas R. Suozzi
County Executive

# PART II

## THE HOLOCAUST MEMORIAL AND TOLERANCE CENTER: 2003-2013

HMTC is moving ahead on many fronts.

*From L to R: NY State Assemblyman Charles Lavine,*
*Stanley Sanders, New York Senator Kirsten Gillibrand, Howard Maier,*
*Steve Markowitz and David Gewirtzman*

# INTRODUCTION

## HISTORY REPEATS ITSELF:
Jed Morey*

I T HAS BEEN stated so often that the answers we seek to the problems that plague humankind can be found in history that the statement itself sounds hollow. Yet nothing rings true more than the wisdom that comes from understanding history, for it is knowledge that prevents us from repeating horrific mistakes and connects us with our humanity.

The educators and docents at the Holocaust Memorial and Tolerance Center of Nassau County (HMTC) are not simply history teachers. They do not approach the Holocaust as a singular event to be remembered through photographs and accounts relegated to the history books. Rather, they bring the Holocaust to life through the faces and voices of both the oppressed and the oppressors, and challenge visitors to see themselves through both lenses.

Just as we cannot appreciate current catastrophic circumstances without understanding the path that led us to them, the Holocaust cannot be viewed as a moment in time. It was a confluence of political and societal events and attitudes that brought about the Holocaust. While our political circumstances may differ today, many of the attitudes that were pervasive in Europe prior to the period we identify as the Holocaust, stubbornly remain embedded in modern culture. Addressing them begins with identifying them and explaining their significance to those who might otherwise ignore them or misinterpret their meaning. That is what we aim to do.

*Jed Morey, publisher, Long Island Press and HMTC Board Member*

# CHAPTER 9

## HOWARD MAIER, CHAIR EXTRAORDINAIRE

**P**ROLOGUE–FEW WOULD HAVE predicted the power and ambition of Hitler and the Nazi forces. Even for those who did, leaving Europe was well nigh impossible for most Jews. Those who could afford to leave and to obtain a visa, may not have wanted to abandon their businesses, hoping for a change in the political situation. Others had the funds but few countries would accept immigrants, including the strictly isolationist United States. Dr. Arlette Sanders, a member of our Advisory Board, recently sent me an interesting article from an unpublished doctoral thesis: "Prologue: LBJ's Foreign Affairs Background, 1908-1948." It appears that Lyndon B. Johnson, while serving as a young Democratic congressman in 1938 and 1939, arranged for visas to be supplied to Jews in Warsaw. He also oversaw the illegal immigration of hundreds of Jews through the port of Galveston, Texas. (1989, by Louis Gomolak a University of Texas student)

Howard's Maier's father, the youngest of 5 children, did manage to leave. He emigrated to America at age 17. As life deteriorated further for the Jews of Germany, the girl who would some day become Howard's mother, also left her family. She went to England to work as a domestic, gaining entry to the United States after 3 years. The two met in the United States and married in 1945 and Howard was born the following year. The family settled in Manhattan's Upper West Side in Washington Heights, as did other German Jewish refugees. A member of what we call the "Second Generation," meaning children of survivors, Howard entered first grade speaking only German.

Several of Howard's relatives managed to escape from Germany. Five family members, including his paternal grandparents and cousin Sonia, were on the Saint Louis, the ship that departed Germany in February of 1939 with 900 Jewish passengers possessing visas to go to Cuba. Arriving at Havana, they were not allowed to leave the ship; Cuba was no longer accepting their visas. The ship then went to Miami and continued to several other United States ports. Its passengers were refused entry at all ports. President Roosevelt was more interested in getting reelected and not alienating the isolationist Southern Democrats, than he was in saving Jewish lives.

The German captain tried his best to find safe harbor for his passengers but after 40 days at sea, running short of food and other supplies, the ship turned to return to Europe. Meanwhile, in the dark periods of the Third Reich and afterwards, the Joint Distribution Committee (the JDC), a Jewish rescue and aid organization, was the symbol of hope for hundreds of thousands of refugees. Only through the Joint could powerless Jews in the United States be able to somewhat help save the lives of the Jews doomed to destruction. Jews in the United States donated funds to help the Joint's frantic efforts to wire money to various European countries trying to get them to allow the passengers to disembark. Dr. Joseph J. Schwartz, a rabbi from Baltimore, had become the head of "the Joint" in Europe. In 1941, on the eve of the "Final Solution," he directed a rescue and relief effort from his office in Lisbon, Portugal. Undertaken in coordination with every imaginable resource, it was an effort that would ultimately play a key role in the salvation of tens of thousands of lives and possibly was joined by Aristedes de Sousa Mendes. As far as the St. Louis passengers were concerned, only those who disembarked in England, Howard's family among them, were assured of survival. Of the passengers who had to return to Europe, 500 perished. In time, Howard's family obtained visas and were able to continue to the United States. Sonia Maier, Howard's cousin, helped Sarah Ogilvie and Scott Miller, researchers at the USHMM, the United States Holocaust Memorial Museum in Washington, D.C., to trace the survivors of the St. Louis who are listed at the back of the book, *Refuge Denied: The Saint Louis Passengers and the Holocaust.*

~ ~ ~ ~ ~ ~ ~ ~ ~ ~

By 1998, the Holocaust Memorial and Educational Center had two able, intelligent men, both retired businessmen, both wanting to do their best for the Center. Boris Chartan, a survivor, had succeeded in his goal of establishing an educational center where survivors and docents could teach school children, teachers, and adults about what happened in the Holocaust. Howard Maier, a member of the Second Generation, was ready to take it one step further. Once he had visited the Center, he began to apply himself to learning as much as he could about the Holocaust. A superb autodidact, in a few years, he was well learned but anxious to learn more. He believed that he could and would raise the funds to install a state-of-art exhibit at the Center, one that would relate the story of the Holocaust in an authentic, clear and dramatic way. He offered his services to Boris who graciously accepted his help and invited him to serve on the Education Committee with David Gewirtzman and Richard Weilheimer. They too, were bent on modernizing the Center's exhibits.

Howard was soon invited to join the Board of Directors. One year later, by November 1999, at the 7th Annual Tribute Dinner, he was awarded the Center's Humanitarian Award. Howard's father-in-law, former Governor Mario Cuomo, was the keynote speaker. The evening was a resounding success with a huge attendance. By 2003, the Board elected Howard to be Vice-Chairman with the understanding that a year later he would  become Chairman. During that one year, between accepting the position of Vice Chairman and until he would become Chairman, Howard became an ardent student of the history of the Holocaust.

In order to formulate his vision for the future of the Center, he set several goals for himself. The first was to go beyond his own family's story to learn more about the Holocaust. Next, he was eager to explore the exhibits of the finest Holocaust institutions in order to guide what he hoped would be our future state-of-the art Holocaust exhibit. He also wanted to learn how, beyond their exhibits, these institutions were serving their communities. He attended Holocaust education conferences and visited almost a dozen Holocaust museums in the United States, sometimes accompanied by board member Marty Levine, including the United States Holocaust Memorial Museum in Washington, D.C. and regional Holocaust centers in Houston, Tampa, Richmond, Montreal, Spring Valley, the Museum of Jewish Heritage in New York City and the Simon Wiesenthal Tolerance Centers in both New York and Los Angeles, developing relationships with the Directors of each. Chairman, Howard, with his wife Dr. Margaret Cuomo Maier and survivor/teacher Gloria Glantz, also visited Poland and followed it with a visit to *Yad Vashem*, Israel's national Holocaust Center in Jerusalem.

Upon becoming Chairman in 2004, Howard presented an action plan to the Executive Committee of the Board of Directors. It was the culmination of his learning experiences during his visits to the other museums. He set himself the following goals to provide leadership and as a guide for himself and the organization. It would also help him estimate the funds that would be needed to accomplish them.

1. To evolve the Board from a "Board of Directors" to a "Board of Governance;"

2. To have a state-of-the-art museum presenting the history of the Holocaust in a compelling manner, incorporating audio-visual testimony from the Holocaust survivors on Long Island;

3. To raise sufficient funds for an expanded staff of experienced professionals who would provide additional educational programming;

4. To train docents, survivors and facilitators to provide consistent accurate teaching of Holocaust history;

5. To augment and improve the types of education provided to children and to adults.

Gradually, it was also decided to change the name of the Center from "The Holocaust Memorial and Educational Center" to the "Holocaust Memorial and Tolerance Center." The change of name recognized the Center's inclusion of tolerance issues, a subject that had long been discussed in Holocaust museum circles. In the book: *Holocaust: Religious & Philosophical Implications*, edited by John K. Roth and Michael Berenbaum, (Paragon House, 1989) various emotions are described among the 11 contributors: Elie Wiesel insisted that a rhetoric of remembrance which is not matched by a practical commitment to human rights is empty . . ." (p.10); Emil Fackenheim, without referring to other historical events, wrote that "remembering the Holocaust is more than an educational necessity, it is a sacred duty."

~ ~ ~ ~ ~ ~ ~ ~ ~ ~ ~ ~ ~

# Goal # 1–The Board of Directors

Howard's fulfillment of his first goal was most interesting. What is the difference between a "Board of Directors" and a "Board of Governors?" The Center has always had a respected and dedicated Board of Directors. I especially remember when Jack Stein, who had advised presidents, sat on our board; we were so proud to have him. Several board members had specific functions. I was the librarian and Walter Stern was the writer and so on. Boris Chartan was the president who informed us of what was happening and what were the future plans. We might make some comments and offer suggestions, but when a vote was taken, I don't remember any disagreement.

The complexion of our present board is different and has grown more numerous. What we had in the past was an interested, intelligent and diligent board of directors who were cooperative and free with their ideas and suggestions, but were nothing like the type of "power" board that Howard Maier organized years later. The by-laws were changed several times to allow the board to grow to 39 members from 15 as called for previously. Over the years, the Board was expanded both numerically and according to influence wielded. Each new member brought something to the mix, either by themselves or by access to others who possessed "power." Howard paid careful attention to what and how each one could contribute to the Center, in wisdom, of course, but also in the realms of finance, influence and profession. This has resulted in a much more diverse and powerful board. Now we are partners, not only followers.

Howard attracted business and community leaders, including Michael Dowling, CEO of the North Shore LIJ Health System, the largest employer on Long Island. Another notable Board member is

the former County Executive Thomas Gulotta, a close friend of Boris Chartan. If you remember, it was Tom Gulotta who was instrumental in securing a property that would be suitable for our purposes. Howard also welcomed Reverend Reginald Tuggle of St. Paul Community Church, the largest Black congregation on Long Island; and when, after serving on the Board for 5 years, the Reverend moved to North Carolina, Howard recommended Reverend Roger William of the First Baptist Church in Glen Cove. Today's Board leadership was largely recruited during this period, including Vice-Chairman David Rosen, Treasurer who has also chaired the popular Golf Tournament, Jerry Sloan; Secretary, Bernard Vishnick, Esq.; and other key members of the Executive Committee, including: Peter Klein, Ron Brunell and Jed Morey.

*David Rosen (to the right) and Golf Buddies*

Howard carefully selected his "Executive Committee," the segment of the board that handles debatable decisions and policy issues before they come before the larger board and also decides if they will. Some board members resent this, but there are times when it may be better to discuss the ramifications of a decision and plan accordingly with a smaller group before it is brought to the whole board.

For instance, many years ago, when the Center and its board were rather new and our funds meager, a board member asked for a donation of $1,000 to another organization. It was to be used to bring a Holocaust exhibit to the Jews of Cuba. No one knew anything about it beforehand and with only a brief explanation we were asked for a vote on this expenditure. What did we have to do with Cuba? Or the other organization? Even though he explained it, his request to an unprepared board for a donation of $1,000 was refused. At that time in our history the project seemed superfluous to our main concerns plus a strain on our budget. Only recently, did I request the entire story of this strange episode. Now, having the time to digest it, I regret my negative vote. I imagine that had it happened with the current board, a full history of the situation would have first been heard and discussed at the executive board, which might have resulted in a different vote. It is a great story and I take the liberty of relating it to you here.

Note: this was loosely translated from the Spanish:

"While in Cuba several years ago, my wife and I visited the president of the Jewish Community of Santa Clara. I became possessed by a desire to bring an understanding of the magnitude of the Holocaust to Cuban Jews. In this I received much help in the United States from the Jewish Museum of Los Angeles, Yad Vashem in Israel, the Organization of Jewish Solidarity and many others. I hope that this exhibit helps Cubans to understand what happens when a society loses its tolerance values."

(Photograph of the monument follows on the next page)

Monumento al Holocausto, Santa Clara, Cuba

It seems that years ago, one of our board members, upon visiting Santa Clara, a predominantly Jewish city in Cuba, through the auspices of the *Jewish Solidarity Organization*, learned that Cuban people, including Jews, had no idea of why Israel should be so important to the Jews. To demonstrate the need for Jews to have an Israel, a land of their own, our board member and his wife offered to supply a Holocaust exhibit for these Cuban Jews that would demonstrate that had there been an Israel as a haven and defender, what had happened to the Jews of Europe would not have occurred. His plan was to have the exhibit financed by several people and/or organizations. Enlisting the help of *Yad Vashem*, he ordered an exhibit of the Holocaust constructed that he intended to bring back to Santa Clara piece by piece. It was very "cloak and dagger."

Each piece had to be carried in separately by different groups assembled by Jewish Solidarity. They hired a curator from a large established Holocaust museum and began the task of putting the exhibit together in Cuba. Funds were collected from various associations and our board member assumed that his Holocaust Center would be proud to be part of this project as well. The project continued, but without our participation. On opening day, some 500 Cubans visited the exhibit and after one month, it was shipped to the Patranato Center in Havana, the second largest city of Cuba.

~ ~ ~ ~ ~ ~ ~ ~ ~ ~ ~ ~ ~ ~

In the meantime, back at the Center, we were progressing towards Howard Maier's Goal #2–to redo the Holocaust Center's exhibits.

## Goal # 2–To Have a State of the Art Museum

The committee realized that before a new museum exhibit could be created, they first had to renovate the building. The Harold and Harriet Pratt mansion was built in 1904 and needed major repairs and upgrading. Among other things, the building needed air conditioning, central heating, upgraded bathrooms, including a "handicapped bathroom," plumbing, a sprinkler system, the electrical system and an elevator. In order to accomplish this goal Howard continued  and improved upon the close working relationship the Center had with Nassau County, the owner of the building. The County agreed to infrastructure upgrades for central heating and air conditioning, and secured federal funds to install an elevator to make the building handicap accessible. Howard's choice of a supervisor for the project was beautiful petite Marlene Ostroff, seen on the previous page with a workman and Marcia Posner. Before Marlene retired to raise two daughters, her profession was to train staff worldwide in the use of her employer's computer programs. So in addition to overseeing the renovation, she was our "computer techie" and soon also our "Accounts Payable" person. She quickly learned the language of construction and before long could be seen discussing problems and solutions with the architect, David Swift, with technicians and workmen. How I enjoyed seeing Marlene in the hall in earnest discussion with a tall broad shouldered workman concerning a construction issue.

When Marlene and I met for lunch, I asked her for a quote for this current book. She replied:

> "I was inspired by Howard's vision to create a world class Holocaust museum. I also wanted to be part of an organization that made a difference in the world."

> *Marlene Ostroff,*
> *May, 2013*

Realizing that he had to raise $2,000,000 from the Board plus other donors to address the remainder of the building renovations and the creation of the new museum, Howard obtained major pledges from Board members Russell Stern, Alan Mindel, Howard Brous, Isadore Mayrock, and Frank Lalezarian. Additional funds were received from many others, including a $100,000 grant from New York State. Howard and his wife, Dr. Margaret Cuomo Maier and Stanley and Phyllis Sanders increased their commitments as well. Then, something like a miracle happened and her name was Claire Friedlander—her emissary—Peter Klein.

Peter Klein was a friend of David Rosen. David Rosen, the Board's current Vice Chairman, had just joined the Center's Board. At his first Center Board meeting, David presented a check for $50,000 to the

Center. It came from his friend, Peter Klein on behalf of Peter's client, Claire Friedlander, a Holocaust survivor. Howard had met Peter Klein a year earlier when David Rosen introduced them. After Ms. Friedlander died, Peter Klein became President of the Claire Friedlander Family Foundation. Knowing the Foundation's desire to promote tolerance and to teach the lessons of the Holocaust, Howard made a proposal to the Foundation for it to provide $1,200,000 to the capital campaign to finish the museum and to create an education center on the second floor that would become known as the Claire Friedlander Education Institute.

*Howard Maier and Peter Klein*

The proposal was accepted. It forever changed the landscape of the Center. It included $400,000 to be used toward the museum renovation: the total

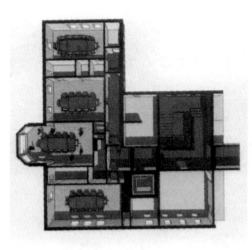

revamping of the entire main floor into a state–of–the–art exhibit space that included video testimony by our survivors, the expansion of the library, plus an archives room for artifacts. In addition, $800,000 would be used to construct the Claire Friedlander Education Institute and to build new offices for the staff in the former servants wing. Peter Klein presented the check to Chairman Howard Maier in a ceremony in the Children's Memorial Garden. It was a never-to-be forgotten event.

Howard had also asked the Foundation to pledge $500,000 over five years towards the Center's operating budget to fund "Education." Peter Klein suggested that this $100,000 annual pledge to the operating budget be used as a "matching grant." The Friedlander Family Foundation confirmed Howard's proposal to Peter; and the Center had its first "Angel."

## Claire Friedlander Foundation

The Friedlander Family Foundation is named for its benefactor.

Claire Friedlander passed away at the age of 98 in 2009. Ms. Friedlander, a child survivor of the Holocaust who was hidden with her parents for 3 years on a peasant family's farm, was well aware that she and her family survived only because of their hosts. Catholic peasants, they were among the "Righteous" of Europe who stepped in at great personal peril to do what they thought was right. This has had a vast influence on Ms. Friedlander and her family. Upon her grandmother's passing, her granddaughter reminded us that we all might take an example from the Catholics who saved her great grandparents and their child. As they were representative of those who, when they see any form of intolerance, step in to help to right a wrong being done, so too can we imitate their actions today, by stepping in to help those being bullied, victims of name calling or slang code words labeling a race, religion, and so on. Recent events on Long Island have demonstrated that we need to stand up and say something, rather than ignoring it and keep going. We need to apply our energy to everyday lives, becoming more tolerant and understanding; making connections with those who are different from us in our workplace, community, and school. We need to pursue the Claire Friedlander family's dream and become what HMTC calls "Upstanders," not "Bystanders." This is the goal of the Claire Friedlander Education Institute.

## Designing the Content for the New Exhibit

Howard assembled a committee to help plan the new museum. He wanted to present the history of the Holocaust in a compelling manner, incorporating audio-visual testimony from Long Island Holocaust survivors. It was a very exciting time. Leading committee members included Stanley Sanders, David Gewirtzman and Gloria Glantz.

The next step was to engage a design firm that would create an exciting tour for the Center. A committee was formed from local community leaders and members of the Center's Executive Board. An architect, David Swift, and a designer were engaged to assist in designing the changes for a new exciting tour at the Center. The firm, "Evidence Design," was selected. Its owners, Shari Berman and Jack Pascara, a husband and wife team of professional designers, had designed the Houston Holocaust Museum that Howard and board member Marty Levine had selected as the best designed museum in their "quest for the best." They had also designed for the United States Holocaust Museum in Washington, D.C.

Marlene Ostroff, reported in our CENTERNEWS, that upon examining the plans, the team's use of space in our old mansion "wowed" all of them.

Even from the plans of the new "Permanent Exhibit," one could feel the progress of a tragedy that was about to befall the Jewish people. The exhibit is designed in such a way as to provide a sense of drama and movement—this in our huge but solidly staid rooms. It is quite amazing. These angular galleries trace the development of the Holocaust from antisemitism to the rise of the Third Reich. They continue to the atrocities of Holocaust ghettos and death camps, and then on to other genocides. At some point, one gallery morphs into another related topic and ends with a plea for understanding and respect in our own communities. Holocaust artifacts were needed to "flesh out" each display; pleas for these are ongoing. Howard and the committee guided the designers to use testimony and artifacts from the survivors and rescuers who were affiliated with our Center and also requested that they have audio and video play a major role in the presentation.

Howard had already arranged for our survivors to be filmed and recorded so that even should they no longer be with us, their experiences and the lessons they taught would be continued. Many of our survivors are now gone and when I see their faces and hear their stories on the video screens embedded in the exhibits, I pause as I approach and cherish the fact that in a way, they are still with us and are still helping to educate the children and adults who come to our Center.

Once the Committee and the Board approved the plan, the firm of Stewart Senter Inc. was hired to do the renovation and construction work and Evidence Design to fabricate and create the exhibits. The Center was closed for the renovation and the installation of the new elevator for the handicapped. It was reopened in January 2010 after 18 months of renovations. Classes were held at other venues with the use of posters and media.

Despite the awkwardness of having to carry the visual components of our lessons to off-site locations, moving our teaching sites had some positive aspects, as well. It afforded the Center with the opportunity to become better known in venues that otherwise might not have heard of us or did not have the funds to bus their classes to us. Sending "portable" visuals and traveling lecturers to sites, in addition to those who are able to visit our magnificent state-of-the art exhibits, allows us to spread our programs further and might even be a project viewed favorably by granting organizations.

As Marlene describes, the galleries are arranged chronologically in an intrinsically exciting pattern of angles interspersed with showcases of relevant smaller items. The exhibit begins with larger than life photographs of the satisfying varieties of Jewish life before the Third Reich. It wends its way in an angular journey through the rooms of the first floor depicting

the Third Reich's escalating punishments rendered upon its "former" Jewish citizens and the step-by-step ruining of their lives. Some of the larger than life photographs mounted in dramatically angled panels have interesting showcases set into their rear. An early showcase depicts satirical children's books with illustrations of ugly money-grasping Jews. Later in the tour, a showcase holds ghetto money, passports, eyeglasses and so on. Televised testimonies by our survivors intersperse the static photographs.

The positive aspects of the era are also demonstrated: the Kindertransport, the "Righteous" Gentiles and Muslims who sheltered Jews, the Allied armies who liberated the camps, and the establishment of the Modern State of Israel.

Preceding the final gallery are photographs of other people who have suffered displacement, torture and death at the hands of their former countrymen: the Balkan States of Kosovo, Bosnia, Sarajevo; and in Africa, Darfur and Rwanda, for instance. This final section of our exhibit includes a televised conversation and tender interaction between an elderly white Jewish survivor of Poland, our inspirational David Gewirtzman and his almost daughter, the equally inspirational Jacqueline Murekatete, a young survivor of the Rwanda massacre. The story of their relationship and deeds will be told in Part III, Chapter 15.

Our mission had evolved unobtrusively from teaching solely about the Holocaust to also discussing injustices in other countries and teaching about how we should respond, how we can fight prejudice, hatred, bullying and apathy. As Irving Roth inferred 20 years ago with his theme: "From Prejudice to Genocide," the Holocaust could not have happened without prejudice. The exhibit demonstrates this. It provides a detailed chronicle of the Holocaust appropriate for visitors from 5th grade through adulthood and also deals with other genocides. The beautiful room where our library used to be now hosts traveling exhibits.

Three of the goals Howard had set himself were already in the process of being realized and the following two, goals #s 4 and 5, were set into action in short order.

In goal #4, Howard set about hiring a new Education Director. The Center's former Education Director, Regina White, was retiring. Howard embarked on a worldwide search for the finest Education Director he could find and her name is, Beth Lilach. Beth, a Holocaust scholar, became the new Director of Education and working with others, directed the content of the new exhibit.

In goal #5, "Education," Howard suggested that educational programs for adults as well as for children be initiated and/or enlarged. Beth Lilach's innovations are described in the following chapter by Dr. Arlette Sanders. Dr. Sanders' contribution is unique to Howard's new vision of Education at the Center. It is a program for adults in a workplace situation with a multicultural staff.

~ ~ ~ ~ ~ ~ ~ ~ ~ ~ ~

We recently received an exceptional archival gift from Nazi Prosecutor, Eli Rosenbaum. An invaluable documentary record of a unique trial and conviction, the Boleslavs Maikovskis case about a war crimes criminal hiding in the United States, is the first of its kind in the history of our country. Rosenbaum was able to have documented and photographed the handing over of the entire files of the Former Office of Special Investigation (OSI) to our Holocaust Center. Although the Nazis kept meticulous records, Eli Rosenbaum was equally meticulous in finding and interpreting them.

For almost every event, there is an interesting side story. Here, are two . . . . Rosenbaum grew up with the family of survivor-testifier Charlotte Gillman. He presented these irreplaceable records to our Center in honor of Charlotte Gillman and her husband Floyd who was Chairman of Music for 30 years at Elmont Memorial High School, in New York, which he attended. These records are a rare and precious enrichment to our archives. There is also a back-story—why Rosenbaum became a Nazi hunter, in the first place.

Rosenbaum became a Nazi hunter because he is a member of the Second Generation. When he was a child, the Holocaust was not mentioned in his home. It was too painful for his parents who had both fled Germany before the war. Rosenbaum's father returned to Germany, however, wearing a U.S. Army uniform. One weekend, a quarter of a century ago, when Eli and his father were driving through a blizzard, his father casually mentioned that he had been one of the first Americans to report on Dachau after its liberation in April 1945.

Eli said: "I asked my father: 'Well, what did you see?' I was looking out at the road and didn't hear anything. Finally, I looked at my father and saw that his eyes had welled with tears. His mouth was open like he wanted to speak, but he couldn't do it. He was crying. To the day he died, he never told me."

Eli Rosenbaum's father was surely on his mind as Eli, now the Director of the U.S. Human Rights and Special Prosecution Section of the Justice Department's Criminal Division, pursued the case, winning the deportation litigation against Maikovskis, enabling him to be deported and tried in Germany. It would be the first time that a Nazi criminal was found outside of Germany and returned to there to be tried. Since the trial dragged on for years, ultimately the German court decided that Maikovskis was not physically fit to stand trial. He died in Germany in April 1996. As Eli was a close friend of the Gillman family, having grown up with them and their children, this valuable archive was given in perpetuity to our Holocaust Center in honor of Charlotte Gillman and in memory of her late husband, Floyd Gillman, Chairman of Music for 30 years at Elmont Memorial High School in Elmont, NY.

~ ~ ~ ~ ~ ~ ~ ~ ~ ~ ~ ~ ~ ~

Joshua Greene, author and filmmaker, wrote the following :

"Since completing its renovations under the extraordinary leadership of board chairman Howard Maier, tens of thousands of students have taken the tour and heard moving presentations by survivors and other docents–including my students at Hofstra University. It is the highlight of the semester."

At the Center's 20th Anniversary we were honored to have Gov. Andrew Cuomo as guest speaker.

*Howard Maier and Governor Andrew Cuomo*

# CHAPTER 10

## EDUCATION: A NEW PHASE
## BETH LILACH

A T HTMC WE bring the Holocaust to life through the faces and voices of both the oppressed and the oppressors and challenge visitors to see themselves through both lenses. A substantial part of this is to be alert to what is happening today in our own communities. Are there echoes of prejudice and harassment in our neighborhoods similar to those found in Nazi Germany? Unfortunately, sometimes there are, and we must be on guard to prevent them and fight them. The Center searched for an Education Director who would be a leader in teaching the Holocaust and its implications.

An international search was conducted, chaired by Dr. Arlette Sanders. Our efforts resulted in hiring an American, Beth Lilach, as Director of Education in 2007. Beth had completed her Holocaust and Genocide Studies courses at Clark University's Strassler Center, teaching about the Holocaust for the past 20 years. Six months later, Sarah Cushman, also from the Strassler program, was hired to assist her as Senior Director of Youth Operations. HMTC programs were separated to better focus on the needs and requirements of each with both Beth Lilach as well as Sarah Cushman employed as full–scale education directors.

*Beth Lilach, Senior Director of*
*Education and Community Affairs*

Beth addresses the needs of colleges, universities, community units and organizations.

In the 7 years since she arrived, in addition to correcting and guiding our exhibits, she has solved troublesome issues and enriched the reputation and accomplishments of the Education Department. Beth has made contacts all over the world, including valuable links with the World Council on Jewish Studies and the Education Director of the new Hong Kong & Macau Holocaust and Tolerance Center who intends to pattern their new Center on ours. In Houston, she initiated creation of a Northeast Alliance of Holocaust Centers including: HMTC, Rhode Island, Maine, and Rochester; others will be invited. Our working partnerships with many prestigious organizations, colleges, and just "plain folks" in far flung locations as well as locally, can be attributed to Beth. She is held in high regard at *Yad Vashem* in Israel. We are very proud of her.

Beth began her term at the Center by making adjustments to former procedures and presentations, for instance, the training of docents. During Irving Roth's time at the Center at least three days of classes were set aside to train new docents. The library supplied them with books written for teaching about the Holocaust and the new docents were urged to attend subsequent events held for teachers and department heads. Dr. Regina White and Linda Finn also had classes for training docents and she and her teachers' council prepared books to refresh their memories and advise on teaching techniques,

## *Renee Katz and Sheila Rind*

Beth trains all docents to be consistent throughout the tour and to match their narrations to what is shown in the new exhibits. An intensive 5-Day Course in the history and background of the Holocaust is held periodically. Workshops train facilitators and survivors in how to present the prescribed narrations. Following this instruction, docents-in-training trail experienced docents until the newcomers feel comfortable and secure. Even though our docents hew to a standardized narration, the very nature of the exhibit calls forth emotion on the part of the docent and viewers. Here are two examples from one of our finest docents, Sheila Rind.

It was a July 4th weekend. Everyone else was away, so Sheila Rind's husband Nate volunteered to be the receptionist. The entrance of a group of 11 rambunctious tourists interrupted the quiet of the afternoon. Here for a wedding, they were staying at the Harrison House, a former Pratt mansion but now a hotel and were amusing themselves by exploring the neighborhood. Looking around and spying the large photograph of Charlotte Gillman and her family, one called out: "Anna Frank" "Anna Frank." The rest then entered the first gallery and so did Sheila. She started to explain that it was not Anne Frank and her family, but our own Charlotte Gilman and *her* family. The problem was that the group spoke in Italian, which Sheila did not. One of their group spoke English and as Sheila took them on a tour in her usual heartfelt empathetic manner, reliving for the group the trials that people were forced to bear, the English speaker translated, evidently just as sincerely. Not a sound could be heard except for Sheila's narrative and its translation. At the end of the tour, all were moved and exhausted. The communication between docent and guests was so clear that one said in Italian: "We thought we could suddenly understand English," to which Sheila replied, "And I thought that I spoke Italian."

*Charlotte Gillman and Family*

The second story that Sheila shared with me was the time she offered to guide a man and woman waiting in the lobby. The wife was a patient at the Helen Keller Institute and so essentially, Sheila was giving the tour to the husband, but he would translate Sheila's narrative by tapping on his wife's palm at each station to communicate with her. Sheila led and explained and the husband tapped and translated for one and one/half hours. At the end of the tour, the husband thanked Sheila and the woman hugged her. Leaning into Sheila's ear, with a great effort, she whispered "Thank you." Sheila has never forgotten such experiences and the great blessing it is to be a docent at this Center. She couldn't help but think, however, that had this woman been in Nazi Germany, she might have been murdered.

~ ~ ~ ~ ~ ~ ~ ~ ~ ~

In her presentation to the Association of Holocaust Organizations, Beth discussed 4 challenges that we face today in Holocaust education, and their solutions.

## Challenge #1-Tackling the problem of the aging of our survivor population

Solution: Organizing second generation and even third generation volunteers to reprise their family's Holocaust experiences has solved the problem of the diminishing number of our survivors. The Second Gens are becoming the heart of the Center.

## Challenge #2–Making the Holocaust relevant to young visitors and teens

To combat apathy and validate the relevance of the Holocaust, we must remind them that prejudice and indifference allowed the Holocaust to happen. The Holocaust has been made more relevant to young visitors by explaining that the challenges of the Holocaust are reflected to a lesser degree by challenges in which some teens feel threatened by their peers from bullying and ostracism abetted by social media. Prejudice and indifference allowed the Holocaust to happen. In our Tolerance Workshops, we teach children not to be "Bystanders" (doing nothing to help the target of abuse), but to be "Upstanders," to join in protecting the bullied victim. "We want to bring our students to the point where they do not bully others and if they are bullied, it doesn't faze them."

Docent Ilise Bernstein tributes Sarah Cushman, Director of Youth Education, for making a delicate, challenging job a joy for those who worked with her. Ilise says: "Her empathy and sympathy permeated our meetings and discussions. Her perception and tact in dealing with sensitive issues were motivating role models. Above all, her sense of humor, *joie de vivre* and wide open smile was infectious, inviting us to join

in on the joke, allowing us to see humor whenever possible, even in a grim setting. She was an inspiration to all of us to make our world a better place. "Owing to Sarah's capacity as a successful mentor of young people who did not hesitate to ask her for guidance, Jenna Cavuto, Adelphi senior, was accepted as an intern at the Museum of Jewish Heritage-a Living Memorial to the Holocaust. The newly minted Sarah Cushman, PhD, recently returned to Clark University's Strassler Institute, specializing in Holocaust Education, in a new executive position.

## *Honey Kern at the HMTC Middle School Conference*

The Center's annual Middle School Conference is a huge inclusive conference that has grown in size and importance over the years. It used to be only about Tolerance, but has now includes issues associated with bullying. Honey Kern has been a central player in HMTC's Annual Middle School Tolerance Conference for the past 12 years. The conference brings together students from across the counties. Inspirational speakers talk to Long Island's middle school students about the short term, long-term implications of tolerance, engaging them in critical thinking skills through small group activities to raise awareness of their role in creating a democratic bully-free society. These have raised awareness and built networks of caring throughout Long Island for more than 12 years. The Center encourages young people to become part of the solution to intolerance and to create a climate in their schools that is welcoming and safe for everyone. Its tolerance activities are quadrupling. We hope that armed with knowledge, awareness, insight and practical skills, children and adults learn equality, compassion and respect for all individuals.

The WALMART Foundation's NY State Giving Program awarded HMTC recently with a check of $25,000. It will be used to launch an expanded model of HMTC's highly effective Tolerance and Anti-Bullying Workshops. Furthermore, HMTC, in cooperation with the Claire Friedlander Family Foundation and the Police Departments of Nassau and Suffolk Counties give an annual "Friedlander Upstander Award" to one student each from Nassau and Suffolk Counties, who has proved to be an Upstander against intolerance in any of its forms.

## Director of the Claire Friedlander Education Institute

We have welcomed Tracy Garrison-Feinberg, formerly with the *Facing History* organization, as the new Director of the Friedlander Education Institute. Continuing and extending Sarah's work, Tracy will be focusing on Holocaust and Anti-Bullying/Tolerance education for Elementary School through High School students. She will also be responsible for the Annual Middle School Tolerance Conference. Tracy will be assisted by her lovely secretary, Emanuella Pean.

# Youth Educating Youth

A group of 30 teens from the Jewish Child Care Association's Bukharian Teen Lounge participated in the HMTC's Holocaust education program. The visit included a workshop, tour of the museum and testimony from Holocaust survivor, Ethel Katz. One of the students, Ariela M. confirmed that she now has the duty of educating other youth on the tragedy of the Holocaust. She said: "During the Holocaust, the Jews were bullied by Hitler and the Nazis. While everybody saw what was happening, many chose not to do anything, to be Bystanders. If more people had decided to stand up to the bully and be Upstanders, the Holocaust may never have happened. Hearing Ethel's testimony, I knew that now I have the duty of passing on her story to make sure that future generations know about the Holocaust and make sure that it will never happen again. Remember to always stand up and speak up if you ever see bullying because if we don't stand up, then no one will. The Center not only has an "Upstander of the Month Award," but also an Upstander of the Year Award, as well.

HMTC has been busy interacting with several different sites. "Long Island Wins" hosted a program with HMTC that included a conversation discussing a fair immigration policy. HMTC also co-sponsored a program with "The Righteous Conversations Project" coordinated by Jen Herz, Co-Chair of the Teen Advisory Board "Remember Us." The program featured powerful testimony from Holocaust  Survivors and discussion about the importance of social awareness and contemporary issues of injustice. As a result of all these activities, we now celebrate an "Upstander of the Month" as well as of the year.

## *Challenge #3–"Ostracism, Taunting, Non-Cooperation in the Workplace"*

Michael Dowling, Director of the North Shore/ Long Island Jewish Medical Complex visiting the Holocaust Center in 2006, was moved by the stories of survivors and impressed by the Center's programs. He saw that these could be adapted to the multi-ethnic, multi-religious members of the hospital complex who also represented a broad scope of ages, educational, and national backgrounds including: the Philippines, Central America and Europe as well as small towns in other locales.

Dr. Arlette Sanders addressed the multicultural character of the modern workplace with a "Tolerance in the Workplace" program that used the history of the Holocaust to promote acceptance and respect for diversity. It was sponsored in 2007 by the staff development arm of North Shore/LIJ, the "Center for Learning and Innovation." Attendees included 25 assorted staff members from their early 20s to 70s or even 80s from the many NS/LIJ hospital affiliates. Most were too young to know what "the Holocaust" meant. It was not a part of their history. The notion that all levels of staff be exposed to examining discrimination among them was a highly valuable idea.

A full day seminar led by Dr. Sanders with Nancy Kaplan, Gloria Glantz and Louise Bobrow was designed to "engage their minds as well as their hearts" and lasted for six hours. They viewed DVDs of Holocaust speakers Jacqueline Murekatate and David Gewitrzman and then wrote their responses to these DVDs. The room was surrounded with Holocaust images, quotations about tolerance and diversity by famous speakers, and posters that described the differences between 'Bystanders' vs. 'Upstanders' (rescuers). After lunch, when participants had learned about the breakdown of "tolerance for diversity" in Nazi Germany during World War II, the program segued into the need for "tolerance in the workplace" based on role-plays or case studies of hospital behavior among professionals as well as patients. The program was well received. Between 2007 and 2011, the HMTC presenters made at least 15-20 presentations to the staff at NS/LIJ. Later, they adapted the presentation for a corporate organization. They met with success and were fine-tuned by every presenter. This seminar is available to business, professional, medical or government groups.

## Challenge #4–Too Brief a Span for Holocaust Education

Referring to the brief time granted to this topic in the schools, Beth remarked: "This is a myopic view of Holocaust pedagogy." Holocaust education is not only Holocaust history, but includes sociology issues because the problems facing our society have parallels to the history of the Holocaust sans Hitler. Added to our courses on the Holocaust are links to the 'Ladders to the Holocaust' that shows how bullying, stereotyping and hate crimes can escalate to become genocides. A stellar cast of our top speakers, testifiers and educators testify and lecture at these courses."

There are many opportunities for educating teachers in summer institutes that are now accredited by the New York City Department of Education. As described in the previous chapter, $800,000 would be used to construct the Claire Friedlander Education Institute. On August 5, 2013, HMTC announced that it had received a $100,000 contribution for a new state-of-the-art classroom in the Claire Friedlander Education Institute. We plan for the Institute to be an off-campus site for college and university Holocaust education for educators, scholars and authors. It would offer a more sophisticated analysis of historical and contemporary issues, much of it dealing with new and timelier information relating to the Holocaust and other genocides. The Institute will accommodate four classrooms fully equipped with current audio visual aids and cutting edge technical equipment for specialized Holocaust video-conferencing programs. There will be a wide variety of workshops for youth, adults, and law enforcement personnel.

In September 2013, the Nassau County Commission on Human Rights acknowledged our accomplishments by presenting us with their Humanitarian Award. The Institute is scheduled for completion in the spring of 2014.

# PROGRAMS

Beth Lilach has initiated widespread relationships within the community, bringing programs on little known subjects to the Center. Each includes an exhibit that usually runs for a month. Recent programs of 2011-2012 include the following:

### *"Portraits of Our Past: The Sephardic Communities of Greece and the Holocaust"*

Martin Elias, who funded the program, is the son of an Israeli mother and a Greek father, He explained: "Not everyone knows about the decimation of Greek Jews by the Nazis." The exhibit described two separate groups of Greek Jews: the Sephardic and the Romaniote. The Jews who came to Greece in the 15th century as refugees from the Inquisition in Spain and Portugal are the larger group and are known as Sephardic Jews, while Jews who arrived in Greece more than 2,000 years ago as prisoners of the Romans and are the oldest Jewish community in Europe, are called the Romaniote Jews. Each has different customs and a different language.

The exhibit was divided into 3 sections; the largest central section was about the Sephardic Jews who continued to speak Ladino, which is based on Spanish with Hebrew characters. Some 60 photographs and 14 artifacts were on display. They showed photos of happy, intact, seemingly prosperous families and beautiful artifacts. This contrasted drastically with photos of the Holocaust and the third segment of the show, a DVD, by Martin Elias' cousin, Beni Elias, now deceased, that shows images of a concentration camp, where Jews too weak to work were immediately taken to the crematorium. There were many pictures of the Holocaust, including images of sobbing people on their way to Nazi death camps. Martin Elias recalled that "Greek Jews got along well with their Christian neighbors;" and the DVD also tells stories of Greek gentiles who helped to save Jews. Many Jews were hidden or were helped to hide in the mountains of Greece. Some Resistance forces in the mountains consisted of both Christians and Jews, sometimes together and sometimes in separate groups. There are 315 Greek Christians named "Righteous Gentiles" by Yad Vashem. Among them are the archbishop of Greece and the police chief of Athens who, together, saved 560 Jews by giving them false Christian I.D. papers.

(The library has several books on the subject, including: *Jewish Resistance in Wartime Greece* by Steven Bowman.) Largely unknown is that between 1943-1944 a number of teenage Jewish girls left their extended families and joined the general exodus of the Greek Resistance to the safety of the mountains. Many of the girls were multilingual, fluent in Spanish, French, Italian, and/or German, which proved very helpful to the Resistance. About 70,000 Jews were sent to Auschwitz; approximately 5,000 Jews live in Greece today.

~ ~ ~ ~ ~ ~ ~

## In the Lion's Shadow: The Iranian Schindler and His Homeland in the Second World War

In 2013, sponsored by Frank Lalezarian, an American-Iranian Jew, HMTC was honored to host Dr. Fariborz Mokhtari, the author of: *In the Lion's Shadow: The Iranian Schindler and His Homeland in the Second World War* (History Press, 2011). The book presents the saga of Abdul-Hussein Sardari, an unsung hero and savior of a certain group of French Iranian Jews during

World War II. Ancient history confirms that Iran was once known as a haven for Jews. As early as the 6th century B.C., Jews who had been exiled to Babylonia found a savior in Persia's Cyrus the Great who helped their return to Palestine. Would Iran still prove a safe harbor for the hundreds of Jews of Paris in the early 1940s with the Nazis on the prowl?

Sardari, a member of a once royal family that lost its power in 1925 when the new regime took over, was now an attorney in charge of the Iranian Diplomatic Mission in Paris. He knew that when the Nazis rounded up Jews, they put them in the Drancy ghetto until they were shipped to Auschwitz and was determined not to allow this to happen to the Iranian Jews of Paris. The matter was even more complicated since in the early 1940s, Iran, while having a flourishing trading relationship with the Nazis, was also a refuge to Jews fleeing Hitler's army. Before the Jews of Paris could travel to Iran, passports were needed that the Nazis would honor and which would not identify them as Jews. It was an impossible situation, but Sardari thought of an ingenious solution. Dr. Mokhtari's book tells how when the Nazis occupied Paris, Sardari defied Nazi orders by issuing thousands of passports and travel documents to Jews after convincing the Germans of two things: 1) that the old passports held by these Iranian Jews were no longer valid as the Teheran government had changed, and 2) nor were these Jews "real Jews!" Instead, they were "Iranian Followers of Moses." They were "Djuguten" and should not come under Nazi racial law. They needed new passports to travel that he would furnish. While Eichmann and others were puzzling this out, between 500–1000 Iranian Jews received new passports from Sardari. It is thought that 2000 people may have been saved, including children. In 1952 he was recalled to Tehran and charged with misconduct and embezzlement, charges that Sardari finally got revoked in 1955. In the 1978 revolution he lost his property and pension. Attendees included relatives of Mr. Sardari and the children of Jews whom he had rescued. The audience was so large it filled an oversized tent that had been installed for the event by Mr. Lalezarian. Dr. Mokhtari's wonderful book has been added to our library.

*(On the left are) Frank Lalezarian and Beth Lilach with relatives of Mr. Sardari and the children of Jews whom he had rescued.*

*Dr. Mokhtari accepting "Thanks"*

~ ~ ~ ~ ~ ~ ~ ~ ~ ~ ~ ~

# The Marcelo Lucero Case

The path to the Holocaust was lined with the passivity or fear of on-lookers who did nothing to deter the wicked from persecuting the innocent, because to do so would have meant their persecution as well. That doesn't happen in this country, nor do we want to be guilty of the crime of passivity, of dismissing injustice. Yet when one ignores news because it did not happen in "one's own backyard," we are echoing the Holocaust where bystanders did nothing to help. Owing to the program presented at the Center, we learned about the victim, Marcelo Lucero, and his younger brother, Joselo Lucero, who would not let his brother's memory be forgotten.

Marcelo Lucero, age 37, was an undocumented Ecuadorean immigrant who worked at a dry cleaning shop to support his mother, a sister and a nephew back in Ecuador. One night in 2008, Mr. Lucero was taunted by a group of 7 young "toughs" on the hunt to rough up Spanish immigrants, and who then attacked him. When Marcelo fought back, one, Jeffrey Conroy, drew a knife and severely wounded him. The police and ambulance responded after almost a half-hour delay and Marcelo died. Why so long? The incident exposed the resentment and hate that local residents and also town authorities have against the large numbers of undocumented immigrants who live there year round. The incident gained the attention of advocates for immigrants and brought to light the negative attitude of town authorities, partially because of Mr. Lucero's younger brother, Joselo Lucero. Now, English speaking, Joselo made a film about the incident and continues to show it and to speak wherever and whenever he can. It caught the attention of the Federal government who investigated the authorities of the town in which the incident happened. The entire nation may have been alerted to the problem and hopefully, in the not too distant future, there will be a solution. Mr. Conroy was acquitted of the most serious charge against him, murder as a hate crime. He was sentenced on May 26, 2010 to 25 years in prison.

Today, March 11, 2014, the day this manuscript is being submitted to the publisher, the *NY Times* editorial page reported on this crime and the fact that "more than a dozen Latino men on Long Island reported being robbed by a Suffolk County police officer" while being stopped on the road. The officer is being tried for this crime and possibly for additional hate crimes in the future. The *Times* then goes on to give the history of Marcelo Lucero's death at the hands of teenagers who made a sport of hunting and harassing Latino men. Where did Marcelo's younger brother, Joselo come to report on the crime and to publicize the persecution of Latino immigrants in Suffolk County? To the Holocaust Memorial and Tolerance Center of Nassau County.

~ ~ ~ ~ ~ ~ ~ ~

# ORT

In late September, 2013, HMTC had a program and exhibit: "ORT: Education & Humanitarian Relief for Victims of Poverty and Racism." The title hardly expressed the drama and miracle of the ORT schools and its teachers.

I remember that in 1964, in our brand new neighborhood, we were shown a film: "The Mellah" as an incentive to join ORT. It portrayed a slum neighborhood surrounded by walls meant to separate the Jews, confined to a "mellah," (which means a "ghetto") from the Arabic population of Morocco. The Jews, while religious, were backwards in other regards, and were also very poor. That was when OR T decided to establish boarding schools and took their children outside the ghetto to be educated and taught a trade. Afterwards, I wrote a play: "The Mensch From The Mellah," using the music of "The Man From La Mancha." But where the

"Man from La Mancha" tilted at windmills, the young people of the Mellah made concrete progress, accomplished much and entered into the 20th century.

ORT rises to every occasion where Jews need their help. Its teachers are the rescuers of a wounded people. ORT's name: "Organization for Rehabilitation Through Training," is derived from "Obshestvo Remeslenofo Zemledelcheskofo Truda," (The Society for Trades and Agricultural Labor) founded in 1880 to instruct Russian Jews in skills or trades that would be useful in the Pale of Russia to which they were confined, and to countries in which they hoped to emigrate.

In World War II, ORT went into the ghettos of Europe teaching Jews the skills needed by the Germans in the hope that these skills might contribute to the Jewish slave laborers being allowed to live. After the war was over, ORT flooded the DP Camps, teaching every imaginable skill that could be useful in the country to which their students hoped to one day emigrate. A neighbor who owned his own manufacturing business in New York's garment center told me he learned about the trade from ORT in a DP camp,

~ ~ ~ ~ ~ ~ ~ ~ ~ ~ ~ ~

# The Holocaust and the Law in Nazi Germany

*Nazi Justice* was an interesting program presented by Congressman Steve Israel. Congressman Israel served as President and CEO of the Touro Law Center's Institute on the Holocaust and the Law, a think tank that explored what happened to lawyers and judges during the Holocaust and how their counterparts in Nazi Germany used the law to take away the legal rights of citizens, codifying anti-Semitism. German lawyers and judges simply rewrote the law. They might as well have rewritten the Ten Commandments as the only verity the Germans recognized was of the Nazi variety. The congressman's first book on this subject was presented to him years ago by the Louis Posner Memorial Library.

~ ~ ~ ~ ~ ~ ~ ~ ~ ~ ~ ~ ~

# AWARDS

Many awards have been granted to the Holocaust Memorial and Tolerance Center ("HMTC.") Among them is the 2013 Video Conference Award by "VC Content Providers Database" for being one of the 2013 Top-Rated Nonprofits. HMTC has many new programs and seminars,

HMTC also grants many awards. A Teacher Fellowship will be awarded for "Echoes and Reflections" (Multimedia Holocaust Curriculum Visual History Testimony-Primary Source Materials.) Beth Lilach is engaged in outreach and collaboration projects across the USA and with Yad Vashem. The Center is also collaborating with other museums in New York City. There is a "Righteous Conversations Project" that brings together Holocaust survivors and teens to speak up about injustice in today's world through new media workshops and community engagements. The program is also open to the public. We are proud and happy to have Beth Lilach and Tracy Garrison Feinberg as our Education specialists.

# CHAPTER 11

## CARRYING THE TORCH—
## SECOND GENERATION

### MISSION STATEMENT OF THE SECOND GENERATION GROUP:

**The 2nd Generation group, affiliated with the Holocaust Memorial and Tolerance Center of Nassau County, meets periodically to explore and share the unique experiences, awareness, bonds, burdens and responsibilities that come with being Children of Holocaust Survivors.**

S URVIVORS WERE AT first loath to talk to their children about their Holocaust experiences. After Elie Wiesel published his book: "Night," the damns were broken. Survivor parents began to reveal their experiences to their children and grandchildren. These children, now middle-aged, are the Second Generation. They have assumed their obligations, becoming our docents and testifiers in their parents' stead. They are also the ones who run our events.

## Meryl Menashe

 This year we celebrate the 20th anniversary of the Holocaust Memorial and Tolerance Center of Nassau County .... From the first moment I drove onto the Center grounds, I was entranced. As a child of survivors, living in a neighborhood surrounded by survivors, the Center was a natural fit. My childhood was filled with memories and stories. Family, friends and neighbors had tales to tell, some open and willing, others reluctant. Some never spoke about it at all even though the scars were visible. We members of the Second Generation feel enormous gratification in assuming the responsibilities of our elders by working to memorialize and teach the Holocaust. Here, Lynda Savyon tells how the Second Generation began to form a viable group:

Adapted from Lynda Savyon's article in the *CENTERNEWS*:

## OUR SECOND GENERATION GROUP, 2010

On a cold winter's night in 2007, the Holocaust Memorial and Tolerance Center brought together a small group of adult children of Holocaust survivors. Our task was to consider the merits of starting a "Second Generation" group. Facilitated by Beth Lilach, Director of Education, and Louise Bobrow, the original group was small and unsure of its footing, not quite certain of how to begin processing our experiences as children of survivors. Many thoughts and ideas emerged from this meeting. Ultimately, we all agreed that it would be a worthwhile effort to initiate such a group. Through "word of mouth" more and more "2<sup>nd</sup> Gens" began to attend the monthly meetings. We started to tell our stories and marvel at our commonalities and differences. We come from many walks of life, most of us skilled and educated professionals. We often see our quirks reflected in the habits and attitudes of our peers, amazed that the others are also always "prepared for the worst," vigilant about even the slightest hints of antisemitism and suspicious of government motives. Most of us felt over protected by our parents and blanketed by an overarching sense of the critical importance of family. Distrust of others and the world-at-large is another quality we seem to have in common. The bittersweet legacy we have inherited has been woven into the tapestries of our lives, often driving us to protect the underdog, fight social injustice, and work hard to achieve financial success. Acutely sensitive to our parents' losses, it has been particularly important for many of us to try and make our parents proud, an attempt to somehow counterbalance the harsh hand that many of them were dealt.

The power of our stories and our parents' stories brings many emotions and insights. Some of us have never been in such company and find the experience to be profoundly moving, even exhilarating. Some of us are children of two survivors; some of our parents never spoke of their history, while others related their chronicles in depth. Some of us are "hybrids," children of one survivor parent and one American parent. Whatever the mix, all of us had front row seats in the theater of the Holocaust, which directly or indirectly shaped our development, sensitivity and world–view. The Second Generation group has allowed us to explore what being a 2<sup>nd</sup> Gen has meant to us and even its possible effects upon our children. There are more than 100 members in our North Shore group; 30 or more attend each meeting. As a result of the success of this group, a new 2<sup>nd</sup> Gen group has recently started in Oceanside. Looking back at that cold winter's night, three years ago, wondering if such a group would take off, I am happy to say that it has been a very positive experience that has enabled many of us to integrate the puzzle pieces of our lives more fully.

*North Shore 2nd Generation–Sid Waxman, Gail Kastenholz, Meryl Menashe and Others Dining Out*

*South Shore 2ⁿᵈ Generation*

*Standing from L to R: Sid Waxman, Estelle Kobilinsky,*
*Sarah Generowicz, Suzanna Litman, Vivian Rick, Irv Miljoner*
*Seated from L to R: Debbi Schalt, Sarah Wexler, Stasie Fishman, Roz Epstein*

Irv Miljoner, a Second Gen active in the LEAS program, agrees that the purpose of the Second Gen groups is to provide a forum for them to explore aspects of their adolescence into adult years that make them different from others, even other Jews. They also have topic and theme discussions including current events as viewed by their families; they invite guest speakers, including survivors; view films, engage in various activities and dispense information of general interest and otherwise collaborate on activities with the HMTC. More and more, Second Generation members are the guardians of the Holocaust story. It is they who have shouldered the responsibility of continuing the saga of what happened to their parents and grandparents.

Gail Kastenholz, a docent, facilitator and educator has chaired the North Shore Group Second Generation Survivor events at the Center from 2010 to 2014, the present time. She recalls that: "All of these were days of remembrance and celebration." Gail's parents survived by being hidden by a Polish farmer, but most of their immediate and extended families perished. Inspired by the courage of her mother and father, seeking more information and looking for connections with other children of Holocaust survivors, Gail joined and became the first President of Generation to Generation, the first North Shore Second Generation Group on Long Island more than 3 decades ago. Originally an awareness group for 2Gs, their mission soon became to educate the community and local schools.

At the June 19, 2013 annual Volunteers Dinner, our docents, many of whom are Second Gen, paid tribute to the remaining survivors with the following unedited writings.

## Introduction by Gail Kastenholz:

Being a grandparent is something you cannot imagine until you are one. Being a child of Holocaust survivors is something you cannot understand or embrace unless you are one. Our future is shaped by our past. For me, these two events are significantly and forever entwined. My father and my precious newborn grandson share the same name, "Raphael." My father and my mother are watching over all of us. I hope they are smiling. As a Second Generation, the past will forever be part of my family through songs my mother sang, through snippets told to me and now repeated by me, but mostly by transmitting these core values: the fight for freedom, the commitment to Judaism and the importance of heritage and history. What came before stays with one forever. That is why we say to the survivors who are here tonight, "You are our heroes, our role models, our family, our friends, our loved ones. You are the "wind beneath our wings" and the wings of future generations. We thank you and we promise we will never forget." The Center's goal is to learn from the past, that there will be a better and more just future for all humanity.

## Lili Zimmerman-Schneider

As a Second Generation, what I find to be your most amazing legacy is your defiance and resistance in the face of death. It would have been so much easier to give into despair and yet you resisted believing that tomorrow you would be liberated from the horrors. You are the resisters who crawled out of the ashes and who chose life over death. You resisted by believing that love triumphs over hatred, so you allowed yourselves to fall in love again, to get married, to create new families, to share in *simchas*; and are now enjoying the *naches* from your children and grandchildren. You resisted by assimilating and adapting to a strange new country and by becoming proud, productive American citizens. You resisted by moving forward. You resisted by showing your determination to never allow your past to be used as an excuse for not vanquishing the new challenges you faced as refugees in a new country, which both you, and my parents, so adoringly referred to as "the *goldene medina*." Tonight we give tribute to you, our survivor friends, and thank you for the lessons well taught.

## Andrea Bolender

When I came to the Center over 8 years ago, I wasn't sure what I was searching for but I do know what I found! My father, my hero, had survived Auschwitz, but passed away from a rare cancer traced to the numbers branded on his forearm . . . I was both sad and angry, but was looking for a way to fulfill the promise I made him to never forget.

## Deborah Brand

My heart aches at the atrocities that were committed on survivors and those killed by Hitler. I thank you and my father for sharing your horrific stories with the world. Your lessons are so valuable to the children whose classrooms you have visited. I thank the second and third generations for teaching me tolerance and compassion. For you, and in memory of those who did not survive, I promise to be an "up-stander" and not a bystander. For you, who work hard to battle evil and prejudice in the world, I promise never to forget.

## Vivian Rick

Shalom—I'd like to say "Thank you," to each of you. Thank you for your courage in sharing your stories and in opening your hearts, for being hopeful and brave, for making a difference to all those you've touched, for trying to put the pieces back together so that they have a purpose and in doing so, I hope you have found peace—Shalom

## Irv Miljoner

My legacy as a child of Holocaust survivors becomes ever more important as the years pass. It affects my perspective, dealings with people, my considerations and actions, and how I approach my work and my life. A photo of my father's family appears in the HMTC room devoted to depicting family life before the Holocaust. On every visit to the HMTC I always spend a few quiet minutes by the photo. It centers me and connects me, not only to my father who passed away 25 years ago, but also to the grandparents, uncles and aunts whom I never knew.

## Meryl Menashe, a 2G, Offers These Amazing Stories

I am the daughter of Leon and Miriam Beck and the daughter-in-law of Nissim Menashe and his Christian wife, Katy Menashe and have two stories to tell. The first story is about the Righteous Gentile, Catherine, my mother-in-law. The second is about my father, the amazing Leon Beck.

Nissim Menashe, my father-in-law, was the youngest of 9 children. He was 30 years old when the Nazi's invaded Salonika, Greece. The family had 60 members. Nissim tried to convince his family to leave while the Italians were still in charge, but as a close–knit family, if one would not go, no one would. The family moved into the Baron Hirsch ghetto in Salonika. Nissim left them and at great expense, boarded a train to Athens where he met the Chalkowsaki family. They were a poor Greek Orthodox family who had already lost a child to starvation. Their 16-year-old daughter, Katy, agreed to marry Nissim, a businessman, who then converted to Christianity and supported her family during the war. Since Jews spoke Ladino, his Greek had an accent that would identify him as a Jew, so he had to learn how to speak unaccented Greek. Once the war ended, the Archbishop of Greece proclaimed that any Jew who had converted during the war, could and should return to Judaism to honor their lost families.

Next, my father's story. My father, Leon Beck, lost his brother, 2 sisters and parents to the Nazi's *Einsatzgruppen* (mobile killing units) in Poland while he was serving in the Polish army. Captured by the Nazis, he escaped only to be captured by the Russians and sent to prison in Siberia. Mercilessly tortured but using his wits, he survived. When the Russians released their Siberian prisoners, Dad had to march across Siberia and then ride in open trains. By the time he reached a Tehran Displaced Persons camp he was almost dying from typhus. Fortunately, he was recognized by a cousin and brought to Palestine where he acted as an interpreter for Jews escaping from Nazi Europe. He joined the Israeli army and fought in the War for Independence. Dad inspired his grandchildren who wrote moving testimonials to and about him, read at his graveside, after his death.

# SECOND GENS ARE THE ONES WHO RUN OUR EVENTS

## The Annual Tolerance Dinner and Auction

*Erika Witover, Roz Abrams and Andrea Bolender*

This enjoyable and profitable evening event includes dinner, drinks, and shopping in a country-club auction atmosphere. The concept was created by Andrea Bolender. Andrea is also leading a trip to Holocaust sites in Europe in 2014. Her pal, Erika Witover, another member of the Second Generation, is sure to be in on the action. While silent bids are written on the cards attached to the goodies, I remember when we bid for items with an auctioneer, which was lots of fun. Goods are donated or on consignment. Roz Abrams, a broadcast personality, shown between Andrea and Erika was the speaker in the year represented by the photo. The theme of the speaker's presentation involves Tolerance, or more recently being an "Upstander," rather than a "Bystander." But the evening's attraction is also that it provides a way for us to socialize with one another and new friends, while doing a good deed. A not to miss event!

## The Upstanders Walk for Remembrance

Silvana LaFerlita Gullo, affirmed that her 4 1/2 years at the Holocaust Memorial and Tolerance Center was a life-altering, life-learning experience that she wouldn't trade for the world. She recalls: "The Center's home took me by surprise, a mansion set amongst 240 acres of a nature preserve. Next to the building was a lovely garden with a sign that read "Children's Memorial Garden." Stopping to enjoy the beauty of the garden, I noticed a brass plaque with impressions of butterflies honoring the children who had perished. Howard Maier interviewed me for the position and described their plans to engage in tolerance work and to expand its programs for children. I hesitated to accept not only because it was a long drive from my home, but also because I didn't know enough about the Holocaust. Howard told me not to make a decision until I experienced a tolerance program. And so began my life-altering experience of learning the lessons of the Holocaust as delivered by Gloria Glantz. I learned more about the Holocaust during that workshop than I had learned my entire life. I accepted the position. I had to translate what I had learned into a program I could share with others. Soon I was able to create a brief, but effective 20 minute presentation that would teach the lessons of the Holocaust to adult groups." *(Gloria's experiences are described in PART III.)*

## The Children's Memorial Garden: A Community Education Opportunity

Raising funds to maintain the Children's Memorial Garden became the focus of a community event that Silvana designed and initiated– the "Annual Walk to Remember." It included musical presentations by inter-religious children's choirs to honor the memory of the 1.5 million Jewish children murdered in the Holocaust and all children who had lost their lives during the war. At various points in the walk, additional information was offered and often discussions ensued. Visitors would learn about children in  the *Kindertransport* and in *Terezin*, the pseudo town that was really a waiting room for Auschwitz, about children who were given away to Christian families to save their lives and children who were hidden by the

Resistance and/or Righteous Gentiles. The walk began and ended at the patio entrance to the Children's Butterfly Garden. There, guests could purchase a paper butterfly to honor the memory of a child and meet a survivor who would share their personal history. Silvana said: "Before I left the Center, a second wall was begun to serve as a memorial wall for family members like Ethel Katz's, who died during the Holocaust. She could finally hold a formal Jewish funeral service and have a place on which to place a burial marker for her entire family who were shot while trying to escape the Nazis, when Ethel was but 14 years old. (Ethel's story is told in Part III). My family also purchased a brick on the Butterfly Wall to honor their loved ones. *Providing the concept for such a place is one of the most fulfilling things I have ever done in my professional life."*

## Helping to Build the Board of Directors

Silvana helped to develop the caring, powerful Board the Center enjoys today, mainly through her friendship with David Rosen. When Silvana was the Director of Ronald McDonald House, she had helped David Rosen to find an age-suitable *mitzvah (good deed)* project for his daughter's Bat Mitzvah. Upon assuming her new position, she invited him to the Center. He visited and soon after introduced Claire Friedlander, a unique woman of blessed memory, who was also a survivor. David also brought in several generous board members including Peter Klein, who was to become the Executive Director of the Friedlander Family Foundation, as well as Alan Foley and Stuart Ball, both honorees at the Center's first Golf Outings. Silvana was also instrumental in interesting Keith Gutstein, the grandson of a Holocaust survivor, who introduce Ron Brunell, a 2nd generation survivor who joined the board. Ron's father published a newspaper in the States for survivors from Germany.

# Telling Our Story: Communicating Our Message

With the assistance of a graphic artist from Ronald MacDonald, Silvana developed a brochure to be inserted into Anton Community Newspapers and other PR materials showing haunting images of children. These provided an opening for conversations with others regarding the Center. The brochure showed Holocaust victims not being helped by bystanders. The legend then led to the intolerance and bullying present in today's world, and implored readers to be "Upstanders: not Bystanders." Although the campaign did not raise a substantial amount of funds, it did help to build awareness for the Center. Once when Silvana was speaking before a group, a wise survivor told her: "You may never have another chance to teach these important lessons to the people in the room so make sure you affect them while you have them." Silvana continued: "I am hopeful that the people with whom I shared this lesson were touched by what they learned and forced to consider becoming an 'Upstander instead of a 'bystander,' making the difference in the outcome for a victim they encounter. I also enjoyed helping the Center's Tolerance Benefit Committee, manned by the Second Generation, to grow into an event that was becoming an important annual activity. I wanted to be a part of everything, not bound by the confines of the title: 'Development.' The Holocaust Memorial and Tolerance Center was very central to my life and always will be."

# WE PLAN TO CELEBRATE
# OUR SECOND GENERATION

To mark the 20th anniversary of the Holocaust Memorial and Tolerance Center, Beth Lilach and our "2Gs" are planning a major Second Generation conference event scheduled for Sunday, June 8, 2014. It is titled:

## "FROM GENERATION TO GENERATION,
## THE LEGACY CONTINUES:
### An Event Honoring Survivors, Rescuers, Liberators
### and Their Descendants."

This single daylong event is a celebration of the lives of those who managed to survive and thrive, to endure and to garner the energy to fashion a new life and a new family. Boris Chartan, Founder of the Center, is chairing it.

The event is being planned by Beth Lilach and will be held at Hofstra University which is its co-sponsor. 1,000 people are expected to attend. We are reaching out to Holocaust Survivors, 2Gs and 3Gs (Second and Third Generations), Rescuers and World War II Liberators and their descendants. The keynote speakers who open and close the event will be innovative scholars, whose insights and research have revealed new vistas of the Holocaust.

Beth Lilach said: "One of the primary goals of this tri-state event is to provide opportunities, services and community for survivors who are without friends, families or resources. We will be making special efforts to bring these survivors and/or their families to the event." Several "break-out" sessions of varied nature and topics are being planned. Some "break-out" rooms will be based on geography so that survivors will be able to meet other survivors from their homeland. There will also be rooms for encounters and socializing between children and grandchildren of survivors, the 2G and 3G (as we term them). Rescuers and their descendants, and World War II Liberators and their families will each have their rooms that will be open to the general public and to all participants. Much attention is being paid to the exhibits and displays of artifacts. Educational lectures will be provided and various service agencies and vendors will make their presence known. *Note: The event was tremendously successful with more than 700 attending.*

## STORIES OUR PARENTS TOLD US

Perhaps some of our Second Gens will tell the stories that their parents told them, such as those that follow.

### Eleanor Blackman

My mother and her father were hiding out in some small town up in the Pyrenees Mountains. On one occasion my grandfather was in the woods gathering fuel for the fireplace when he ran into some Nazis. They asked him who he was and he, not speaking anything but German, pretended that he was deaf and dumb. The soldiers unable to get any information from him roughed him up and let him go. On another occasion my mother took the bus down the mountain as she did once a week to get food. On one of these trips, Nazi soldiers boarded the bus and asked that all Jews get off. My mother did not get off. The Nazi officers walked around the bus asking everyone questions in German. My mother, who was from Germany originally, pretended not to understand German and spoke only French to the soldiers. She said everyone on the bus knew who she was but no one gave her up.

The second story was told to me by one of my French cousins.

My mother's family had a furniture business in Trier, Germany. On Kristallnacht the store was ransacked and burned. After the war the family opened up a furniture store across the border in Metz, France. My cousin Raymond tells me that when he was about 8 years old, he was walking with his father and a man came up to them and asked his father: "Do you remember me? His father did not respond to the man and kept walking. When the man left, my cousin asked his father: "Why did you not talk to the man? His father answered: "Before the war he was our employee. On *Kristallnacht*, he was there helping to burn the store down."

## Franklin Small

Soon after I retired from teaching, I made an appointment to volunteer at the museum. I'd listened to the stories of my mother and her family from an early age. A kaleidoscope of images rattled in my mind: my Mom's *Kindertransport* stories, the deportation and eventual murder of many of her relatives, the heroism of a brave Viennese doctor who hid my uncle, and my grandparents last-minute visa that allowed them to come to America . . . I understand now why these impelled me to write a Brotherhood essay at age 14, influenced me to enter the Reform Rabbinate at age 21, goaded me to write a soulful essay about the Warsaw Ghetto uprising and stoked the fire to work most of my life in an African-American and Latino school, where I often chaired the Martin Luther King Celebration Committee. I felt a deep sense of identity with the Holocaust and a strong desire to contribute. It had been "background static" in a lifetime journey lived in the largely unrecognized shadow of the Holocaust. With maturity, increased ethical awareness and perhaps a higher spiritual development, a new insistence grabbed hold. Facing my own mortality and wanting to make a difference, I look to the Holocaust and its web of literature, history and testimony as an indispensable matrix from which to summon the humanity needed so that we will not, in the prophetic words of Dr. King, "all die as fools."

~ ~ ~ ~ ~ ~ ~ ~ ~ ~ ~ ~ ~ ~ ~ ~

*Lillian Gewirtzman once asked some 2Gs to write about whether their homes were different from those of their non-2G friends. Here are their replies:*

## Andrea Bolander, Second Generation, born in Queens, NY 1961

I was never allowed to go away to summer camp or to sleep at a friend's house, although many were welcomed at mine. My father cried when I left for college. I am the image of his mother, a burden yet very much a privilege. Devoid of all the family that my friends and neighbors enjoyed, no grandparents to spoil me with special treats, no aunts or uncles to visit on holidays, I always felt quite empty. It was a curious mix of both the American influence of my mother and the accent laden adopted family that my father cherished as siblings. My three siblings and I were his sole reward for having survived Auschwitz. The responsibility weighed heavily on my young shoulders, although I did not at first recognize it. Only later in life did I realize that I had made many critical decisions prefaced by the thought "how will this affect my father?" Education, denied to him, became my focus as well. While my friends were off backpacking in Europe over college summers (an option I *never* would have been allowed) I was taking extra courses at university–enabling me to graduate ahead of all my classmates. At the time it seemed like I had a firm grasp on life. Today it sometimes feels like a life half-lived. Like a life that was rushed . . . . to get to where? I wasn't running out of time, was I? I *wanted* the memories of a misspent youth that my friends possess so clearly. I *wanted* to pause dreamily and remember "the time were at the *Arc de Triomphe*." I married young, again eager to begin a successful life. I worked hard; I achieved financial success and all its trappings. I had control of my life, or so I thought. My father's childhood lacked that control, so I would make it my mission to control mine. I am sure that I evidence some remains of his tortured childhood. Why else would I stress over something as inane as throwing out leftovers? Why is it that I torture my children with my expectations? Why do I force feed them a steady diet of perseverance? Am I still trying to live up to the lofty heights I never feel that I achieved, but that my father deserved? Am I living vicariously through the children he never had the opportunity to watch grow up ? I stayed in an unfulfilling marriage for possibly the same reason. I couldn't bear to present my father with my failure, as though he might take it personally . . . All my life, I believed that I would be able to give my children what I never had, wonderful grandparents, a plethora of aunts, uncles, and cousins. When my parents passed away just a few months apart, my dream died with them. I had everything I ever needed: the unflagging support of parents who cherished me and declared their pride with every ounce of their being; their willingness to forego their own creature comforts to provide for their children's and their boundless love for their grandchildren. When my father fell ill, it was Hitler's final revenge. My father had a rare cancer of the liver that was traced back to the tattoo on his arm. His attempt to regain that coveted control over his life was thwarted once again. They gave him a grim prognosis, 3-6 months survival. In his heavily accented English he answered "I'm not ready; I'll let you know when (or as he pronounced it VEN)." It was vintage Benek Bolender, attempting to exert control even when handed a veritable death sentence. It was then I saw him in an entirely new light. My father wasn't trying to control his life so much as he was trying to live it vigorously, perhaps regaining his stolen years in the process. My father lived for six years, a medical miracle they all said. It was nothing less than I expected. He was not going to give up any more time to Hitler's whims. Those six years were both bitter and oh so sweet. He had five more grandchildren, including two sets of twins! He traveled the world in between debilitating chemotherapy treatments. He never felt a moment's pity for his lot in life. It was then that I stopped feeling sorry for my lost experiences, for what my father taught me was priceless. Survival—a lost art, a skill so many lack, a skill of necessity. A skill that my friends with the youthful memories I coveted, do not possess. I learned from my father to become attached to people-not to "things." I am the child of a survivor. It was the best gift I ever received.

## Carly Hanft, Third Generation, daughter of Andrea Bolender

Hi, my name is Carly Hanft. I am a 3rd generation Holocaust survivor. My grandfather, Benek Bolender, survived 4 years in the most horrific of all concentration camps, Auschwitz. Although he passed away when I was young, I am fortunate to be raised in a family that both remembers and uses the lessons of the Holocaust to teach me the importance of tolerance. As young as age 6 or 7 years of age, I wanted to help fellow students with disabilities. When my mother got involved with the Center, it was only natural for me to be working right along side her. In 5th grade, my school came to hear a survivor's testimony. Although I had heard my grandfather's stories many times, hearing it in the museum solidified in me the need to be proactive in spreading the important lessons of the Holocaust. It is easy to be tolerant when we think the same and share the same values, but what happens when this is not the case? Standing up for what is right may not be the popular thing to do, but it is the right thing to do. The study of the Holocaust will be extremely important to these students' lives as they make connections between history and current moral decisions with which they may be faced. They become aware of the importance of making choices and realize that one person can make a difference. I am currently training to become a museum docent. I am proud to be the youngest docent here! I can't wait for my classmates to visit the awesome new exhibit and spend time in our amazing library. It contains all the resources a student could ever want when researching both the Holocaust and all genocides since. I hope that you like the new exhibit!

## Debbie Loeb Cohn

I was a very young girl when I first heard my parents' stories. I remember my mother recounting the moment when she was only 13 years old and had to go on a train to a foreign country all by herself. She had to say goodbye to her parents at the train station, and that was the very last time she ever saw them. "Imagine how you would feel if you were only 13, having to say goodbye to your parents forever," my mother would say to me. "How did I have the presence of mind at that young age to speak up to a Nazi officer on that train ride, who did not want to let me cross the border that day?" she would say. She ultimately had to go into hiding in Holland, and would tell me, "My story is similar to Anne Frank's and her family, with one big difference–I wasn't caught."

My father would also remind me often of his terrible experience as a young German man, being arrested on *Kristallnacht* and being sent to *Dachau* Concentration Camp. He recounted his ordeal, still not believing that his own countrymen could have turned on him as they did. It was his own country, a place where he had grown up and gone through all his schooling, a place that he had been proud of. But many of his countrymen followed Hitler blindly. I have always felt different somehow, even different from my Jewish friends. When my parents were speaking to me of their experiences, many of my friends didn't want to be reminded of such difficult times. But I knew that my parents were giving me a gift. They gave me the gift of compassion, and of appreciating life and not taking anything for granted. My mother never wanted to waste a morsel of food, even saving one used tea bag for many cups of tea. She would tell me, "I was starving during the war," and it had more impact on me than if she had told me that some other people were starving in some far-away land. I also sensed a great feeling of loss, never having known my grandparents, and having very few relatives. I found my parents treating many of their friends like family, welcoming them into our home on holidays, almost naturally extending our family circle.

## Barbara Kupfer Murray, Second Generation, Samarkand Uzbekistan, 1945

My parents Liba and Leib Kupfer, survived WWll as prisoners at a labor camp in Archangel, Siberia. They had fled Poland for the Soviet Union in September 1939 to escape the Germans and wound up spending three years in a camp, deprived of food, living under extreme cold, and fearing for their lives. Freed in 1943 when Poland and the Soviet Union agreed to release Polish citizens, they were permitted to live and work in Uzbekistan. I was born in Samarkand in 1945. After the war, we returned to Poland with my mother's uncle Joseph, his wife and their baby *Moishe*, who was born on the freight train that was returning them to Poland. They soon learned that most of their families had perished in the Auschwitz and Treblinka camps, and that Jews were not welcomed back to Poland. Returning to her grandparents' former apartment, it was obvious that Poles had stolen all the possessions in the vacated apartment, as well as theirs, and were found using her grandparents' furniture and belongings as their own. Then, when her parents learned the horrible news concerning their families, there was no longer any reason to remain in Poland. They traveled to a Displaced Persons Camp located in Vienna. While in the DP camp, a reporter from *The Forward*, a Yiddish newspaper, took their picture and my parents explained to him how we had emigrated from Uzbekistan where I was born, to Vienna. My father treasured this article and to this day, I have it framed and hung on a wall in my house. When the DP camp closed, we were able to move to France because my parents had lived there in 1937. In 1951, we were able to immigrate to the United States when my mother's older brother, Meyer Moskowitz sponsored us. Our first home was a three room furnished apartment in Coney Island. At age the age of 6 I would sit for hours watching people walking on the avenue and Imagine what their lives were like. My parents kept to themselves. When friends would come-by, my mother would say to me "don't answer the door." I don't remember ever having friends or a relative visiting. I can still recall that even during our stay in France mother would tell me to stay away from the window and not to respond when people rang the bell. This behavior continued into her late years. While she was friendly to people outside, her home was private. When I was younger, my mother shared many emotional stories of her experiences during the war, but when I was young I didn't want to hear them. We didn't have a television set until I was 9, or a telephone till I was 12. If I asked "why?" my parents would say "This is not important; we have what we need. You should be happy with what you have—food to eat and clothes on your back. For years we were hungry and had nothing. You are lucky!" Safety was definitely a very clear concern for my parents. They were always worried about me. In elementary school, I was never permitted to go on class trips. I can recall my class going to the Statue of Liberty, and my mom too worried that something would happen to me to allow me to go. It is ironic that as an immigrant my mom did not see how relevant it would be for me to see it—the symbol of our journey to freedom. Ultimately, I was able to have my own room complete with photos of my music idols on the walls, and after much nagging, a Royal typewriter and phonograph. With these items I became an American—able to leave, at last, the *Shtetl* of my parents. Reflecting on how I was raised, I know that I was loved unconditionally and taught how to live a life of good moral values and concern for others. My parents were not demonstrative with words or actions. They rarely kissed or hugged me, nor did they say "I love you." But I always knew it. When I would bring home my report card, whether my grades were in the 70s, or 90s, they'd always say "that was a good grade." I was their total focus of attention. My father, a garment worker, was always there for me. Once when I had an assignment to go to a concert at Avery Fisher Hall at Lincoln Center for a college music course, my father insisted on accompanying me. Since I had purchased only one ticket, he was prepared to spend the evening in the lobby. At this time of my life I can better understand how their difficult experiences shaped my parents' personalities; why their concerns centered on the essentials of life: a roof over our heads, food to eat, and a meaningful Jewish life. In their humble way they prepared me for life in a country that they never truly understood and that never understood them. As I grew older, I yearned to know more about my parents' thoughts, feelings and experiences during that painful time but I worried that retelling them would be too sad for them. I wish I had asked. My parents are now deceased and I have a void that I cannot fill. I thought that by volunteering at the Holocaust Center I would reconnect with my past and keep my parents close. The staff and volunteers at the Center were warm and welcoming from the very beginning. I soon found a home working with Gloria Jackel in the library.

## Meaghan Murray, Third Generation–Daughter of Barbara and Frank Murray

This was written 9 years ago, in 2004, when Meaghan was in Junior High School. She is now a teacher.

Usually a child thinks of her parents as heroes, but my heroes are my *Bubby* and *Zaida* (Grandma and Grandpa) whom I have never met. Their determination to survive despite endless tragedies and to see their family again, gave them hope that they would one day live a life without persecution. Their story gives my family the determination to defeat every challenge and has allowed my mother, my sister and I to teach others by way of my grandparents' example. My introduction to the

Center was the day my mother brought me to sit at the front desk with her. After growing up with parts of my grandparents' story in the back of my mind, I wanted to learn more about what had occurred during those nightmare years. That afternoon, I took a tour of the Center and was amazed by the pictures, the artwork and how hard all the survivors had worked to be able to survive the Holocaust. From then on, I was hooked. I started to read more and more about different people's stories. I was very connected to a book my mom helped to write, "From Generation to Generation," when she was a teacher at Abraham Lincoln High School in Brooklyn. It had an interview with my mom about her experiences as a Second Generation survivor as well as a moving poem by my older sister about her experiences, and some of our family history. The sad part is that I could never pick up the book. It was such an emotional experience for an 11-year-old who is the granddaughter of survivors. That year was my happiest in school because we read "Night" and then "Dawn" both written by Eli Wiesel. I was so moved by his words and story. We were then given the opportunity to read 1,000 pages of whatever subject we pleased and then to write a paper or do some creative activity on it. It didn't even take me 5 seconds to think of what I was going to read about: the Holocaust. I was finally able to whip out my mother's book and read it from cover to cover. I told my parents and they showed me countless other books that they owned, which I could read from cover to cover. I thought a lot about the creative project I would do. First, I thought about writing about my cousins who were deported by Klaus Barbie when they were hiding in a French orphanage. As I thought about Auschwitz where my cousins were killed I thought that I should tell a story about convoy 71, which took them to their deaths. Two months and about 956 pages later, I realized that my story should really be set around the life of *Tzerel*, my grandmother's sister, who also died during the Holocaust. At the end, I was so proud of my writing and how hard I worked to write in memory of my family. It gave me the desire to come to the Center every week with my mother as a volunteer. I wanted to help educate others about the Holocaust as my mother has done as a docent. I feel so honored to be here with such a wonderful group of people. I realize that I am able to be here only because of the strength of my grandparents. Unfortunately, my grandparents died before I was born. I was never able to hear their stories, listen to them talk Yiddish, attend Temple with them or even just to sit down and have a cup of tea. If I were able to go into the past, my one wish would be to meet them and to feel their strength. I see how much my family loved them and how much of an impact they have had on my life.

## Rena Schwartzbaum, daughter of Lillian and David Gerwirtzman

On the surface, our home did not appear different from those of my peers. My parents, having immigrated when they were relatively young, were well assimilated. The Holocaust was rarely discussed, and my mother spent most of my life denying that she was a survivor at all, since she had escaped into Russia. My father did not share his complete story with me until I was 13 years old, and even then, I got the "Holocaust-lite" version, more like a fairy tale where the child heroes prevail over the evil witch, and everybody lives happily ever after. English was the primary language spoken by my parents, but my father had a fairly pronounced accent, which I only discovered after a playmate asked me where he was from. I took guitar lessons and played field hockey; we took summer vacations together, played tennis. My parents entertained in the house. My brother and I graduated from high school, college, and professional schools and went on to marry and have children of our own. On a deeper level, however, my home was different. As a child I was often confused by these differences. There was a powerful, unconscious, unstated, expectation for me to be happy. It took many years for me to comprehend the impact that this perceived obligation held over me. Sadness was something to eradicate like the plague. For my parents, especially for my father, there was no such thing as allowing an opening for unhappiness. The magnitude of his loss would be overpowering. According to my father everything was "absolutely terrific." How could I possibly undermine his positive spin? If sadness could not be expunged, then at least it could be contained and locked away in the far reaches of the mind's Siberia. I suppose that this reflects the sense of protectiveness that I felt regarding my parents. I saw how hard my parents worked and if anything, wanted to ease their burden. My friends would ask if my parents made me work. To the contrary, my parents were afraid that I was working too hard. I was also unable to relate to the blasé attitude of some of my peers toward their extended family. Sometimes friends would bemoan that they could not get together with me because their grandparents were coming over again. I felt so lucky to have four surviving grandparents. I was so proud of them for having survived, venturing to an unknown land and starting over. My deep connection to my family, and the stories that eventually leaked out, despite my mother's best efforts to shield me from the horrors, did seep into my unconscious thoughts. I would have daydreams and fantasies that I am quite sure were not shared by my friends, but later learned were typical of children of survivors. I remember once playing a video game called *Break Out*, which my friend had lent me. I was trying to motivate myself to beat my previous score. To my shock I became aware of the following fantasy: "I am in a concentration camp. A German guard informs me that I have to obtain a certain score in order to keep my family from being sent to the gas chamber. One by one they would select my brother, mother and father; I would play for their life." When I "came to" it was 2:00 am, and I was sweating. I did not play that game again, nor did I share that story, or other similar disturbing thoughts, with my parents. As much as my parents truly wanted us to be Americans, my brother and I clearly received mixed messages. They loved our freedoms, but they could not relate to our pastimes, especially our innocence. Both empathic by nature, but having lost their youth, they could not make sense of ours. At times I felt that my struggles and concerns seemed "cute" to them. How could they not? For my parents, education was tantamount to survival. My mother, at age sixteen, would leave her displaced persons camp in Germany, by herself, would take a bus to a German high school, still replete with anti-Semitism. The message again? Education at all costs. It was terribly painful for my parents to see me taking education for granted when they had been deprived of their aspirations. I unconsciously decided to make them proud. My college acceptances felt, in part, shared with my parents; my achievements and awards, not totally mine. Although my parents did everything possible not to burden me with survivor guilt, I definitely felt a pull to do something "meaningful" in order to compensate for the many family members who had not survived. Although my brother would probably deny it, I do not think that it is coincidental that he became a pediatrician, nor that I became a child psychologist. As might be anticipated, separations were not easy in our family. My parents owned a pharmacy and worked together every day. They were never apart. My brother and I handled our separations in different ways. I believe that the adolescent struggle to find my identity was especially difficult. I did not feel as American as my friends. In my early twenties I attended a Second Generation survivor's group. Some of their experiences did resonate with me, but I felt that the focus was negative, too heavily weighted towards pathology as opposed to resiliency. Yes, there is a persistent theme of loss in my family, but also one of strength, survival and future. As an adult I have grown more comfortable with this dichotomy and not having to fit neatly into a niche. What I am is an American daughter of survivors. As I write this, I wonder if, a generation removed, my current home is "different" than those of my peers whose parents are not survivors. I believe that it is.

# PART III

## LIBERATORS AND SURVIVORS

❄

WE HONOR ALL OF OUR LIBERATORS AND SURVIVORS, NOT ONLY THOSE WHOSE WRITINGS APPEAR ON THE FOLLOWING PAGES.

# CHAPTER 12

## LIBERATORS: JIM VAN REALTE
## AND HERMAN HOROWITZ

O UR MOST IMPORTANT volunteers are those who testify–the liberators and the survivors. I think of them as "old souls," messengers who have been to hell and back, traveling from place to place with their tales of warning and foreboding, stories that frighten and teach. Later, it would be their children, the second and third generations. Below we introduce two of our valiant liberators: Jim Van Realte and Herman (Hy Horowitz).

# Jim Van Realte

The Kuperferg Holocaust Resource Center and Archives of Queensborough Community College recently had an exhibit: "Their Brothers' Keepers: American Liberators of Nazi Death Camps." It describes the U.S. Army liberators who were usually from 19-25 years of age. Although they had already experienced the ravages of war and the death of comrades, none had any idea of what they would find in the concentration camps they would liberate. Some could not handle it. Others would tenderly lift up the sick and dying and carry them to the newly erected hospital tents. For many prisoners, it was the first time they had ever seen an African American close by. Prisoners were known to fall on the ground and kiss the hands and boots of their liberators. One GI married the barely alive young woman whom he carried to a hospital tent and visited throughout her convalescence.

Jim Van Realte, the man with a twinkle in his eye and a ready joke on his lips was also a talented actor in our "Becoming the Pratts" plays and a member of our speakers' group. Jim had been one of the liberators of the camps in World War II. The letters he wrote home describing the unimaginable tragedy he was witnessing became one of our first exhibits. They are part of our current exhibit, as well. Jim wrote:

"A former prisoner who had starved so long that he could hardly eat anything showed us around the camp. He still wore around his neck a little disk that once entitled him to a 'meal'. If it was lost or stolen, it was not replaced. That little disk meant a prolongation of life, but only a prolongation, for every prisoner there was slated to die."

Jim wrote that 200,000 people had died there. "Last February, 2,000 died. The average per day was 675. Now that we are taking over that rate had been reduced to from 20-40 a day."

## Herman (Hy) Horowitz

Hy, now in his mid 90s, is our second liberator. He lectures to students about his reactions when entering a concentration camp. He is also a talented writer. Here he describes some of his other experiences in World War II.

*Me at Camp Polk, LA in March 1942*

**BURNING BERGEN BELSEN**–On April 15, 1945, precisely at noon, while my Battalion was attached to the British 3rd Army, we crashed the heavy iron fences and saw the heavy iron gate on which were the words BERGEN BELSEN. In my mind and in the minds of my American and British comrades, it was the closest thing to entering hell. On the ground, piled on top of each other, were the bodies of Jewish men, women and children. Young boys who had been turned into men in less than one year, cried openly and unashamedly. Our eyes were not yet accustomed to seeing Nazi brutality. A young British soldier, all of 17, kneeled beside me with his rosary in his right hand. Looking up at the sky, he said in a shaky, but loud voice: "Please Lord, tell me that what we are seeing is just a bad dream." We both knew it was not. But the saddest of all were those inmates, barely alive, staring into space not knowing what lay ahead. They wandered aimlessly, shredded lice-filled clothes on bodies that were almost translucent. They were too weak to hug us and unable to put food into their shrunken stomachs. We were afraid to lift them into trucks and ambulances for fear that their frail bodies would break in half.

I stood there, not knowing what I could do for these poor souls. There was nothing. So I went back to my tank and from my knapsack took out the small Hebrew Prayer book that my rabbi had given to me on the day I left for the army and recited *Kaddish*, the prayer for the dead. They fitted some tanks with blades and we dug deep ditches, then pushed the lifeless corpses into them. Then a team of British flamethrowers torched the remaining buildings, buildings that once held misery and death. And in a matter of hours, Bergen-Belsen was reduced to a pile of smoldering ashes as though it had never existed. But in the minds of the liberators and survivors, Bergen-Belsen did exist. Forever indelible in our minds are visions that time will never erase, permanent recollections of man's inhumanity to man.

**THE STAMP**–In August 1944, my Division, the 7th Armored, spearheaded General Patton's drive from Normandy to Germany. On August 15th after a week of heavy fighting, we liberated the city of *Melun*, 35 miles south of Paris. After the war I made several returns to France, sometimes with my wife, Sally, and other times with veterans from my Division. We always made sure to visit *Melun* where we had made several friends including a teacher who happened to be friendly with a teacher in Freeport. Over the years we paid each other visits, and one year she sent us a card from the French Riviera and something about the stamp caught my attention. On the stamp was a Star of David and barbed wire. I knew there had to be a story and after my rabbi saw the stamp, he did also. I sent a photocopy to a friend in another city we had liberated, Chezy-sur-Marne as he was a stamp collector. He passed it on to a major stamp dealer in Paris. Weeks went by and I heard nothing. Then one morning I received a phone call from a man who identified himself as Robert Abrami. He was visiting his daughter in Montreal and was planning to spend the weekend with us and tell us about the stamp. He happened to be writing a book, but as the publisher did not like the last chapter he wanted my story to be the last chapter. He told us that the stamp was a replica of a picture he painted that took him four years to convince the French government to make the commemorative stamp. When he revealed what the stamp represented and why he painted the picture, Sally and I were both taken aback. You see, between July 15 and 16, 1942, Robert Abrami's entire family was rounded up and thrown in the *velodrome*. His entire family perished and he was the only survivor. The painting was to commemorate that horrific event. Just before leaving, he handed me a large mailing tube and said not to open it until after he left. When we opened it, we were stunned to find the original painting.

I brought it to the rabbi the next morning to see if I should donate it to the East Meadow Jewish Center. He said "No," it should go to the Holocaust Center in Glen Cove where many more people could view it. The next week, I did. That's when Boris Chartan approached me and asked if I knew anything about baseball, and if I did–this was a home-run. He asked if I would loan it to the Center and I said: "no," I would present it to the Center. When he asked how the painting came to be in my possession, I repeated the story above. He then asked me to become a docent at the Center, which took me by surprise. Two weeks later, I delivered a hastily assembled testimony to a group of 20 Freeport High School seniors. When I finished, almost every student gave me a hug and a handshake. Boris said that the only thing he saw moving on those seniors were their eyebrows. I have spoken to more than 50,000 students since that day. Books have been written and movies made about *Rafle du vel d.'*

~ ~ ~ ~ ~ ~ ~ ~ ~ ~ ~ ~ ~ ~

The Babes in the Barn—After landing on Normandy, we began a lightening advance across France. When we reached the outskirts of the city of Metz on the German border, Headquarters realized we were running low on fuel. Sent a distance to replenish our supply, we got lost and were running low ourselves. We decided to spend our night in an abandoned old barn. After one of our team checked out the barn and gave the O.K., I entered the front door. I had taken a few steps when I suddenly heard what I thought was a baby crying. Why would there be a baby in a barn in the boondocks? I was afraid it was a ruse so I clicked the bolt on my rifle to make a loud metallic sound and in my best German and French yelled "Come out or we shoot!" Suddenly, in the hayloft above, I heard children sobbing. I found a ladder and went up to the hayloft. There were two young boys sobbing and shaking. I told them not to cry because we are American soldiers and they are free, but to them any uniform was a danger and they continued to cry. In my high-school French, I conversed with the boys and learned they were ages 9 and 7 and Jewish. A Gentile French farmer and his wife on a farm about 3 miles away from this barn had hidden them until a stray shell hit the farmhouse and the farmer and his wife were killed instantly. The boys were saved because they were living in a dirt cellar under the house in a niche carved in the wall. They ran for safety and found the barn. Despite my reassurance, they continued to cry. Suddenly, I got an idea. In our box of dehydrated rations were two wonderful things, a bar of Hershey chocolate and Wrigley's chewing gum. The older boy vaguely knew what chocolate was, but neither knew how to chew gum. We gave them all of our chocolate that they devoured instantly. God only knows when they had eaten last. It was early morning by now and I took two calmer boys down the ladder and got ready to head for our Division. A few miles down the road I saw a sign that said: "MP Station (Military Police). I stopped the convoy and made a hasty decision to take the boys into the MP station with a request that they be taken to a Displaced Persons Center with the possibility that they might find their parents. As we got out of the jeep, Jacob, with tears in his eyes grabbed my hand, looked up at me and said: "Could you please find my mother, father and younger sister who we haven't seen for almost three years?" It bothered me then and bothers me yet, wondering if I made the right decision. Hopefully, I did and they are both alive and well, raising a family of their own.

*Editor's Note: Hy Horowitz has recently been granted France's most prestigious award: The Legion of Honor, designed and created by Napoleon Bonaparte in 1802. On June 8th, 2009, Rep. Carolyn McCarthy read the notice of this honor and Hy's dedication to the Center's mission read into the Congressional Record. We congratulate him.*

*Hy Horowitz, now a "Chevalier" of France's Legion of Honor*

*April 30th, 2009*

*Ambassade de France
aux États-Unis*

*L' Ambassadeur*
N. 970

Washington, April 30, 2009

Dear Mr. Horowitz:

I am pleased to inform you that by a decree signed by the President of the French Republic on April 16, 2009 you have been named a "Chevalier" of the Legion of Honor.

This award testifies to the President of the French Republic's high esteem for your merits and accomplishments. In particular, it is a sign of France's true and unforgettable gratitude and appreciation for your personal, precious contribution to the United States' decisive role in the liberation of our country during World War II.

The Legion of Honor was created by Napoléon in 1802 to acknowledge services rendered to France by persons of great merit. The French people will never forget your courage and your devotion to the great cause of freedom.

It is a personal pleasure for me to convey to you my sincere and warm congratulations.

Sincerely,

Pierre Vimont

Mr. Herman W. Horowitz
506 Oakdale Road
East Meadow, NY 11554

# CHAPTER 13

## SURVIVORS:
## POETS & WRITERS GROUP

UPON BECOMING RETIREES, survivors began to volunteer to testify about their experiences for the Center. Although they were coached at the Center on how to describe what had happened to them to students, I wanted to help them record their experiences in a written form. An organization named "Poets and Writers" sent us a poet named Veronica Golos as a writing coach. Each week, she assigned the entire group an innocuous phrase and told them to use it in their writing. I had thought that they would write fuller testimony, but the phrase acted like a key that unlocked their memories and emotions. They wrote more than the practiced deliveries told to their audiences. They wrote about their feelings in prose and poetry. Lillian Gewirtzman and I took their writings and edited them for a book. This chapter contains only pieces written for the class.

# ANNIE BLEIBERG and DAVID GEWIRTZMAN

*ANNIE BLEIBERG*
*Born in Oleszyce, Poland 1920*

Annie Bleiberg, whose testimony, stories and poems are found throughout this chapter, moved from Pelham Parkway in the Bronx to Long Island to reach her speaking engagements more easily. Alerted by her daughter, Dr. Susanne Seperson, of the opportunity to tell her story at the new Holocaust Center, Annie was eager for an audience. She especially relished talking to youth. She wanted to convince them to cherish what they had and to not waste it.

Annie, who claimed that she couldn't write, surprised everyone in our Poets and Writers group with her moving stories and poems. Annie has even received fan mail from a Lieutenant Colonel of the U.S. Marine Corps. It can be found in the Index under "Letters to Our Survivors."

# THE TRAIN IS ME

Little guys and big ones gather in the living room. The mission is to assemble a "choo-choo" train. In time, the whole train is put together with passenger, train cars and caboose. The "choo-choo" train turns its wheels and moves on the tracks. It moves to the right, to the left, straight ahead and in circles. The room fills with laughter. Everyone is happy. And there are trains in real life. The real train turns its wheels too. It moves and speeds, covering distances and carrying goods and people from place to place. Thousands of people are traveling daily. They hurry to catch the train on time. People are always going places. This is life. There were other trains with other assignments. They puffed their steam and blew their whistle, ripping through the night air in horrifying anguish. They were panting, hauling long lines of cattle cars. The doors were sealed shut, the windows were gated with heavy barbed wire and nailed down with board. Each car was guarded by a Gestapo. Inside were people; resigned, some half dead; some dead already. All standing, packed like sardines. They were forsaken, marked for death. Jews, their destiny, *Belzec*. When the train came to a screeching halt and unloaded its human cargo, it was death on arrival. I was once one of the human cargo on such a train. *600,00 Jews were murdered in Belzec, including my family!*

# AN ODE TO NISELE

I see this little face,
your beautiful little face
with twinkling blue eyes,
carved little nose,
pink cheeks and little red lips
surrounded by blond wavy hair.

It is you, little baby.
It is you, little Nisele,
the first baby in the third generation,
the only baby in the family.
You had a throng of admirers.
We all loved you and
indulged your every whim.

You smiled in response
and made us forget
the gravity of the times
for a split second.

It was war,
a brutal war,
especially for Jews,
even on two-year-old angels
like you.

You knew so much.
You never cried
but you shrunk at the sight
of a German soldier
or Polish policeman.

You clung to your mommy.
Your beautiful eyes
weren't smiling any more.
They turned grey, half closed.
Your little mouth
into a thin straight line.

You didn't cry.
You didn't say a thing,
Not a single word,
But you knew it all.
Your face said it
And your body too.

## THE THINGS I CAN'T REMEMBER

What am I searching for?
I am thinking long and intensely,
but I can't remember.

So what is it,
that thing I am looking for,
but can't remember?

Sometimes I can't remember
where I left my keys,
the name of a friend . . .
But these are minor things,
or so I think.

But the real things,
the important things
those I can't remember . . .
Are they too painful?
That I never understood,
nor wanted to?
I can't remember . . .

~ ~ ~ ~ ~ ~ ~ ~ ~ ~ ~ ~ ~

*DAVID GEWIRTZMAN*
*Born in Losice, Poland 1928*

# DEPORTATION

It was early in the morning. The window was shut tight and covered by a dark curtain. This was mandated by the authorities to prevent light from showing at night. It also kept the morning rays out. With the doors bolted, it gave us a false sense of security. We didn't sleep. The hot air of a midsummer night in a living room turned bedroom for ten people did not allow for restful sleep. The smell of sweating bodies and urine was overwhelming. The lack of sleep was not due only to the discomfort of tight quarters, we had become used to *Kartoshki*. It was Saturday, August 22, in the ghetto of the small town of *Losice*, Poland. The evening before, rumors had spread but nobody knew how and from where they originated. Some were based on former German so called *"Actions"* in neighboring towns, others on pure speculation. Foreboding spread like a black cloud hanging in the sky. I, a 14–year-old boy, lived in an apartment with my parents and a younger sister and brother. Three more families forced upon us by the overcrowded conditions in the ghetto, shared our rooms. Somehow my father managed to feed us, and so far to keep us safe unlike most of the remaining unfortunate ghetto residents. Shots rang out followed by more shots. Shots were often heard in the ghetto. There was no need for an excuse for Germans to shoot Jews. Only the week before I saw my friend's father shot on the sidewalk below the window of our apartment. I pushed aside the curtain and looked out. A wave of fear like an electric current passed through me. In the square below dozens of men in assorted uniforms aimed their rifles at any person who dared appear in the open. A number of corpses lay on the pavement. The shots continued.

"Every Jew in the ghetto is to come down into the square within one hour," loud voices called out in Yiddish and Polish. "Any Jew remaining inside a building after that time will be shot."

Cautiously, some individuals started to enter the square. Then, like a rushing river a multitude of people, singly and in families, poured in from every corner of the ghetto. Old bearded men, mothers with infants in their arms, grandmothers holding on to small children–each family trying to stay close together. Few young people were to be seen, most were away in forced labor camps. Many carried bundles in white sheets knotted on top, some too heavy to hold on to. People, forced to choose in minutes from what took a lifetime to collect, threw any item close at hand into a bundle and went out into the square. Many wore heavy coats, on the assumption that they would be needed later on in the winter months. The hot sun beat down on them as if nature itself conspired with the Germans, to increase their suffering. The square, too small to accommodate all the people and their belongings, erupted into wild chaotic disorder. Whips came into action with ever more vigor. Neither were pistol shots spared. Grandfather *Shlomo* came to say good-bye. He had no illusions. No matter the destination, there would be no place for old people. He encouraged us to attempt to do everything in our power to survive. He hugged and kissed me, turned and walked away.

"*Berl,* everybody, let's pack and go. There's little time left" I heard my father's voice.

"Go where?" I asked.

"Where everyone else is going", he answered.

"Is Usher, my cousin going too"?

"No. He is in the attic, the hiding place, the one we built a few weeks ago."

"I am staying too. Usher is my teacher; he knows what to do."

"But the Germans will kill us if they find us".

"I don't care." I responded. I ran up the stairs to the top floor with my parents and siblings in pursuit. In the corner of uncle Abraham's room, I slid under a bed and pushed myself through a trap door into the hiding place, followed by my family. The door sprung shut. The 80 square-foot space was dark, its walls bare. It had been converted from an old storage space thanks to the foresight of my cousin and financing by my father. A small jagged hole was its only source of air and light. Through it one could see part of the square below. Twenty-seven of us were crowded into the tiny room. Extended family members, neighbors and a few strangers who had found out of its existence, all hoped to find shelter there. Under the tin roof, the temperature must have been well over 100 degrees Fahrenheit. We gasped for air. Although tense and edgy we kept quiet, as did the children of whom there were several. In haste, nobody thought of bringing in water. Squeezed close together we perspired profusely. Some started to disrobe. No sanitary facilities were available. No longer able to hold it in, some relieved themselves where they stood or sat.

Those closest to the hole had a chance to look out and see below. Sheer chaos reigned. The sheet-wrapped bundles lay abandoned, their owners no longer having the strength to carry them. The cries of separated parents and children blended with the rising voices of parched people screaming: *"Wasser, Wasser!"* (Water, Water). Crazed with thirst and fatigue, people no longer cared about their possessions, or even the wounded and the corpses on the cobblestones. The order to march was given. Slowly the square spilled out its wretched contents; the mob moved in the direction of the railway station. Silence descended, the silence of midnight at a cemetery. As if a wild hurricane, death had passed, sucking out life. Neither sound nor moan could be heard. We felt nothing; numb to touch, smell or sound, we were lost in a world we no longer recognized.

# THE JAIL

"It is time to go!" I heard my father's voice. I had woken up from a restless night. Nightmare had followed nightmare. Several days before, I witnessed the deportation of the Ghetto Jews from our town, *Losice,* Poland. Now, hidden in the attic of our building for three days without food or water, among 27 people crammed into a small cell-like place, it took me a while to clear my head. The previous evening, my parents decided to send me, a boy of 14 and my 11 year old sister, *Rywka,* to a Christian farmer in the nearby village of *Swiniarow* where we were to seek refuge. Known to us for many years, we thought the farmer was sure to help. We were told to ask him to come the next evening to the Ghetto and guide the rest of my family, my parents and my 10-year-old brother Itzek, out of the Ghetto. The decision was made in spite of the occurrence of the night before. A family of four had attempted to escape from the hiding place but ran into a German patrol. Watching through a hole in the wall, we saw *Szmulek,* one of their sons, shot and the rest of the family led away under guard. My sister and I got dressed in old, worn clothing and were told to act like village kids looking for lost sheep. I was given a long stick and told to walk barefoot with my sandals hanging down my belt. Blond and blue-eyed, we could pass as non-Jews. For the first time in my life I was given the responsibility to make decisions not only for myself but also for my sister and the rest of the family. Their life now depended on the success of my mission. *Can I do it? I am only 14 years old, only 14.* The thought kept on passing through my mind. *You are a coward, a coward,* echoed another voice within me. The face of *Szmulek,* lying on the sidewalk moaning for hours before he died kept reappearing over and over again. *Dad, how could you do it? How could you saddle me with such a mission? Did you consider the consequence of your decision? Will you be angry if I refuse? What if I fail?*

"It is time to go!" Father repeated. We descended the stairs to the first floor. Outside was dark. *Szmuliek's* body had been removed a short while ago. "Please, please, let it stay dark a little longer, just a little longer!" We ran across the street, *Rywka* at my heels. We didn't look back. We ran as fast as we could—out of the building, crouching behind a wall, into an open lot, another building and finally into a field. Out of breath, we found ourselves outside the Ghetto, out of town. *How did we get through the barbed wire?* I wondered. We ran into a field of rye, tall at the end of August, ready for harvest. Hungry, we picked at the kernels and chewed greedily. We rested, listened. Only an occasional crow of a rooster, a bark of a dog, disturbed the stillness of the morning. *Was it possible that such mornings still exist?* For three days my sister and I had been without water. We came upon a stream, a place where we used to swim in the summer and skate in the winter. It was not considered drinking water, but we couldn't be choosy. With nobody in sight we approached the edge, crouched under a tree, put our heads into the cool liquid and like horses at a trough we gulped and gulped till we drank our fill.

"To *Swiniarow!* Let's go!" I called out, assuming the role of big brother bestowed upon me by my father. Some farmers appeared on their way to work in the fields. "*Niech bedzie pochwalony!*" ("May He be praised!") I recited in my rustic Polish, learned years ago while vacationing in the countryside. "*Na wieky wiekow Amen!*" ("Forever and ever, Amen!") came back the answer. *Jozef,* the farmer we were to see, lived in the first house at the entrance to the village. As we opened the gate to the farm, he and his wife came out of the house screaming: "*Precz! Uciekaj!*" (Get lost! Run!") "I do not want any Jew-kids here! The Germans will find you and kill us all!" "*Chwilke, poczekaj*" (wait a second!) his wife called out, addressing my sister: "Little girl, you are wearing gold earrings; the Germans will soon find you; why don't you let me have them?" She removed the earrings from her ears and sent us back.

We returned to the rye field. The angry, cruel sun beat down on us, adding to our discomfort. Hungry and tired we fell asleep. We woke up late in the afternoon still hungry and tired and decided to visit a former teacher of mine, Mr.Golombek. A Christian, with faith in the future and the daring to come into the Ghetto to instruct us in order to keep our education up to standard. I judged him trustworthy and hoped he would help us. At sundown we approached his house. I knocked at the door. Mr. Golombek appeared and with a look of shock and surprise invited us in. He never asked what happened to us, he guessed. He placed some milk and bread in front of us that we proceeded to ravenously swallow in large bites. Mr. Golombek, a dove in Polish, lived up to his name and to our hope. His wife began to cry. "The neighbors must have seen them come in. Some may have already notified the police in order to be compensated for denouncing Jews." In spite of Mr. Golombek's hesitation about letting us stay, I had to agree with her. I didn't want to harm him. We left.

Late in the evening we started on our way back into the Ghetto. "At least, we will be back together again with the family" we reasoned. In the dark it was hard to see anything. Turning a corner we heard a loud scream: "*Stoj bo strzelam!*" (Stop or I shoot!). A large dog appeared in front of us followed by two policemen, a German and a Pole, a local collaborator. "Where did you come from?" the Pole shouted. Shocked, frozen with fear, I could not seem to get a word out. I raised my arms.

"Put your arms down and speak." he shouted again. In a shaking voice I said we were separated from our parents during the deportation and decided to return home. He believed me. We were marched to the police station. The front room of the police station was familiar. It had belonged to my paternal grandfather, *Schlomo*, before he was evicted from his home. On Saturdays after prayers I would visit him and recite portions of the Bible I had learned the preceding week at Hebrew school. He would then ceremoniously open the cabinet, extract some candy and while presenting it to me would say in Yiddish: "*Du wakst a Talmud Chohem!*" (You are growing into a Torah scholar!).

A tall obese official entered the room. He proclaimed that we broke the law by not following the orders given during the "relocation." We were to be punished. I asked whether we could keep the chunk of bread that Mr. Golombek gave us. His answer: "You will not need it where you are going." In darkness, under guard, we were led through the streets of *Losice* to the town jail. We walked up the steps to the third floor and were pushed into a cell. The iron door slammed behind us. A shameful moon sent in weak rays of light through the barred window, but no hope.

I failed. I failed myself. I failed my sister. I failed my family. How was I to explain to my father that the trust he placed in me was in vain? *Didn't I follow his instructions? Dad! Was it reasonable to expect such wisdom from me? Am I to be blamed? Did I do something wrong? Dad! We are going to be shot tonight, do you know?* Fear, terror, fantasy mixed with reality. Past and present memories kept crossing my mind. The myth of Leonidas, the Spartan, the defender of Greek civilization against the Persians, suddenly entered my thoughts. Near Thermopylae, while dying from his wounds, he wrote his own epitaph with a bloody hand on a nearby rock. I found a piece of broken glass. I cut my finger. In the dim light, I scratched on the wall my name, my sister's, the date and a note that we were to be executed. We embraced, shed some tears and exhausted fell into slumber. Steps on the cobblestones woke us. Our ears caught only a fraction of conversation between a German policeman and the Polish jailer. They had difficulty communicating. One spoke German the other Polish. Minutes later we heard the clanging of doors on the second floor. Young voices of a girl and a boy kept repeating: "*My nie zydzi, my nie zydzi!*" ("We are not Jews.") Their pleas were answered with the screams: "*Raus, raus!*" and the sound of cracking whips. More clanking of doors followed. Again we heard steps outside. Like an echo of crazed witches, slowly dying in the distance we could still hear "*my nie zydzi, my nie zydzi.*"

A while later, like exploding bombs, shots pierced the eerie stillness of the night. Glued to the floor, Rywka and I stood motionless. We remained in that position for what seemed like hours, holding on to each other without saying a word. We waited all night for our guards to come back. They didn't. Two days later, a Polish policeman showed up. After days without food or water, devoid of any feelings, hardly able to walk, we were marched in the direction of the cemetery gates but continued walking. After some distance we were led into a narrow street in the former Ghetto, surrounded by barbed wire. We were now inmates of a newly formed labor camp.

## MY BAR-MITZVAH

It is the day of my Bar-Mitzvah. Saturday, May 1941. Prominently displayed on the right sleeve of my jacket is a white armband with a blue Star of David. Pimple-faced, my voice cracking, wrapped in my father's *tallis*, I recite the prayers and read from theTorah. Not from the scrolls. We are not allowed to have those in our homes. From the *Chumash* I read the week's Torah segment (the *Parsha)*. My teacher, Semiatycki, a transplant from the prestigious Hebrew *Gymnasium* of Warsaw, had prepared me well. My Hebrew is more than adequate. I am able to speak in the language our ancestors spoke 3,000 years ago. I roam the sands of Sinai with Moses, listen to the grumbling of the Israelites and watch them build the "Golden Calf." Next, I deliver my *D'var Torah*, a speech rich in Jewish history–Samson, King David, the Maccabees–the culmination of months of intensive study. The more the Germans try to suppress us, the more we learn. After the prayers, we celebrate. Our banquet consists of a murky liquid in lieu of wine and saccharine-sweetened bread. But nothing dampened the spirit of the day. Suddenly, the door flies open and a squad of German soldiers burst in screaming at us: "*Alle manner raus!*" (every body out!) We run downstairs and line up as ordered. Women, young children; the elderly are left behind. The rest of us are marched to the *Sarnaki* highway. We are given hammers and shovels and ordered to break the stones into gravel to fill the holes in the road. We are not surprised. It happens often. Our whole area is filled with thousands of German soldiers, members of *Guderian's* Second Panzer Army ready to attack the Soviet Union ten miles away. In the meanwhile, they amuse themselves with harassing Jews. The soldiers guarding us are not interested in the results of our work. They smoke, talk among themselves and occasionally look in our direction. As long as we work they leave us alone. Our teacher, Semiatycki, hammer in hand, is surrounded by us, his students. He softly suggests that we make use of the opportunity to continue our lesson. We are going to study the poems of Bialik. He knows most of them by heart. To the cadence of banging hammers and scraping shovels, he begins to recite:

> "If thou wouldst know the mystic fount from whence
> Thy brethren going to the slaughter drew
> In evil days the strength and fortitude
> Immaculate, thy nation's spirit was
> Whose hoary age, though sate with shameful life,
> Did not disgrace its gracious, lovely youth.

*David Gewirtzman and his extended family, about 8 people, spent the Holocaust hidden in a bunker underneath a Polish pig farmer's pig sty.*

*LILLIAN GEWIRTZMAN*
*Born in Graboviec Poland 1934*

## A MEAL WITH LENIN

I cannot recall the name of the film, although I saw it over and over again. I paid little attention to its beginning or its end. It was 1941. We were living in Agdam, the Republic of Azerbaijan, in the former Soviet Union. Arriving on evacuation transports of refugees from the besieged Ukraine, we had been dispersed among the native population whose Muslim religion and Turkic language were alien to us. Eight of us occupied one of the two rooms in a hut belonging to a woman called *Zachra* and her younger companion—both widows of a man called *Akhmed*. A seven-year-old at the time, I hung around *Zachra Khalla* (auntie *Zachra*) hoping to be offered a wedge of bread from the fragrant flat loaves she baked in her *Tandur* pit. Sometimes she shared. At other times, ignoring my wanton stares and watering mouth, she would offer me a lesson in

Azerbaijani arithmetic instead: *Bir, Iki, Utch, Dort, Besh* . . . and with that, disappear behind her door.

I would then head for the local *Kino* which always showed the same Russian film: Comrade Lenin steps down from the train onto the platform at Finland Station in St. Petersburg and addresses a crowd of rowdy sailors. I suffer through yelling, endure the rifle-wielding and flag waving scenes, and wait for the good part: Lenin is partaking of a meal with an assembly of peasants. Ignoring all dialogue regarding the suffering of the proletariat, the ills of capitalism, the call to revolution, I wait for the moment where Lenin, in peasant garb, seated cross-legged on the floor, is taking hearty bites of boiled *Kartoshki*. I follow his every move as his hand reaches into the pot, extracts a steaming potato, dips it into the salt-cellar, and without interrupting the discourse, carries it slowly and deliberately towards his mouth. I swallow my saliva, open my mouth, shut my eyes, and chew along with him. Drawing the starchy vapor into my nostrils, I crush the lumpy pulp against the roof of my mouth. The rest of the movie is of no interest to me. In time, I learn to arrive exactly at mealtime and manage to carry the flavor on my tongue for hours.

*GLORIA GLANTZ*
*Born in Wegrow, Poland, 1939*

## WHAT SONG DID YOU SING, MOTHER?

What song did you sing, mother,
When you left me behind?
When you walked with my brothers
you were driven; you ran to the beating whip.
As you hung your pajamas on the hook,
did your thoughts wander off to your *Gitele* at all?
Did the smallest hope that she would not perish,
that perhaps she would go on, go on to live,
ease a bit of you brutish hell?
Did you scratch the wall with your gentle fingers
till your blood oozed out?
Did you comfort *Zelig, Yitchak,* and Mendl?
Chant *Kaddish* in advance, for yourself, and for them?

*Ai-lu-lu,* you sang
to one child, to the children,
to a roomful, to a people
never to wake from this eternal sleep.
Your voice could soften any heart.
Your song could sooth a grieving breast.
But did it?
Did your tears invade your throat
as the gas seeped silently into the "shower room,"
assaulted your body, clamped-shut your voice?

No more melodies for the children of Israel.
Your black upsweep, turned white, now swept up
soft as your voice once was, floating as your image floats,
through the poisoned clouds of remnants of a people,
cleansed by the memory of your sweet melody.

~ ~ ~ ~ ~ ~ ~ ~ ~ ~

# FOR MARIANNA AND MICHAL KOWALCZK

I came into the world at an inauspicious time in an unwelcoming place for a Jewish baby to be born. It was during the unnatural eclipse, the darkness of 1939-1945. The place was *Wegrow,* Poland. When the Germans entered Poland they had a specific agenda in mind. Take over that country for *Lebensraum* (living space), get rid of the Jews and kill the Polish intelligentsia. They certainly did not want bright Poles to initiate a resistance against them . . . therefore they annihilated the educated clergy, professors, and all political and intellectual leaders. On that count, Maria Kowalczyk would not qualify as she probably only attended school up to 3rd or 4th grade–exactly the level the Nazis considered necessary education for all Slavs who they claimed didn't even need to know numbers past 100 . . . because they were going to be slaves in the 1000 year Reich. It was also a time when much of the world had lost its moral compass. What we think of today as ethical and moral behavior was turned on its head. Helping someone might result in your being killed. Betraying someone would be a reason for reward. Nations could use excuses to turn away our people–"We don't have a Jewish problem and we don't want to import one." And yet, there was a Denmark. There was a Wallenberg, a Sugihara. Books have been written about them, movies made. And there, among the famous and revered, was a simple woman, my "*Matka*", Maria Kowalczyk. You will not find her in film, in your library computer catalog, in a movie, or on u-tube, yet Maria Kowalczyk embodied the pinnacle of heroism.

I, Gitl Przepiorka, the baby daughter of a Jewish couple, Esther and Mendl Przepiorka, was then a cross-eyed, curly dark-haired little girl renamed Gucia Kowalczyk whose height was measured by the sunflower stems my M*atka* (mother) made me stand in front of. "Look how big you got, Gucia!" she used to say. The sunflower stem was my yardstick. I remember the sunshine, the warm rays and the gravel under my bare feet. I see scraggly randomly growing, purple, white, yellow, and pink wild flowers. I make crowns from these for my *Matka*. The flowers died in a day, or two or three. The child lived till no longer a child

"*Matka*, what made you so astute about guiding my behavior in front of those German soldiers who came looking for Jews in the middle of the night? How wise of you to make sure I knew my prayers to the Blessed Mother, Mary, the *Matka Boska*." You were so patient when I was learning my alphabet. I cried and *tried*. You encouraged me patiently, made me repeat the letters and rejoiced with a big smile when I learned them. You made me feel loved. What made you love me so? I remember you teaching me the prayers to the *Matka Boska* so I would sound like a good Catholic child. You even had me say these prayers in front of the German soldiers who held a flashlight to my face in the middle of the night . . . .

The pounding on the door was relentless. It was the middle of the night. I was four years old, fast asleep under my warm down comforter, my *perinah*, a remnant of my other long ago home. A picture of Holy Mother Mary with her son, Jesus, hung above my bed. The banging ceased. Two gigantic men directed a flashlight at my head. I could see only the tops of their leather boots. One of the men passed the light over my black curly hair, my nose and my face. The other held my chin, roughly turning my head. I rubbed my eyes open and held my breath. I was wide-awake now. He shined the light into my eyes. My heart was beating rapidly, I was sure it was audible.

"*Jude! Jude!*" The shrill voice shouted. Whatever did that mean? *Matka* (mother) stood there in her frayed green pajamas trying to calm me. Choked up inside, she had a hard time uttering a sound. "*Gucia, moya kochana,*" she called my name endearingly, "show these soldiers how you say your prayers." I was slow to respond.

"*Schnell! Mach Schnell!*" one of the booted men barked. He pulled my cover off, leaving me exposed as I lay there curled up with my knees to my chest. I felt him grab my shoulders and suddenly I was standing there on the icy floor. I caught a glimpse of Jesus on the wall. His long hair, his mild smile and familiar face had been a comfort to me before. Forcing a faint smile on her face and looking directly at my disbelieving eyes, *Matka* repeated slowly: "Gucia, show them how well you can say your prayers . . ."

My toe hit against the gray pail standing at the foot of the bed. It was my toilet, to keep me from having to go outside in the night frost, a relief I might have welcomed at this moment.

For the third time, *Matka* spoke–this time to the soldiers: "She's a Christian . . . you'll see–my granddaughter." My trembling knees thumped down on the icy wood floor, my damp palms pressed together in prayer . . . My eyes roamed the serene face of the Holy mother above my bed. Slowly and tentatively I began to recite: "*Matka Boska* . . .–Mother of God . . .

The men shut their flashlights, snapped their heels together and walked out. They found no *Juden* in that house that night.

~ ~ ~ ~ ~ ~ ~ ~ ~ ~ ~

On a Yom Kippur afternoon, when we are exhorted to beg forgiveness of those we have willfully or inadvertently wronged, I ask *her* to forgive me. Yes, I have memories, but also regrets. *Matka* did not know Gucia after her childhood. *Matka* no longer got flower crowns; nor did she have anyone with whom to create them. She had only her memories. So it came naturally for me to speak about her when, in 2007, I was given a phrase from the Yom Kippur afternoon service of the *Pirkei Avot*, Hillel: 2:6 (in the Hebrew Liturgy) on which to comment.

*Bamakom sheein anashim, hishtadel lihiot eesh.*

"In a place where no one behaves like a human being, you must strive to be human."

~ ~ ~ ~ ~ ~ ~ ~

What would the proper good-by have been? We could have had some conversation. I would have asked her some questions. How long did it take me to call you "*Matka*"? What kind of child was I? Did I talk about my original family to you?

What thoughts could she have had on the day I was taken from her so brusquely? Would she have thought: "*Gucia, moya kochana*, how I will miss you! I know I made a promise to your mama and papa. Your father was good to us. How could I know I would grow to love you so deeply! I did not think of the danger to my family and me when I took you. I only knew it was the right and Christian thing to do. I will look for your shining, dark eyes, tangle of black curls, your little dancing feet, your sweet voice singing. Who will make crowns of flowers for me now! I will always pray to our Lord, Jesus, for your safety. Do not forget me. Will I ever see you again?"

I would have looked into your eyes and explained why I considered myself a miracle wrought by her. Perhaps by then I might have known about the red-headed little *Worim* girl, who lived in a non-Jewish neighborhood, didn't look Jewish and was outside playing when her parents were rounded up for Treblinka. When she was seen wandering around helplessly at night she was reported by her neighbors, so the Germans could pick her up by her legs and shatter her head against the concrete wall. I could have been such a little girl . . .

If I had been 15 instead of 6 when I was taken from *Matka*, I might have been more thoughtful, acted differently. I might have asked some questions . . . . "What did you do not to have your neighbors betray me?" I would have asked her. "What did you tell them? What influenced you? Didn't you know you could be killed!?"

"Thank you" sounds so inadequate for what you accomplished. But 'thank you' is all I have." I would have said "thank you for your kindness, for your patience, for your good sense, for your affection, your sacrifice, your risk-taking, your love—for my life. Thank you for being a mother to me. I will not ever forget you. I will make your name known so others will always recognize you for your pure goodness!"

Why didn't the adults let me write to her? What harm would it have done? I don't remember my reaction to their reasoning. But I wasn't forceful enough. I should have insisted! I should have had tantrums.

On the other hand, I was taught to be obedient. I always had to be polite. I couldn't disobey. There was so much forgetting. Each day I was blossoming, learning, feeling, growing, catching up. Unfortunately, these regrets can't be addressed now. I was so busy becoming more normal, less fearful, Canadian, American. I was becoming a child, a teenager. The psychology of the time was to "move on. Don't dwell on the past! Forget the past. Be here now." When I wanted to write to her (at age 8 and 12), I was given the standard excuses. "We don't have her address." "You have to go on with your life." "That was in the past, forget about it." "You're here now."

I would have gone back to visit her when I was an adult. I would have sent her money if she needed it. How deeply I regret never having contacted her all those years. I know you saved two other people. I met them 25 years ago. They had communicated with you. At that time they showed me a slide of you. Your face was wizened, wrinkled. It had the look of kindness upon it. They told me you still had an oil painting of me on the wall . . . . I don't remember anyone painting my likeness . . . They told me you asked them to see if anyone at their daughter's upcoming wedding might have some knowledge of me. In their house I took a picture of my family and asked these people to write you that I am well and have 2 children. I had lost all my Polish so I couldn't do it myself. They promised to write to you on my behalf.

I felt like throwing daggers at them when I found out 2 years later, that they hadn't kept that promise. "Why?" I asked. "We felt it would be harder for her to hear from you now especially since you never got in touch with her before. She'd be even more hurt!" . . . They took it upon themselves to make that prediction. I could have gone to the Polish consulate or to the Polish Museum in my town and had someone write it for me! I should have done so! But you had already died in that 2-year period. I missed that opportunity! You would have welcomed a word from me any time, wouldn't you, Matka . . . At least I could have thanked you . . .

Last month, after a wait of two years, I was overjoyed when a notification arrived from the department: "The Righteous Among the Nations," of Yad Vashem in Israel, that Maria Kowalczyk and her husband Michal, have been honored for their wartime record of saving Jews at great risk to themselves. Perhaps she would forgive me for my past slights. At least now I have made her name known for others to recognize her sacrifice and courage.

Neither the Kowalczyks nor their next of kin are alive now to attend the usual ceremony at Yad Vashem where they would have been presented with a certificate and medal. However, there will be an honoring ceremony in America. On Sunday, Nov. 24, 2013, the event, co-sponsored by the Holocaust Memorial and Tolerance Center of Nassau County and the Polish Museum in Port Washington, will take place at the Community Synagogue in Port Washington. It is only fitting that this religious Polish Catholic woman who saved a Jewish child be honored at an event where the community of all faiths is welcome. I will do my utmost to make the occasion worthy of her.

# YAD VASHEM

יד ושם

רשות הזיכרון לשואה ולגבורה

המחלקה לתמידי אומות העולם
The Righteous Among the Nations Department

Gloria Glantz
8 Linda Road,
Port Washington NY 11050
U.S.A

Jerusalem, 29.4.2013

**Ref: Kowalczyk Marianna & Michal #12517.**

We are pleased to announce that the Commission for Designation of the Righteous has decided to award **the title of "Righteous Among the Nations"** to **Kowalczyk Marianna and Michal**, for their help rendered to Jewish persons during the period of the Holocaust at the risk of their life.

They are entitled to a medal and a certificate of honor which will be presented to their nearest relative at a ceremony organized by the Israeli embassy listed below, as soon as we receive an address of her next of kin. For this purpose, we kindly ask you to provide us with the address of the honored nearest relative.

In the future her name will be added on the Righteous Honor Wall at Yad Vashem.

Irena Steinfeldt

**Director**
**Righteous Among the Nations Department**

cc: 1. Maryla Starr, 40 Overlook Drive, Woodelif Lake, NJ 07677, USA
2. Morris Friedman, 116 Madison Green, MG 116, Pompton Plains NJ 07444 USA
3. Shirlez Ginsberg, 5955 Wilderton Ave. Apt E3, Montreal, H3S2V1, Canada
4. Dr. Mordecai Paldiel, mpaldiel@gmail.com

*HERBERT LAUNER*
*Born in Austria, 1925*

If the plural of "tooth" is "teeth," why isn't the plural of "booth," "beeth?" If the teacher "taught," why hadn't the preacher "praught?" And why on earth is it one "goose" but two "geese?" There was no "ham" in "hamburger," nor "pie" in "pinapple." Nothing made sense. It was May of 1939. I was a 14-year-old boy in the 7th grade in Cleveland, Ohio, where I had arrived alone from Austria a few days earlier. My English vocabulary consisted of only a few words and phrases, including "hello," "goodbye," "How are you?" and "My name is–" Had I know the story of "The King and I," I would have concluded, in the King's words, that the English language is truly a "puzzlement."

I was born in Vienna in 1925, the only child of middle-class parents. I was attending an elite high school when Nazi Germany annexed Austria in 1938. As a Jewish student, I had to sit in the far corner of the classroom wearing a badge emblazoned with the word "Jew." Then came November 9, 1938, *Kristallnacht,* and the beginning of the terror period for Jews. That evening I was almost kicked to my death by my closest non-Jewish friend, and my parents and I were beaten by 4 hoodlums who invaded our apartment, smashed our furniture and dragged my father out to the street to scrub the sidewalk.

Due to the immigration laws at that time, we could not come to America as a family so my parents sent me off alone at the age of 14 with only the $10.00 I was allowed to take. I left Vienna on April 30, traveled through Switzerland and on to France where I boarded the Queen Mary for New York. I still have my passport marked with the red "J." When I arrived in Cleveland, I moved in with relatives. Almost immediately after starting school, I met 10 other kids who were also recent immigrants. One of them, a Romanian, proposed that we form a "Refugee Club." We decided to band together as a way of dealing with our insecurities. But there was a catch. In order to hold meetings in the school, we were required to get the permission of our principal. Gentle and soft-spoken, Mr. Goodwyn was the kind of man who could make a point without being dogmatic. He was a wonderful educator and the person who started me on the road to becoming an American. "If you really want to start this club," he said, "I will give you my permission. I only ask that you hear me out first before making any decision." He offered us an alternative. Instead of forming a group based on our common bond as outsiders, he suggested that we concentrate instead on learning American customs, American colloquialisms and American sports.

"Don't forget your heritage," he counseled, "but try not to maintain an Old World ghetto mentality. Make it your business to study 10-20 new English words a day and I will help you with pronunciation and the correct usage."

Despite Mr. Goodwyn's sincere advice, the group decided to form the Refugee Club anyway. I was hesitant to join it at first, but one of the girls in the group was beautiful and she let me kiss her–so I immediately became a member. But our principal's words ultimately proved more powerful than those kisses. The more I thought about what Mr. Goodwyn's had said, the more I understood that a great lesson lay within our principal's words.

# CHAPTER 14

## MORE SURVIVOR STORIES

$I$N THIS CHAPTER are writings of our colleagues at HTMC (the Holocaust Memorial and Tolerance Center) who did not attend the Poets and Writers course. Some writings are family chronicles, while others are drawn from their published autobiographies.

### *KRISTALLNACHT*

On November 18, 2013 the New York Times carried this article in the column titled: *Link-by-Link*. The account, "9 Nov 38," is a Twitter account set up by German historians as if it were an up-to-date account of the widespread violence and destruction of synagogues and Jewish owned businesses across Germany and Austria at the current time. The article said that It was practicing what could be called 'historical tweeting', using the brevity and immediacy of Twitter to recreate events from the past as if they were playing out before our eyes. The five historians who run the account said that they got a lot of responses from people who actually wanted to research their own families' historical role in Kristallnacht– their own story in their town," he said, adding "which is all I want."

Following, we have personal reports from our own survivors of the horrors of *Kristallnacht* that 75 years ago in Nazi Germany, culminated in a night of anti-Jewish terror which plunged the country on a path to the Holocaust.

*Karl Heiman*
*Oberdorf, Germany*

## THE EVENTFUL HISTORY OF
## THE HEIMAN TORAH

Karl Heiman was one of our most colorful survivor-speakers. He always alluded to his father's sterling German military record and the medals awarded to him for his achievements while fighting on the German side during World War I. This resulted in Karl being allowed to attend German public schools far longer than other Jewish children, but ultimately his family, too, had to flee from the Nazis. Below, Karl describes *Kristallnacht* and why . . . "Our Oberdorf synagogue never burned down . . ."

"It was a night of absolute horror throughout Germany. Synagogues, Jewish homes and shops went up in flames. Frequently, Jewish men, women and children, were tortured, shot, or otherwise slain trying to escape from burning to death." But Karl's family escaped the worst of it and below he describes perhaps why that was.

"Oberdorf is nestled in an extremely scenic and historic landscape about 60 miles southeast of Stuttgart, the capital of today's State of Baden-Wuerttemberg in southern Germany. Our ancestors had lived there since Roman times. The Heimann families were always regarded with the highest esteem for their philanthropic, cultural, historical and even environmental contributions to the local and surrounding communities in word and deed. One of the more important ancestors of the Heimann families, H.L. Heimann, Chaim Loeb Heimann, presented a beautifully written Torah to the Jewish community synagogue in his home town of Oberdorf, Germany in honor of Germany's victory over France in the war of 1870-71. Chaim Loeb Heimann had this Torah commissioned in Vienna, which at that time was renowned for its great Torah scribes. Not only is it a beautifully written Torah, but it is also an exceptionally richly decorated one. It remained in constant use in the Oberdorf synagogue, well into the Nazi era.

In 1938, 5.5 years after Hitler's ascension to power, *Kristallnacht*, descended upon German Jewry. It was by far the worst pogrom, but best organized. Man's inhumanity to man had reached its lowest depths. Most historians agree that this horrendous event signaled the beginning of the end of European Jewry as we knew it. The Holocaust had now started in earnest, mercilessly and vengefully. During the night of November 9th to 10th, a very well organized nationwide mob of Nazi storm troopers and henchmen set fire to every synagogue in Germany. Well over 1,000 synagogues were burned and destroyed.

In Oberdorf, the hometown of the Heimann families for many generations, something very extraordinary and unexpected occurred. The relationship between the Jewish and Christian citizens was always extremely cordial and respectful. The local Nazis refused to participate in this orgy of destruction and hatred. Other Nazis were then recruited from different towns to set the synagogue afire. When the Christian neighbors realized that the synagogue was burning, they promptly extinguished the flames. Our Oberdorf synagogue never burned down, to the great surprise and relief of the whole community. The Torah scrolls were rescued and saved, although the Nazis had already stolen the valuable ornaments and religious adornments. The various Torahs were given to the individual Jewish families whose members or ancestors were instrumental in donating or presenting these valuable parchment scrolls to the Oberdorf Jewish community synagogue. Among the righteous citizens of Oberdorf, the most outstanding ones were the family of Mr. Daniel Schwarz. They excelled in their very active support and help of Jewish causes, Jewish families and Jewish history. During the Nazi tyranny they did their utmost, often under great personal danger, to help and assist their fellow human beings of the Jewish faith.

When our family was finally able to emigrate to the United States in August 1939, the Heimann Torah traveled with us. We landed in New York on August 17, 1939, just two weeks before Hitler attacked Poland and ignited World War II. Coincidentally, August 17, 1939 was also the 30th wedding anniversary of our parents, David and Bertha Heimann, the parents of Heinrich (Heiner), Martin Udo and Karl. We arrived on the American passenger liner "Manhattan." The Statue of Liberty in New York Harbor seemed to radiate an exceptionally bright glow on the memorable day.

During World War II, the Heimann Torah became the Torah in Fort Dix, New Jersey. The Heiman families, residing at the time near Lakewood, New Jersey as hardworking successful chicken farmers, jubilantly answered the Army's call and search for a Torah to be used at the chapel in nearby Fort Dix. It was perhaps the greatest and most glorious time for this historic Torah when its stature was elevated to serve and inspire untold thousands of Jewish soldiers, servicemen and women, nurses and doctors, who were eager and ready to excel and help liberate Europe from the evil of the Nazi scourge. History proves how well we succeeded.

The Bar and Bat Mitzvah of Howard and Elizabeth Heiman, first generation Americans were joyously celebrated in the presence of the Heiman Torah at Temple Emanuel in East Meadow, Long Island, New York. With the permission and encouragement of our parents, the Heiman Torah was presented to Temple Emanuel in East Meadow in memory of the six million martyrs who perished in the Holocaust, the most cataclysmic event in our Jewish history. The Heiman Torah's illustrious saga speaks for itself. May it inspire future generations to a life of peace and prosperity, patience, wisdom and fortitude."

*JANET ETTELMAN*

Janet, a volunteer at HMTC for 20 years and a native of Mannheim, Germany, also recalls *Kristallnacht.*

One evening in 1938, there was a knock at the door. My family was at dinner. My father looked at my mother and she looked at my father. My mother said she would go to the door. Since I was nosy, I said I would go with her. There stood a woman who worked in our house. She told my mother "Something is going to happen tomorrow; I don't know what, but you must tell your husband to leave town." The next morning I got ready for school. My father was not there, but he never was in the morning. He owned a cigar factory in a small village near Mannheim and always left early in the morning to go to the factory. I met my cousin to go to school. We walked on a large avenue that was a pedestrian street with trolley tracks running down the middle. We saw a group of men marching five abreast, each carrying a household tool like a rake, shovel or some other tool over their shoulders. I asked my cousin if he knew who those men were and he said "no." Finally, we went on to school. As we approached the synagogue, we saw the synagogue windows smashed, a large fire burning in the courtyard in front of the synagogue, prayer books and Torah scrolls burning and the entire synagogue damaged. We ran home. I told my mother what I had seen at the school. My mother said: "We can't stay here; we'll go to the park." We stayed at the park until it started to get dark. Then we started to go home. First we went through the business district. We saw all the stores owned by Jews had their store windows smashed. Next, we went through the residential area. Fires burned in front of all the homes owned by Jews. There was no fire In front of our house. The house was owned by my maternal grandmother. She was known in the entire city as a philanthropist. There was no light on in the entire building. When we got into our apartment, we could tell that people had been there. The dishes from the dining room cabinet had been neatly taken

out. Not one dish was broken! Still, my parents realized that we would have to make every effort to leave Germany. With great difficulty, my father and I were able to leave and go to America on the last ship out of Italy. My brother and mother were able to escape to England on the *Kindertransport.*

Krystallnacht precipitated the flight of Jewish children to England and to a lesser extent, to Switzerland, that is known as the Kindertransport.

It was the largest and most poignant rescue of endangered children from the brutal clutches of the Nazi empire. Over a nine-month period before the outbreak of World War II, Britain heroically brought children from Germany, Austria and Czechoslovakia to England in an effort to save their lives. Forced to leave their parents behind the children were torn apart from their loved ones and said their last goodbyes. With few instructions they boarded trains, sailed by boat, crossed the English Channel and traveled distances that they could barely comprehend while their parents remained trapped in Nazi territory. After seven decades, the stories are being told, both in their own words as child survivors and also by their grandchildren.

# KINDERTRANSPORT

*ANITA WEISBORD*

Anita came to the Center with a B'nai B'rith group. They had been touring Long Island mansions on a fundraiser for B'nai B'rith. The last locale on the tour was the Pratt home that had become the Holocaust Memorial and Education Center. They never knew it existed. Jay Feldman was the tour historian. The survivor who spoke to them was Eddie Weinstein who described how he escaped from Treblinka. Anita was so impressed that she went over to Jay and said that she would like to volunteer. Then she added: "I don't know if my story is as dramatic as Mr. Weinstein's as I came on the *Kindertransport.*" Jay replied: that "Every story is important," and he invited her to the Center's training session. Later, when she observed how they led the school children on the tour went right into the history of the Holocaust after talking about "*Kristallnacht,*" without ever mentioning the *Kindertransport,* which

followed it, she was surprised and a bit dismayed. Frantic parents had tried to get their children to safety in England. Anita recalls: "I waited a few months because I was new, and finally, I gathered my courage and went over to Regina White who was the Education Chairman at that time and told her the story. She agreed with me and asked me to bring in some photos and history, which I did. I brought in photos and articles that explained the *Kindertransport* and they made a display and included it in the exhibition and the tour."

Anita, being fifteen years of age, was too old to be allowed to go to school in England. Most children on the *Kindertransport,* upon reaching the age of 15, had to go to work. In her case, her hostess requested that she stay at home with her. She was a very religious woman and supported the missionaries in Africa. Perhaps she had volunteered to host a Jewish child solely to convert her but nevertheless, another child was saved. Anita said: "She wanted to convert me too, 'to save my soul.' We went to church every day and twice on Sundays. If I had been younger and not from a traditional Jewish home, it would have been very easy for me to be converted: after all—a new country, a new language, why not a new religion?"

In "A TRAGIC PAST," Anita's granddaughter, Chelsea Weisbord, writes about a Passover tradition they have each year.

Chelsea writes: "My grandmother's rabbi suggested that the survivors add their flight from persecutors as part of their Passover tradition. Perhaps it will become part of yours, too. Throughout the *seder* there is a lot of fidgeting, whispering and wandering eyes, but when my grandmother speaks everyone looks up and gives her their undivided attention. Every year she tells the exact same story and when she completes it, we all stare at her completely mesmerized. Here is what she reads:

'Tonight, as we tell the story of the Exodus from Egypt, we add the story of our own miraculous escape from a

slavery much greater than in Egypt—from terror and death. We were the condemned of Hitler in Germany. Had we not been brought forth, we would have perished. We would have had no husbands or wives. Our children and grandchildren would not have been born. We are the *Kinder,* the Children of Israel of 1939. We represent the 10,000 saved from the flames, our children and their children, and also the hundreds of thousands of our generation who were not saved.

The burning synagogues of the November 1938 pogrom were our "Pillar of Fire." The flames, seen in Britain, roused our fellow Jews and Gentiles to save us few. They sent for us by trains and transports, *Kindertransports,* to Berlin, Vienna and Prague. Like the Children of Israel in Egypt, we packed in haste, chanted as we crossed the border, passed over the sea dry shod. Unlike Israel in Egypt who marched out a whole people, fully armed, with great leaders, we children were but a fraction.

We marched out alone, unarmed, some as babies in the arms of other children. Our parents stayed behind. Our story is not one story, but 10,000 stories. How we endured; what we accomplished.'

My grandmother was an ordinary 15-year-old girl living in Vienna, Austria. No life could be more perfect. She had friends and family and anything a girl could ask for. On March 13, 1938, her world came crashing down. That was the day that Adolf Hitler and his troops marched into Austria and started to exile Jewish families from their homes. From that day on she knew that things would never be the same. After watching several families vanish, her family decided to run away while they had the chance. Shortly after, the entire family split up. Her parents thought that it would be best to send their youngest child on a train that transported Jewish children to England. She describes it this way:

'–––It was May 15, 1939, the night that my parents decided to send me away. That was the most treacherous night of my whole life. I sat on the train alone and we didn't actually leave until early the next morning. I spent the entire night staring out the window watching my mother who was on the other side. Not once did we stop looking at one another not knowing if I would ever see my family again or even if we would survive. I never understood why my parents sent me away until I had children of my own. The time I spent in England was devastating and brutal because I still did not know if I was ever going to be able to see my family again.'

To me, Passover isn't only about the Jews' freedom from Egypt but it is also about my grandmother's freedom and the freedom that I have today. My grandmother's past is a big part of who I am today. She has made me more selfless, understanding and brave. She tells her story again and again so that her children and their children should know why the Passover *seder* is so precious."

# KINDERTRANSPORT

*MARGARET GOLDBERGER*
*Berlin in 1926*

No matter what religion you practiced at home, the religion you followed in England on the *Kindertransport* often depended on one's hosts. Life in Germany had deteriorated severely but we managed to adjust, that is–until November 9<sup>th</sup>, 1939–*Kristallnacht*, 'the night of broken glass.' In addition to the fright and damage we suffered, my father was one of the many men who were taken away to a concentration camp outside of Berlin. It was a life-shaking experience from which he never recovered. A few months later he was released. My mother managed to bribe Nazi officers with money obtained from an aunt in New York. We soon had to vacate our apartment and went to live with another aunt in Germany. In the meantime, my mother registered me for one of the *Kindertransports*. In early June of 1939, we were notified that I was to leave Berlin within the next few days. I was very excited about this great adventure and did not view it as a permanent separation from my family, since I knew that my mother's relatives in the United States had sent them an affidavit to emigrate there and presumed that eventually I would be sent for. Six weeks after my 13<sup>th</sup> birthday, with my rucksack on my back and suitcase by my side, I stood in the station with about 100 other children. Although other parents and children were in tears, my parents showed no anxiety so I felt confident.

 The train left from Berlin and took us to Bremerhaven where we boarded the *S.S. Europa,* which would deposit us in Southhampton, England before continuing to New York. My stomach was no match for the North Sea and I soon became sick. The next morning, we were in Southhampton and on a pleasant June afternoon, boarded a train to London and were assembled in a large hall at the station to await our hosts. One by one, children were claimed by families who had volunteered to take care of them or by committee representatives. Relatives who had escaped to England earlier claimed the luckiest ones. I sat in the dingy hall for a long time and was one of the last children still awaiting my fate. Finally, a representative of the refugee committee approached me, looked at my name-tag and took me by car to my first home. This was like heaven. The Wolfsons, a wealthy couple with adult children treated me like a princess. They gave me a beautiful room and breakfast served by a maid on fine china and crystal. Mr. Wolfson even took me to the movies occasionally on weekends. My idyllic time came to an end after a month's stay when the Wolfsons left for the United States to rejoin their children. My next stop was a girls' hostel in the East End of London, a poor area with many slum buildings. I roomed with two other girls, one of whom, Lottie, cried for her parents constantly and rebuffed any attempts at friendship. The other, Ruth, is still my friend and we are as close as sisters.

Having come from an assimilated home and enjoyed the Easter and Christmas holidays along with the rest of the Germans, it was difficult getting used to the rules of Orthodox Judaism. Our matron demanded absolute obedience to many rules: meal time, bed time, lights out, assigned household duties, permission to leave the house—but most of all obeying the religious laws strictly: not doing anything that constituted work on Saturdays—switching on lights, writing, opening letters, even if the letters came from home! We were also treated as specimens for the visiting *B'nai B'rith* members who had furnished much of this hostel. The oldest girls were allowed to stay up to serve them tea, the English way. They were instructed to pour the milk into the cup first and then, the tea. The rest of us were sent to bed early on those evenings so the committee ladies could walk from room to room to see the children and point to their beds, each of which had the name of the donor above the headboard. Being treated like this, on view to potential foster parents, was a humiliating experience. We didn't really want to be separated from one another or to be put in another new situation.

At the end of the summer holidays, we were all sent to school. Most of us did not know much English and understood little of what was going on. The classes were large and there was no special teacher to help us. Somehow, we muddled through. Our English classmates spoke Cockney English that made it even more difficult for us to understand. They viewed us as strange creatures. Some confused us with Nazi Germans. As the end of August neared, we received gas masks and prepared for a possible evacuation out of London. The good news from my parents was that my brother who was scheduled for a *Kindertransport* and had run into technical difficulties, had overcome them before World War II was declared. On the Friday before the beginning of the war, we were told to bring our luggage and gas masks to school the following day to be evacuated. When we came home that Friday afternoon and informed our matron of these orders, she panicked and told us we could not possibly travel on the Sabbath. After consulting with the rabbi, who gave his permission—on the basis of the Jewish law, which permits the breaking of the Sabbath in the face of a life-threatening emergency—she relented. Being a teenager, I viewed another change in residence with my whole group of friends as an additional adventure.

However, the term "war" did give me pause and evoked some feelings of fear, especially for what war would mean to my parents who were trapped in the enemy country. How would we continue to communicate? Saturday, September 1, 1939, the day of our school's evacuation from London, was a trial for me. We arrived in school with all our belongings early that morning and were transported to a railroad station to board the waiting trains. Children were sorted into groups, and each group would eventually be transported to a different village in the County of Norfolk. Approximately 30 children, among them 14 of us, hostel girls, eventually arrived at Cockley Cley, a feudal village. My trouble was that I had begun to menstruate shortly before leaving Germany, and the whole procedure was still uncomfortable and somewhat unmanageable to me. My period had begun just the day before the evacuation. On that Saturday we had to change trains several times and each time there was a long wait for the connecting train. We had to stay with the group and there were no bathroom facilities available to us. By the time we arrived at our destination, it was evening. My underwear was soaked. I have never felt as miserably uncomfortable as I did on that day.

We waited in the Village Hall, a small building on the Village Green, while volunteer villagers selected the children they would house. The British government paid small amounts of money for room and board to these people. Naturally, they selected the English children first. Families finally selected four of our girls, who spoke fairly good English. The rest of us were taken to the "Hall"—a huge mansion, almost a castle, three stories high with more than 30 rooms. It was reached by a path through a forest and had a small lake behind the lawn in back of the house. We were given two bedrooms with five beds in each. We woke early the next

morning, a Sunday. It was September 2<sup>nd</sup>, 1939. At approximately 11:00
A.M., as we stood on a balcony overlooking the front lawn, we heard a
radio playing music. It stopped suddenly. In grave tone, the announcer
read a statement of the war declaration against Germany.

Standing on the balcony of this beautiful country mansion, with lovely
trimmed hedges, expansive gardens around us, it seemed impossible that
we might soon hear shooting, or see soldiers marching in. Every girl
on that balcony was shaken, worried about what would happen to her
family. Would they be able to escape Hitler's clutches? Would they be
imprisoned as enemies of the regime? Would they be tortured? We were
afraid to hurt each other by talking too much about it. After that morning,
most of us kept our worries to ourselves. In a few days, our Orthodox
matron arrived. She was given a small bedroom of her own. We also
had a sitting room and a kitchen/dining area. The rest of the house
was absolutely out of bounds. Occasionally, Lady Roberts, the owner
of the mansion, would visit during one of our meals. She would pat the
youngest child on the head, inquire of the matron whether everything
was well, and we would not see her for a week or two, nor would we
see her husband, Sir Samuel. Our London hostel cook and her daughter
also arrived quite soon. They were housed in a nearby villager's house.
Our matron insisted on keeping kosher. The matron soon started making
rules, as she had done in London and we were assigned our weekly,
albeit rotating chores, including cleaning the previous day's ashes out of
the grate, lighting the fire in the cooking stove, scrubbing the floor on
hands and knees, etc. When we were asked whether we would like to
earn a few pennies by helping with the harvest in the field, we welcomed
this opportunity.

We attended a no-longer used two-room schoolhouse. Each English
school day began with a prayer, the singing of a hymn and the national
anthem. One of the hymns had the same melody as the German national
anthem. Soon there was a complaint from a villager that the German
children were singing "their" national anthem. We laughed about this

confusion. It clearly showed that a lot of people did not know what we were about. I realize now, that in the village setting the villagers, remote from the big city, were unsophisticated and unworldly and did not really understand what the war was about.

The letters from our families in Germany had ceased. My mother's oldest brother and his family had emigrated to Holland and so my parents sent letters for me and my brother to our uncle Wilhelm and we corresponded with out parents in the same manner. This communication route came to a drastic end when the Germans overran Holland in the spring of 1940. My brother, however, was in England attending the ORT school in the city of Leeds, so we wrote to each other regularly, but did not see each other for more than two years. On a beautiful April morning, as the daffodils were blooming all over the gardens of the Hall, I received a telegram from my brother informing me that he had received a postcard from our parents who had reached Lisbon, Portugal and were awaiting passage to the United States. This news was wonderful for me, but I hardly dared to mention it to the other girls. Most of them had not heard anything from their parents since the war began. In the absence of their parents, we, the older girls, felt that it was our duty to instill morals and to teach good manners to the younger children.

Although we imposed strict rules on our group, we ourselves did not like the matron's discipline. In spite of all our worries, we were kids after all. We made fun of her behind her back and had secret hiding places in the woods where we made up funny names for her and plotted all kinds of nonsensical things that never came to pass. For the holiday of Purim, we decided to put on a play of the story of Esther. We composed some songs, made our own costumes and invited all the adults in the house to be our audience. It must have been a strange performance for the servants and Lady Roberts, who also attended, since our self-written script was in German. With the onset of the bombing in London, the local police confiscated all cameras; again the fear we might be German spies. Miss Kohn and Mrs. Reissner, our Jewish matrons, were given notice to leave the area because the county of Norfolk was too close to the coast and they might perhaps give signals to enemy planes. The paranoia of the British was understandable. Many Jewish refugees were interned, some on the Isle of Man; others shipped to Canada and Australia.

My rather comfortable life at the Hall came to an end when I voluntarily switched places with my friend Lottie, who had been located in a mean, cold environment. Throughout this time, though I felt close to several of the girls, I generally kept my feelings to myself. If I felt sad or unhappy, I did not talk about my feelings and always presented a cheerful appearance. Since those days, I have rarely shared my emotions. Eventually, by the end of the summer of 1941, five of us, who had reached our 15th birthday, were told by the London Committee that we had to return to London; our school days were over and that we would have to find jobs and start to support ourselves, at least in part. On a warm summer's day, I received news from my brother who had received a telegram from my mother in New York that our father had died of a heart attack. I believe that the horrors of my father's time in the concentration camp and the subsequent years of hardship in his life and in the lives of Jews in general who still lived in Berlin, contributed to his ill health and early death. It was the first time I sat at the window and stared for a long time out into the dark London streets. I could not come to terms with the fact that I would never see my father again. At the beginning of October, 1945 my American visa was finally issued and the next chapter of my life would soon begin.

# KINDERTRANSPORT

## *INGE GUREVITCH*

England had voted to accept 10,000 children and so the *Kindertransport* was born. My mother went to enroll me. The rules were: Only children between 3 and 17 years old would be accepted; a deposit of 50 pounds was required for each child; and each child must have a sponsor.

I did not have a sponsor and so, was rejected. Mother was now desperate. She wangled a temporary visa for herself so that she could go abroad and find me a sponsor. She had little money, nor did she speak English. Upon arrival in New York, she took a subway to the Bronx because she knew that many Jews lived there. Mother stood at the top of the subway stairs and speaking Yiddish only, tried to persuade passers-bye to help get her child out of Germany. Eventually, a lawyer who spoke Yiddish listened to her and took her to his home. She lived with his family and looked after his little girl while he got in touch with the charity that ran the English summer camp in England where I had spent the summer of 1934. They agreed to take me temporarily until my travel papers and visa to the Philippines (where the rest of my family was waiting out the war) had arrived. Now I was able to register for the *Kindertransport*.

The transports started on December 10th, 1938 and lasted until September 3rd, 1939. My turn came in May, 1939. We were allowed to take one small suitcase, no money, jewelry or photographs. Before we left the station, 6 Gestapo police boarded the train and warned us that if we "Jewish swine" were smuggling anything out of Germany the whole train would be turned back and we would all be taken to a concentration camp. There was dead silence. Even the little 4-year-olds felt the tension and there was not a peep out of them. Hours later we arrived at the border of Germany and Holland, but only when the Gestapo left the train did we feel safe. As soon as the train crossed the border, chaos erupted. We sang, shouted, cried and laughed with relief, hugged each other and danced around. At the first stop in Holland, a group of ladies handed each of the 200 children a hardboiled egg, chocolate milk and cookies. I had not eaten an egg or cookie in years, so this was the best and most unforgettable food I had ever tasted. In the morning, the boat docked in Harwich where many children were met by their sponsors, and the others spent hours or days in a sort of camp. Every Sunday, families would look them over and decide who to take home with them. The little kids were easy to place. The older ones, especially the boys, were left behind and ended up in camps being trained to work on farms or to join the British army when they turned 18.

Part of my family was "safe" in the Phiilippines. My half-brother Walter, 14 years older than I, from my father's first marriage, had gone to Italy to study medicine. When Italy became an ally of Germany and Hitler persuaded Mussolini to expel the Jews from all universities, Walter had to leave. He was finally able to obtain only one visa and left Germany by ship in 1938 with his bride, Lily, to go to Shanghai, one of the few places that was issuing visas to Jews. En route, on a layover in Manila, the Philippines, Walter—who spoke 5 languages—was offered and accepted a job as interpreter for the many refugees living there. As soon as they were settled, Walter started the visa application process for father, mother, and me. He was finally able to obtain 1 visa, not 3 and it had to be used for my father who had been imprisoned on *Kristallnacht* and would only be released if he left Germany right away. Now that I was safe, Mother joined Father in Manila and hoped that I would be able to join them when I got my travel papers. But it was not to be. After camp closed, I was in limbo. I moved to a suburb of Manchester where Mr. Levy, the summer camp's treasurer, lived with his family. Less than 1 week later, in September 1st, 1939, Germany invaded Poland and two days later, England and France declared war on Germany. Any chance of traveling to join my family was dashed. Transportation was reserved for the war effort. It was an anxious and very sad time for me. Now I would not be able to go and help my parents in Manila. I was loveless, stateless, hopeless and homeless, afraid of being returned to Germany or sent to a group hostel. Mr. and Mrs. Levy agreed to host me. While some of the *Kindertransport* girls were abused by their sponsors, some treated as maids (although most have good memories of their foster families), I was treated as the 3rd child in the Levy family. At first I felt I was a burden. I cried a lot and felt ashamed of my shabby clothes. But most of all, I felt guilty because I could not help my family and I was safe and lived in comfort. I knew that they were having a difficult time in Manila. Living conditions were abysmal. After the Japanese invaded the Philippines and we could no longer correspond, the news was full of the atrocities people suffered during the Occupation.

I soon adapted to my new life and began to feel at home and one of the family. Indeed, this family became my own. I learned English and English ways, went to high-school, to nursing school and then, met my future husband, Hyman Gurevitch. Hy was a handsome American lieutenant whom Mr. Levy had invited to our Friday night dinner. When the war was nearing its conclusion in 1945, Hy and I married in Manchester with plans for me to come to New York the following year. When the time came, I was very excited, but also sad. England, its people and my new family had become my life and were very dear to me, but I had made my choice and here I was in Southampton, at the pier. In 1946, I sailed on the Queen Mary to join him in New York and to begin my new life. It included meeting my new family, who were wonderful, and adapting to American customs and language, earning my Masters degree in nursing at New York University and raising our two sons.

When the American army retook the Philippines, mother weighed 90 pounds. My father, who had returned home after *Kristallnacht*, a broken old man, had not survived long in Manila. Walter and Lily had babies who had been raised on rice water. Lily was too undernourished to nurse them and they could not buy milk. After World War II, Walter and his family moved to Australia. When mother arrived in the United States, she realized that she had lost the little girl of 14 whom she remembered from Breslau. In the 9 intervening years, we had become strangers and now I was a grown woman with a family of my own.

# FLEEING THE GERMANS

*DAVID AND MIREILLE TAUB*
*Paris, France 1938*

## MIREILLE'S STORY
## LAST TRAIN FROM PARIS

I came to the Center about 10 years ago after Beth Lilach came to my department at Nassau Community College to discuss the museum's programs, I having arrived in the United States from war-torn France as a 2-year-old.

I was born in Paris, on October 7, 1938. Both my parents were born in Poland, They met in Paris and were married on New Years Eve, 1931. My sister was born on October 26, 1934 and I followed four years later, on October 7, 1938. My father, mother, sister, and I arrived at Ellis Island, on August 12, 1940.

The years preceding the invasion of Poland by the Nazis were filled with uncertainty anguish and turmoil, both in France as well as in Germany, Poland and other nations. My parents, filled with apprehension, began their search for visas that would allow them to come to the United States.

My father could be issued a "Nansen Passport" named for the Norwegian diplomat who sponsored these papers. Approximately 2000 in total, they were mainly issued to White Russians by the League of Nations who, after the Russian Revolution needed to immigrate to safe places; in other words, they were issued to people who were unable to prove a national identity. The village in which my father was born was on that fluctuating border between Russia and Poland and fit into that category.

My mother, well on her way to becoming a French National, was able to obtain visas under the French quota, as were my sister and I. Although my sister and I were both born in France, my parents had to petition the French Government for citizenship status, which was granted, but not without filing numerous papers and fees.

The years between 1934, my sister's birth, and 1938, when I was born, were filled with increasingly serious international, political and economic crises. War became inevitable in spite of Chamberlain's optimism. Papers, affidavits, visas were submitted, returned and recognized. Passport applications were filed, received, and placed within rapid and accessible safekeeping.

On September, 1939, while my parents were on vacation in Fontainebleau, Hitler invaded Poland. My family immediately returned to Paris.

With the advent of hostilities, my father began to prepare an escape route via Bordeaux to Spain. He traveled to Bordeaux hoping to be able to send for us or send us along during the beginning stages of the phony war. Paris was under constant bombardment alert and although not many bombs had actually fallen, the citizenry, terrified, sought nightly refuge in makeshift bomb shelters built under apartment building cellars and in the Metro. Gas masks, resurrected from the First World War, and some, re-issued, were constant companions. Ration tickets for supplies such as food, coal, and clothing were issued to prevent stockpiling, looting, and black marketeering.

France was quickly losing the war. In the last days of French fighting, my father was at last mobilized and told to report to a command post in Paris. He came, equipped with his visas and exit papers, requesting permission not to serve because he felt, not only did he risk being killed in what was now viewed as a totally futile war, but, because of imminent surrender, his wife and family were at extreme risk. Compassion won, my father was told to get back to his family. In the meanwhile, my mother packed a small suitcase with several changes of clothing and other necessities such as a small sewing kit, important papers, etc. and waited for my father to return. They managed to get to the railroad station and were able to take the last train from Paris hours before Paris surrendered to the Nazi forces. Our train, under attack, disgorged frightened refugees who hid in the bushes, expecting to be hit by strafing fighter-bombers intent on killing the civilian population. We survived the attack and joined the long march of refugees walking to anywhere in France looking for safety in small communities. We walked, walked, and walked.

When we were tired, we walked slower, but we continued walking away from the war zone. My father and mother alternated between carrying me. My father tried to get us to Bordeaux, as per our original plan, however the Nazis declared the area a "forbidden zone" because of its strategic position, not far from the Atlantic Ocean and Spain.

Through one of those amazing, inexplicable coincidences in life, while waiting on line, in Bordeaux, perhaps to re-validate a document or receive information about other travel possibilities, my father met the American consulate officer who had helped him in Paris. She remembered him because of his highly unusual Nansen passport. She needed to get to Marseilles where the American consulate in Vichy France was to be established. They pooled their resources, rented a truck, picked up refugees, driving across the French Pyrenees towards the Mediterranean. She was protected by her American status as a Consulate Officer; my father provided the language, expertise and some ready cash to buy gasoline, supplies, etc.

We finally arrived in the small city of Perpignan, which is about 100 kilometers from the Spanish border. My parents took stock, looked at my sister, and realized that she had outgrown or worn out her shoes and before they could continue, they would have to replace the ones she could no longer wear. They stopped into a shoe store, located on a large plaza. After a short while, they realized that I was nowhere to be found. They were in a total panic; hundreds of refugees were milling around in that square. As a not quite two-year-old toddler I could have wandered off anywhere. However, within a short period, I was located in an empty shoe carton and was seen and heard happily playing with all the shoes left in the carton.

Once in Spain, we traveled by train to Barcelona, allowed only to travel through Spain, but not stay in Spain. From Barcelona, we traveled to Lisbon, embarking on a Greek merchandise ship. We spent three weeks crossing the North Atlantic, trying to avoid U-boats looking to torpedo ships heading towards America. We arrived in America on August 11, 1940. My father's journal records a terrible voyage.

Six weeks of travel across war zones in France, Atlantic storms, U-boats, grossly inadequate and horrible food had finally taken their toll on me. Upon our arrival at Ellis Island, immigration doctors told my parents that I was too ill to be taken off the Island. I had a fever, broken out in hives and was a very unhappy child. My mother successfully convinced them that there was nothing more serious than the accumulated stress of our experience. While on board the boat, my father had sent cables to various family members that we were scheduled to arrive. When we finally disembarked at the pier, there was no one there to greet us. No one had received the telegrams. My father hailed a taxi, who in true NY style, instead of taking us directly to HIAS, which was a short distance away, took us on the proverbial taxi ride around Manhattan Island, leaving my father with only $10.00. We stayed in the shelter at HIAS for several days. Finally, "cousins" returning from vacation, found the telegrams, and came to rescue us. (It wasn't until several years ago that it dawned on me that cables would not be delivered because of the embargo on shipping news.)

With so many relatives living in New York, my parents decided not to go to Chicago. With their help, we rented an apartment in Williamsburg, Brooklyn. One of the "cousins" provided my father with an introduction to a handbag manufacturer in Manhattan. My parents enrolled in school to learn English. My father joined the Civil Defense League, doing night-time patrol, warning citizens of air raid alerts and black out regulations. We were on our way to becoming Americans. We were extra-ordinarily lucky to be able to escape France. Most of our families in France as well as Poland were not so lucky.

When the war ended, my parents had already made a decision not to return to France. My father started his own business, becoming a well-known, successful handbag manufacturer.

After Beth's talk, I realized that I could combine my family history and educator skills as a docent or a facilitator for our newly developing anti-bullying and tolerance programs. The first part of the training consisted of a number of days immersed in the significant details and events of the 20s and 30s, followed by intensive training in anti-bullying strategies. This was further illuminated with age-appropriate literature. During these years, the museum programs and our outreach approach changed from static exhibits to new and exciting displays that tugged at our heartstrings and stimulated our brain.

My husband David Taub was also a survivor. His story follows mine. He was a hidden child in France during the war. Nobody goes unscarred from those events and David, dealing with demons, found his outlet through the museum. He served as a museum docent for at least 15 years, sharing his terrors and memories with Nassau County school children, using museum artifacts as springboards to discuss his knowledge of those tumultuous times as well as his personal connections. Even before the buzz words of "Victim, Perpetrator, Bystander and Upstander entered our working vocabulary, he would stress how he and his family were saved because of the "kindness of strangers." These words were the key concepts he attempted to communicate to all who came into his range.

# HIDDEN CHILDREN, FRANCE

*DAVID'S STORY*
*Paris, France 1932*

## THE KINDNESS OF STRANGERS

The year was 1939. Our family was on a vacation in *Fountainbleu* with our extended family, which by the way included *Mireille*, who was younger than I. Germany had just invaded Poland and France, as a Polish Ally, joined the war. We returned to a Paris at war. Food was rationed, as was coal, fuel, gas and other necessities. Everything was diverted to the war effort. My father tried to enlist and was turned down because of age and health issues. My 18 year-old brother, Jacques, also tried to enlist in the French Army. He, as well as our parents, were considered by the French as Polish citizens. I became a citizen, by way of application upon my birth in Paris. The only way my brother could defend France was by enlisting in the French Foreign Legion as non-French native combatant. The Legion, because of the crisis situation, had a special enrollment policy. This meant that his service was limited to the duration of the war. He fought for his adopted country, protecting the retreat of the French army. It was a slow war. Many months passed without military achievements.

**1940** Under threat of air alerts, my parents and I looked for safety from possible bombardments. Parisians were afraid that bombs would destroy Paris, like Rotterdam, Warsaw and other cities. The air raid sirens would blast into the night sky; my parents would gather blankets, recently issued gas masks, water and hurry down to the cellar of our building. The cellar was very dark, poorly lit filled with shadowy spaces storing household goods and belongings of the various tenants in the building. Stacks of coal, suitcases, trunks, and unused furniture were stacked in corners, angles and various spaces. Each family had its own territory. The space was small, crowded and smelled of stored foods, wine, and something else. Almost all the families would gather there, but this was no time for playing with my friends. Safety from possible falling bombs could also be found in the underground metro stations. In addition, we were issued gas masks in case the Nazis launched poison gas attacks. The masks were very uncomfortable, the lens steamed up and vision through them became almost impossible. We would remain there for what seemed like an eternity, but was most likely hours; time passed very slowly until the "all clear" signal was heard.

Fearing for my safety, my parents sent me to live with family friends of our neighbors where I had spent previous vacation time when I was a bit younger. They lived in a small village, *Laguepie*, in the *Tarn* and *Garonne* district of southwestern France. *M.* and *Mme. Mercadier* had farm lands outside the village and also owned a small *"pension"* or boarding house within the center of the town. People from neighboring cities such as *Toulouse,* visiting family who lived in the area could stay there during the pleasant summer months. *M.* and *Mme Mercadier* were able to send their daughter to take me back to her town. From the windows of the train, I could see long lines of refugees traveling away from Paris to what they hoped would be safe refuge in the country. The roads were clogged with thousands of families walking, household goods piled into cars, wagons . . . moving almost like robots down the road. We were very lucky to get through. After the war, I found out that German bombers strafed the railroad lines, forcing people to disembark, walk, and clog the roads. This was an effective way for them to stop critical supplies from reaching French soldiers and also served the double purpose of further terrifying a civilian population into submission and acceptance of what would be German victory.

On June 6th, 1940, France surrendered to Germany. This is what occurred as a result of the armistice agreement: the country was divided into a northern occupied zone and a southern *libre* (free zone). Vichy

France collaborated with the Nazis' occupation of the north. This new government was, in fact and in actions, in full agreement with the Nazis, although calling itself a "separate" state.

Through the efforts of *M.* and *Mme. Mercadier,* my brother, *Jacques,* was released from the army not very far from the town where I lived. He spent several months with me in *Laguepie,* working for an electrician in order to pay for our room and food and to buy me a much-needed warm sweater for the oncoming winter.

Following France's surrender, we had no news about the fate of our parents, therefore we decided to return to Paris. To return to Paris from *Laguepie,* we were obliged to traverse areas that had been bombed and were devastated—bridges destroyed and communication between towns and cities limited. We arrived in the Occupied Zone to catch a train to Paris. A panel at the railroad station stated the following: "No Jews or dogs allowed on the train." While I was sleeping, a German patrol on the train checked our papers and asked my brother "Who is David?" David was considered to be a "Jewish" name and not at all typically French. In addition, because of my red hair, freckles, I didn't look "typically" French, although my brother, darker skin tones, dark hair certainly did. My brother pointed to me and they let us pass because this was the beginning of the Occupation and they wanted French people to know that they were being "correct." "Correct" was the word to describe polite, efficient and appropriate. It was not unusual to see an open-air concert with Nazi soldiers playing classical music in a public square. Needless to say, these concerts were part of the propaganda machine highlighting the kind of behaviors the local citizenry could expect. Bitter reality had nothing to do with the perception of the moment.

**1940-41** Paris was declared an "Open City," therefore no bombings, except for the rail areas (the area in which we lived) occurred. Our parents faced the daily problems of the occupation, in particular, the lack of food. Butter, potatoes, and other food staples were sent to Germany and waiting on line for food supplies became the daily activity.

My mother was very friendly with the *Gnuchis* who owned a wholesale bakery. They were able to get flour and other baking supplies because they were permitted to bake their specialty of *"beignets"* (jelly filled cream puffs) that were supplied to the German army. They generously shared some of these needed staples with my parents. Of course, all of this was done in secret because if the occupiers knew of the diversion of these products (and to Jews, no less) they would certainly have been arrested and worse. After the war when these friends were arrested and charged with collaboration with the enemy, my parents testified on their behalf telling of their extreme generosity and kindness, and they were acquitted instead of being imprisoned.

As before the war, my brother was called down to the local police precinct to renew his work permit as an electrical engineer. He was immediately arrested, as was the case with many foreign Jewish veterans of this war, and was imprisoned in a French-run internment camp near *Orleans* (*Beaune la Rolande*). We later learned that his allotted diet had fewer calories and nutrients than the amount of calories allowed in *Dachau*. My mother, hearing many rumors and bits of conversations about the lack of food and poor conditions in the French-run concentration camps, resolved to see if she could help *Jacques* escape. A note she received from him with a chocolate bar for me reinforced her determination. Jacques wrote telling her the barest of information about life in the prison camp. Carefully unwrapping the candy bar, she found another note that described the harsh reality of extreme food rationing and deprivation. Convinced now of the desperate conditions in the camp, she was determined to do whatever she could to help him escape. She and I left the apartment very early in the morning. She carried her handbag over her chest so that no one would notice that she did not wearing her Jewish Identity Star. I held a book, in the same position, also disguising the fact that we were without the required star. Although I was about 10 years old at this time, I was a very robust child. No one (we hoped) would stop an attractive French woman traveling with her child.

I was both a distraction and meant to help. Leaving early in the morning because of erratic train schedules, we traveled across Paris hoping that we wouldn't be stopped. We arrived at a central train station in Paris and were able to take a train to the nearest train station located in the vicinity of *Beane La Rolande.*

When we arrived, we sat in a café, the object of somewhat curious glances, and surveyed the area. The town was tiny and after a walk around the main square and perimeter of the town, my mother asked a pork farmer who also had a store near the center, if we could sleep in their barn, explaining the purpose of her visit. The farmer's wife (*Mme. Demarrais*) appeared to refuse but after she heard why my mother and I were in this village, she sympathetically offered my mother a room in the house. Nobody questioned us because I think that the local village people were somewhat used to strangers hoping to visit loved ones detained in the camp. The farmer's family promised to help and enlisted the assistance of their daughter's *fiancé,* who as a *gendarme,* was assigned to guarding the camp. We stayed for several weeks developing an escape plan.

This was the plan: My brother, *Jacques,* would be assigned to an outside work detail consisting of assisting the local electrician. As a result of the *gendarme's* intervention and influence *Jacques* was given permission to leave camp on a daily basis to help the village electrician. Each morning, after he showed his exit pass, the *gendarme,* also named *Jacques,* smuggled in extra rations because my brother had to build up his strength, as he was currently too weak to escape. My brother would return each evening to the camp; no one checked passes. *Jacques,* the *gendarme,* knew that my brother would have to surrender his exit/work pass at least a week before the attempted escape so that the Germans wouldn't take reprisals against the electrician and the farmer's family who were helping him. Roll call and numbers wouldn't be checked for several hours, giving escaping prisoners a few hours head start. The week before the planned escape, *Jacques* returned his pass card, knowing that on the day of his escape, the guard on duty (the farmer's future son-in law) would allow him to leave without an exit pass. In addition, he was able to maintain the strength that he had rebuilt by eating the rations that had been smuggled in with the help of this *gendarme.*

Because we lived between the *Gare du Nord* (North Station) and the *Gare de L'Est* (East Station) many of my mother's customers worked for the French railroad system and were among the first to organize into Resistance Units fighting the Germans. My mother was told about a "safe place" for the first night he would be in Paris and through a relay of resistance fighters, was told about other safe places. In addition, my mother was able to get him false ID papers that were made by resistance workers. These false IDs were prepared by using fake stamps made by inked potatoes. Unfortunately, many of the fake IDs had errors which, in *Jacques'* case, almost proved fatal.**

The night following our return to our Paris apartment, heavy pounding on the door awakened us. The *Brigade aux Questions Juives* (French Gestapo) were looking for my brother. They began by asking my mother if she knew where my brother was. She answered, "In prison camp at *Beane La Rolande.*" They informed her that he escaped. I remember her comment: "Thank you for giving me the good news, but surely you don't think he's stupid enough to hide behind the skirts of his Maman?" They ransacked the apartment, ostensibly looking for my brother in corners, under the bed and even in the furniture drawers. While looking for him, they found several of the papers that I brought from the village which contained anti-German writing.

The policemen slapped me around, hoping that I would tell them my brother's whereabouts. My mother showed extraordinary courage during this confrontation. She ran to the window yelling into the courtyard, attracting everyone's attention, screaming, and hollering "Stop slapping my son!" The police, frightened at the thought of crossing a hostile crowd, stopped hitting me, however they made my mother open the closed store. When the neighbors saw my mother with the keys, they asked if she was about to open the store again. She replied that she would do so, only when "these *messieurs*" leave (a euphemism describing the hated German occupants.) They searched the store and didn't find my brother there as he was hiding elsewhere in Paris.

*Jacques* escaped from Paris using false papers. In fact, he was caught in a dragnet. A French police officer noticing the glaring error in his false ID papers told him to get out quickly. My mother obtained new, correct papers and he made his way to *Toulon*. While he was in *Toulon*, he worked for an electrician, and because *Toulon* had been bombed, his apartment included, he asked the electrician for a small increase in salary. The electrician suspecting that *Jacques* was Jewish, replied, "You are lucky to be here." *Jacques* took that as a signal to leave before he was denounced and, at that point, joined the *maquis* (the French Underground, the secret army fighting the Germans.)

The farmer's family provided a man's bicycle that I hid in the woods near the prison gate. *Jacques* used it to get away from the town. My mother and I returned to Paris the following morning. *Jacques* pedaled to a nearby village and hid on a farm. The following morning he left for *Orleans* and boarded the train to Paris. We were in the same train, but did not see him.

In Paris, he hid every day, in a different place. The reason he had to change hiding places so frequently was so that the apartment custodians (*concierges*) could be aware that there was a stranger staying in what seemed to be empty, vacated apartments since not only could they hear footsteps, the pattern of the footsteps might be different from the apartment residents. Every tenant had a distinctive footfall and a curious *concierge* would certainly note a "guest" and differences in sounds. (The *concierges*, from the time of Napoleon 1 were known for telling the police about anything new, different or unusual taking place in their apartment building.)

**1942**–Daily life and conditions in Occupied France become increasingly difficult for the civilian population, especially Jews. Initially, only the foreign Jews, refugees from other occupied countries were targeted; eventually however, the French Jews also came under the newly posted racial purity laws.

### Anti-Jewish Laws impacted on our lives in the following ways:

Jews were forced to register their religion with the local authorities. All Jews were forced to wear a flimsy rayon Star of David as public identification. 3 were issued per person with coupons that were needed for clothing. Each time a garment was changed, cleaned or laundered, it necessitated the removal of the star that deteriorated with handling. The badge had the words "Juive/Jew" written in pretend Hebrew lettering that clearly would identify and isolate them from the rest of the population. Early curfews were imposed. If you were caught on the streets without a special permit, you were likely to be arrested. Food, clothing and heating ration cards were issued and there were ration lines for everyone–longer lines, lack of food, heat, and other essential supplies including medicines–were common.

Food was scarce, mostly available on a rationed, limited basis. Families were issued food coupons that one had to use to purchase basic necessities ranging from pantry items to clothing and fabric coupons. Long lines were everywhere, seemingly springing up like mushrooms as rumors flew that a certain store had a delivery of needed items. France, with its fertile lands, grew food in abundance. However, with the need of feeding the Nazi army, as well as the occupying forces all goods (often plundered) were sent back to Germany and their families. French citizens suffered from a lack of everything.

Friends and family members become involved in the armed resistance. Periodic roundups and captures under guise of checking identifications and as reprisals for attacks on Nazi officers were common. I know of two family friends who were heavily involved with the rapidly developing French Resistance movement. One was my brother's friend. He, with his best friend, attacked German officers on the streets of Paris. They even made a pact not to separate and to help each other should either one come under attack. His friend was shot and he stayed behind to help him. Then, he was wounded and captured. Imprisoned in the hospital, he later died of his wounds. My father attended his funeral. This was very brave and very risky, as the Gestapo was certainly watching who attended the funeral and could or might arrest anyone on the spot.

My father calmly walked several miles to the synagogue and back home. After France surrendered to the Nazis and new laws were enacted, it took great courage to face life in occupied Paris. My father persisted in attending services at our temple located on *Rue Notre Dame de Nazareth*. Of course, he had to walk there, visibly wearing his identification as a Jew because he was not allowed to take public transportation. Attending services on any Sabbath and especially the high holidays, and other occasions, was filled with danger. Both the building, as well as the worshippers, were obvious targets and could be rounded up with great facility. The saying, "You can run but can't hide" was probably the theme for those dangerous times.

Another acquaintance was *Pierre Georges,* (*Resistance* name: *Colonel Fabien,*) He was related to one of my friends who lived in our apartment building. He was among the first to organize violent resistance against the occupying army. I later learned that on August 21st, 1941, he killed a German naval officer on the subway station right near my home. In fact, this occurred when *Jacques,* on the run after escaping from *Beane La Rolonde,* was caught in a round up immediately after the assassination. *Colonel Fabien* was eventually caught, arrested, tortured and yet, somehow, managed to escape in June 1943. Whenever we saw each other, he always politely greeted me when I met him on stairs of the building. I, of course, had no idea of his "extra-curricular activities." Perhaps it was just as well. After the D-Day landings occurred, he was killed on December 27th 1944 in *Alsace-Lorraine.*

Schools become battlegrounds as Jewish students were attacked. We fought with our backs against the wall, but I remember that many neighborhood friends ("Up-Standers" as is termed in HMTC parlance) always stood with us as we were attacked in the courtyard during recess time. Jews were not allowed to attend movies, theatres, or use the parks. Life in public places became impossible, both by edict as well as the danger of being caught in dragnets. Nor were they allowed to practice their professions. Lawyers, professors, doctors were not allowed to work in public sectors, however, Jewish doctors continued to treat their Jewish patients even though they had no medical supplies. Jews were told to surrender their bicycles, cars, and radio sets. French radio broadcasts, controlled by the Nazis, broadcasted propaganda extolling the benefits of life under the Nazi occupation. Notable French celebrities appeared on Nazi controlled radio, apparently happy to collaborate with Nazis. (After the war, some of these notable people were brought up on charges as collaborating, some were made to pay a fine, others disappeared from public view.)

My mother wanted to continue to listen to the Free French broadcasts from London. She refused to surrender our radio, but, instead, brought a shoebox filled with radio parts left over from my brother's pre-war job and said that because of my brother's imprisonment he had not finished repairing the family radio. If they wanted a working radio, he should be liberated to continue his job. Aryan managers were appointed to manage Jewish owned businesses and stores; many stores closed. My parents refused to work for an Aryan manager. My mother defied this man by telling him that she wouldn't work for him and immediately closed the store. During that confrontation, she bravely told him, "You are a "*bon a rien*" (good for nothing) a play on the words, "bon Aryan" or good Aryan, the Nazi ideal. Continuing, she also said, "You might be a pimp, but we are not prostitutes." He didn't report her; the store was locked and only reopened after the liberation. After the war, we discovered that he protected a number of large Jewish businesses under the guise of being an Aryan manager, returning to the surviving owners accounts of all transactions and profits. We didn't know that at the time, however.

## 1942: THE MASS ROUNDUP OF JEWS, AUGUST, 1942

My father, warned of the impending mass roundup, arrest and subsequent deportation of Jews to be scheduled in mid-July, made arrangements to hide and escape from occupied Paris. One of his clients who worked at Police Headquarters told him that a mass arrest of Jews was in the works; however, she didn't know the date that this might occur. The only thing she knew and so warned us, was that a definite "action" would occur in the very near future. It would be best if he and his family could hide in a safe place. What place in Paris could be considered safe?

We hid in the recently vacated apartment of cousins for two weeks. Food was brought by the *concierge* of our building, and by neighbors and friends who knew where we were hidden. While in the apartment, we were only able to move at night so that no one would know we were occupying what was supposed to be a vacated apartment. That meant that if, during the day, we had to move from one room to another, we had to crawl on the floor *below the long ceiling to floor level windows* so that we wouldn't be noticed by someone who happened to be looking at the apartment windows. For us, in effect, it really meant almost no movement, as we didn't want anyone to hear any sounds of movement (or talking) at all. The French police went to the *concierge* (superintendent's wife) asking for information about our cousins (who unknowingly to them) had left Paris six months earlier. The *concierge* stated that the apartment was uninhabited for the last six months. If the police had doubted her statement, they would have broken into the apartment and found us. What stopped them from breaking into the apartment to search was the portrait of her dead husband in full Nazi uniform!

Our cousins, Olga and Joseph Rozen, had escaped into the country, taking refuge with farmers who had been recommended to them by neighbors. They spent the rest of the war working on the farm, successfully hidden by this family. After we returned to Paris shortly before the end of the war, my parents, once again, concerned for my safety in case the Germans were successful in their attempt to salvage the situation, sent me to the family that owned the farm where our cousins had found refuge. I was given everything that I needed to eat and stay well (food still being scarce in Paris, allowed to read all the books on the shelves, and taught all the fine points of competitive chess by both the farmer, his sons and one of my cousins). I felt that I still retained my childhood in spite of the difficult years.

Before the 16$^{th}$ of July, my parents began to put an escape plan into effect. With the help of our friends and neighbors *Monsieur* and *Madame Piogeais,* (the butcher and his wife), *Monsieur* and *Madame Trefour,* (the wine merchants) and (*Monsieur* and *Madame Legendre*), the baker and his wife, who were able to smuggle in food and money, we decided to leave the apartment and venture into the streets after hiding for two weeks. My parents and I left our hiding place in the apartment, dressed as suggested, in several layers of clothing including winter coats. Carrying suitcases would have made us too conspicuous and could have led to our arrest. Winter coats under the July sun hardly appeared to be less suspicious, however.

We were to make contact with underworld "passers" who, for a fee, promised to take us to a farm located on the border between Occupied France and Unoccupied France. We were to enter the farmhouse located in Occupied France and leave through the rear door that was located on the Vichy or "unoccupied" part of France. Our "*passeurs*" tried to betray us by taking us to a subway line that did not connect with the main line. They repeatedly announced to one and all that they were "secretly" involved with helping Jews cross the border between Occupied and Unoccupied France. We were in constant danger of being caught at any time. We finally linked up with a main railroad line and my father threatened not to pay them at all if they continued trying to jeopardize our escape. After a very long and difficult voyage, we arrived in *Mont de Marsan*. The "passers" told us to wait for them in a public park nearby. They would meet us later for the actual crossing of the demarcation line. We crossed about 1000 feet from the location of the official point of crossing and hid behind bushes from the Nazi soldiers patrolling the area.

After having received 2/3 of the pre-negotiated fee, the "passers" refused to honor our agreement. Initially, they refused to guide us through the passage. My mother appealed to their "manhood" by taunting them that they were not real men because they wouldn't honor the arrangement. After being taunted by my mother, one of the younger thugs decided to help us and reluctantly assisted us through a railroad tunnel.

We could hear the Nazi sentinels chatting as they passed each other on patrol. In running out of the underground passage, we were detected and shot at. We heard bullets whizz past us. We crossed the railroad track running through a hail of bullets. My mother's shoe heel was broken and her heel was grazed and bleeding, but we couldn't stop. We ran through the forest encountering what appeared to be visions of hell as we saw the charcoal burners, with blackened faces staring at us. Once on the other side, we couldn't board the bus as we didn't have the right papers . . . and of course, there was another ID check by French *gendarmes*. Once again, we went into a *café* to think about our position and what we should do next. My mother confided in the *café* owner who listened carefully and then called in the *gendarme* that had been in the back room. We were horrified until we understood that he was to help us. He took us to the bus, telling other *gendarmes* that we were his family and rode with us to our destination where he waved us through the ID checks being conducted by local police in *Villeneuve de Marsan*.

We stayed there for one night and then traveled to *Pau,* a city not too far from the Spanish border. After a week in a run-down scruffy hotel, we ran out of funds. My father happened to meet a friend from Paris who commented on my father's very dejected and depressed mood. "Maurice," she said, if it's only money that you are worried about, that's nothing." She pulled out an enormous wad of bills and handed the money over to my father. Then she said, "You will pay me back after the war. If we don't survive, this is meaningless. Feeling somewhat better, my father appealed for a reduction in hotel fees. The manager said that he would give us an answer later. The following morning, my parents were arrested by the police and brought to jail at the Palace of Justice. They were to be judged at 2 PM.

I went to the restaurant where we ate our daily meal. (They accepted us without food ticket rations.) I asked the owner to call the office of an Alsatian lawyer who ate at the table next to us. He accepted to represent my parents at their trial without payment. Upon my return to the Palace of Justice I met a friend of my brother from Paris who had just found a job with a butcher. He introduced me to his new boss who offered me a job as a butcher's apprentice so that I could survive without my parents if they were to be kept in jail or sent back to the Occupied Zone. My parents were not deported, however, but were instead sent to stay in *Lacaune les Bains,* a village serving as a temporary "holding pen" until the Jews could be "resettled" in the East in German death camps. In order to travel to *Lacaune les Bains,* we had to spend the night in *Toulouse.* We found a room at the *Hotel Jeanne D'Arc* and tried to sleep.

We were awakened by a heavy banging on our door. In spite of my parents' legal transit papers, we were taken by car to the headquarters of the Police in Charge of Jewish Affairs. (French Gestapo) We were kept in a very hot, sunny and airless room. After waiting two hours, my father requested the right to make a phone call to the only person he knew in the area. This person was a member of the most influential family in town whose son was my brother's friend in Paris. The senior *gendarme,* passing through the corridor, hearing the family name, immediately asked the police officer in charge to return us to the hotel for our luggage and then to the railroad station to catch the next train to *Lacaune les Bains*. We literally caught the train as it was departing. Had we stayed in *Toulouse*, we would have been in default of our transit papers and then, most certainly sent East and then North, to the death camps. Once in *Lacaune*, my parents were not allowed to leave the village and signed a daily register to prove they were in residence. They also noticed that periodically, foreign Jews from Belgium, Holland and other European countries were transported from the village to unknown destinations.

**1942-1944** To save me, my parents sent me to *Laguepie* to stay with the same family with whom I had stayed at the beginning of the war. I was told, both by my parents as well as my adoptive family, to pretend that I was Catholic. As a stocky little red-headed child with green eyes, I didn't look typically "French" and was considered to be different from the other children, not because I was Jewish and circumcised (which they may or may not have known) but because I was from Paris. I served Mass and was the head of the Catholic Boy Scouts during the two years that I stayed in *Laguepie.*

After my departure from *Lacaune* to *Laguepie,* my father was arrested, taken to the military fort in *Castres*. From there he would be shipped to Germany. He was the first down from the truck. He walked straight through the main gate. He was able to do this because he very much resembled the typical plainclothes French policeman. The two uniformed gendarmes at the gate saluted him. He returned their salute and walked out. He went into hiding with the *maquis* (resistance) in a desolate area of the mountains and stayed with local farmers until the end of the war. My mother received a message that told her that her husband was alive and well, protected by the local people but hiding in the mountains not far from the village in which she was forced to reside. My mother remained in this area until after D Day in 1944.

During this time period I became part of local village life. I attended school, passed the state exams with the highest possible scores, but in order to protect me, my grades and name were not posted. It might attract too much attention. This was a small price to pay for safeguarding my liberty. I helped my host family in the hotel, restaurant, garden, vineyard, fed the livestock and ran errands for everyone. The grandmother loved me as one of her own, but *M* and *Mme Mercadier* were very busy running their hotel-restaurant and their fields and vineyards, and, they were not my warm, cozy, loving parents. Everybody in the village of 3,500 people knew that I had come from somewhere else, but nobody denounced me as the little red-headed Jewish boy from Paris.

My life was hard and lonely, but no different from other children raised in rural France. I was fed, although not well, deprived of my sugar rations, and most of all, protected from war and death, infinitely luckier than my French and Polish cousins. At the liberation of France, my parents came to get me, returning to a city devastated by four years of occupation. My brother, having survived as an underground resistance fighter, participated in the fighting for the liberation of *Toulon* and eventually made his way back to Paris. We were reunited as a family in 1945. We have lived to tell our story, individually and as a family, because of the kindness of strangers. Life goes on and along with other survivors, we picked up the threads of our former existence, but missing those who were not as lucky as we and did not survive the Holocaust.

# HIDDEN CHILDREN

*CHARLOTTE MENDELOVITS GILLMAN*
*BELGIUM*

# 10 CUPS OF COCOA

It all started in Antwerp, Belgium where I was born in 1933. In 1938 there was a worldwide financial depression. My father, a skilled master-craftsman, was forced to give up his custom-made furniture shop on the *Lange Kievitstraat* in Antwerp. Our father had to find a job In order to support his family: my mother, my 8-year-old sister Flora, my younger sister, Betty, age 2 and myself, age 5. He took a job as a ship's carpenter on a ship that delivered goods around the world. It would serve two purposes. The ship traveled to many exotic ports in Africa and South America, but he hoped that it would ultimately reach a port in the United States or Canada. He was not going to return to the ship when he was given "shore leave." He would "jump ship."

His sister and her family lived in Astoria, New York. They had not seen each other in 25 years. He planned on reuniting with her with the intent of one day bringing his family to the United States. Although he did make it to his sister, his goal of bringing us to America had to be postponed for 8 years.

Because Papa was no longer working on the ship, his income ceased and we were forced to move from the *Lamonierstraat* to *the Lange Kievitstraat* where the rent was more affordable. Fortunately, the apartment backed up on a street with stores and restaurants and Mama was able to get a job as a cook. Not so fortunately, the back windows of the apartment overlooked *the Beukelaer Chocolate Wafer* factory where the aroma of the fresh chocolate was tantalizing. We, however, were much too poor to buy any chocolate biscuits and had to be satisfied only with the aroma. Perhaps this is where my yearning for cocoa began.

At the beginning of May, 1940 I was sent to a camp for "weak" children. While I was in camp, on May 10th, Germany invaded Belgium. Mama feared the Germans. She made the very hard decision to leave Antwerp with Flora and Betty, leaving me behind in the camp. She was convinced that with the heavy bombing I was probably dead. She made her way to *Le Havre*, France, under horrendous conditions. There was heavy bombing and the car she had paid to transport them abandoned them mid-way. She walked with hundreds and hundreds of other refugees, pushing Betty, age 4 and ill with measles and a high fever, in a wheelbarrow. Mama finally made it to *Le Havre*, but with no tickets, no papers, nothing but fear and the urgent need to escape the war and save her children, her plan was to get on a ship and go to America where Papa was. There was a ship in port and the desperate refugees climbed on board any way they could, even scaling the sides.

The ship, however, turned out not to be sea-worthy, so everyone had to return to shore. With no place to go, Mama started to make her way back to Antwerp. She came upon a church where other refugees were entering, and it was there that the three took refuge for several days. Regaining some of her strength, she continued on her journey and again took refuge in a small hotel. The round-trip to and from *Le Havre* had taken six weeks. Meanwhile, when the bombing began and Mama was making her way to *Le Havre*, the director of my camp decided to return all the children to their families. Because I was only 7 years old and we had no telephone, a counselor accompanied me home to our apartment building. As we left the railroad station imagine my shock to see totally deserted streets—no people, no traffic and all the shops closed, gated and locked. When we reached our apartment building, we rang the bell to our apartment and getting no response we began banging on the locked gate.

An elderly neighbor stuck her head out of the window, recognized me and very bluntly told me that Mama and my two sisters left for America. The counselor became very irritable because she just wanted to drop me off and return to her own family. She told me that she would take me to an orphanage. Frightened, I implored her to take me to my Aunt Leah, who lived four blocks away, but when we got there—that apartment was also uninhabited. Like Mama, Aunt Leah, Uncle Alex and my cousin Nounou were also on their way back to Antwerp. We were now off to the orphanage. I was only 7 years old, without a mother, sisters, or aunt and uncle. The streets were deserted. The stores were closed and I was being taken by a stranger to a feared orphanage. I can feel my fear and tears to this day.

Suddenly, like a mirage, my friend Harry appeared before me! He was the only person on the street. His family was the first to return from attempting to flee Belgium. The counselor agreed to let me ask Harry's family to take me in. At first, they hesitated but I begged and promised that I would be the best little girl, and perhaps having only one son, they agreed. During the day I was the best, most helpful child. But at bedtime I cried my eyes out. Six weeks later, my mother and sisters returned. When I saw them walking down the street, I thought it was only a vision. I ran up to them calling "Mama, Mama, why did you leave me?" Her answer was: "I thought you were dead and it was better to have two children than none."

We remained in Antwerp for about a year. It was during this time that all Jews, adults and children alike, were summoned to City Hall to register and receive their yellow Jewish stars, stamped in the center with a large, black J. The Jews were also given exact instructions in centimeters about where to sew the star. The horror was just beginning. Decrees were issued daily—evening curfew for Jews, no public school for Jewish children, eligible Jewish men had to report for transportation to labor camps and on and on.

Antwerp had a large Jewish population and early one evening we heard the sound of stomping Nazi boots, Nazi singing, people screaming and crying and glass breaking. When we looked out the window, we saw the Nazis breaking into Jewish storefronts that had been officially designated as Jewish-owned with a highlighted Jewish star. The Nazis destroyed everything in sight. They dragged the Jews out by their beards, hair, clothing, and anything they could grab hold of, and stomped and beat them to death. We lived in terror.

Jewish restaurants closed. Mama, who worked in one of them, lost her job. To feed Flora, Betty, and me, she was forced to resort to smuggling. Goods that were in demand in France, she smuggled from Belgium to France. On the return, she smuggled goods that were needed in Belgium. She was always accompanied by either Flora or me, as Betty was too young. The purpose of our presence was two-fold. First, we could hide extra goods under our rain capes. But more importantly, we created distractions, bordering on havoc, when approached on the train by a German official for our papers. Mama had covered the red letter "J" on her identity card with red cellophane and that seemed to work.

We, however, were always prepared to make a fuss if too many questions were asked. At Customs, I remember being asked what was under my rain cape. When I said it was my doll and the customs official asked to see the doll, I would start crying that the official wanted to take away my doll. A crying 8-year-old holding up a long line of people always flustered him and he let us pass. We were able to use this ploy because we went to different border crossings.

The raids on the Jewish neighborhoods became more frequent. Uncle Alex, who had returned to Antwerp after six weeks in the labor camp, said we needed to move to Brussels where we could get lost more easily within the Christian community. He left for Brussels with Aunt Leah and Nounou with the promise to find us an apartment. While we waited to hear from Uncle Alex, we heard a knock at our door. It was from Papa's former furniture store apprentice. He had joined the German army and because of the previous family relationship and his warm feelings for us, he came to warn us that there was a raid scheduled on our street for that night. He told us to leave immediately—not pack, to just go with the clothes on our back. Mama dressed us in multiple layers of clothes and we headed for the train station on the *Pelicanstraat*. With beating hearts, not knowing what would await us on the train, we boarded and arrived in Brussels without incident. We made our way to Aunt Leah's apartment and fell into each other's arms with the thrill of all of us being alive and together.

The following day, Uncle Alex took us to our own apartment, #83 *Rue Navez,* where we settled in as Gentiles. We removed our yellow stars and started life with our new identity. Mama took the three of us to the local primary school on *Rue Capronier,* where we met with the principal, Madame Evens. The principal explained to her that it was against German proclamations for a Jewish child to attend public school. Our Flemish accent made her suspect that we were Jewish, but Mama insisted we were Christians from Antwerp and begged her to enroll us. With permission from an elderly neighbor, we used the name of "Fiers" and were enrolled under that name. After our admission was approved, Mama sought the help of Madame Evens in finding work. Madame called

George Ranson, the head of the Parent-Teacher Association. He was a wealthy industrialist whose factory was taken over by the Germans and so he could not place Mama in the factory. Instead, he put her to work evenings in the basement making transistors for the Underground. We continued life in this way for several months until an incident at school precipitated a change. At recess, one day, a classmate called me a dirty Jew. My teacher reported this to the principal who immediately called George Ranson.

The father of this classmate was a known Belgian Nazi and Mr. Ranson and the principal became fearful. Mr. Ranson came to school and took Flora and me to his home. Betty went to the home of his secretary. We remained there for several weeks while Mr. Ranson made arrangements for us to leave Brussels for a safe haven. We were escorted to the train station where a recent widow who worked for the Underground met us. She accompanied us to our first Catholic Convent where Sister Odonia, a cousin of George Ranson, was given permission by the Reverend Mother to take us in. We were there for three months when again, an incident precipitated yet another move. Flora and I were tutored in the procedures of receiving Holy Communion. The priest, knowing that we were not Catholic, always bypassed us when giving out the host at the altar rail. Betty, who was too young, sat in a pew next to the Reverend Sister. One day, Betty questioned the statue of Christ on the Cross that was on the wall. Reverend Sister, not knowing that Betty was Jewish, said: "You have one of those at home." Betty insisted that she did not. This made the Reverend Sister extremely suspicious of our Jewish birth. She confronted the Reverend Mother, telling her that there were rumors that these children were Jews in hiding since they never left the convent on weekends. Reverend Mother then called Sister Odonia (they were the only two at the convent who knew that we were Jewish) and said that it was becoming too dangerous for the girls to remain and that her cousin, George Ranson, needed to come and get us.

We left the convent under cover of night. Traveling was extremely dangerous. The authorities were always looking for Jews, smugglers, and run-away soldiers. There were many roadblocks. The truck was driven by a man from the Underground. Fortunately, we made it safely back to our apartment in Brussels where Aunt Leah and her family were living since their apartment was raided. They had escaped because of a warning by the owner of the bakery across the street that Germans were waiting for them. It was not long before all three, including 4-year-old Nounou, were picked up, never to be heard from again. Miraculously, Mama, in order to give her sister and family privacy, had been staying at a safe house provided by the Underground. One evening, on her way to visit her sister, she was warned by the proprietor of the bicycle store beneath our apartment, to keep her composure and turn around with him and to keep walking. As they walked away, he gave her the devastating news of their seizure. In the interim, George Ranson learned of a Benedictine Monk, *Pere* Bruno Reyenders, who was placing Jewish children and adults in safe places. Mama insisted that her three children not be separated and so it took a while for *Pere* Bruno to place us. Finally, we were placed in a suburb of Brussels called *Etterbeek*.

My sister Flora recalls this as an orphanage, but I recall it as a correctional institution, particularly because of the very harsh treatment of all the children. The daily food consisted of a slice of moldy bread and watery soup. We were so hungry all the time that when the nuns brought out their garbage, we would sneakily raid it for scraps of potato peels and carrot tops. We had one "bath" in 13 months. The bath consisted of a small basin of water and 60 children using the same bath water. Because I was so small, I was third on line. The lack of sanitation caused an infestation of lice and ringworm. Our heads were tarred to control the lice. At least the tar controlled the itching and scratching. The worst punishment was when there was an infraction of the rules. Then, we were given a "paddling," were locked in a wet basement and told to kill rats. We lived this way for 13 months.

One bright spot was when during the confirmation of some older girls, I was chosen to portray an angel, wings and all. I was given a cup of cocoa and a cookie. Again, the cocoa—it meant that you were special. I ate the cookie, crumb by crumb, and slowly sipped that cocoa to make it last as long as possible.

We had occasional visits from *Pere* Bruno and George Ranson. They would call Flora, Betty and me in for a private talk in the presence of the Mother Superior and whisper to us that our mother was safe. On their last visit, we looked so emaciated that *Pere* Bruno decided that we must be moved elsewhere and new arrangements were put in motion. *Pere* Bruno contacted Reverend Mother, Marie Chrysostome at the Convent of *The Sisters of the Seven Sorrows*. Once again we were we were placed there, transported by the Underground under the cover of night in a truck carrying crates of vegetables. It was a stormy night with heavy rain and hail and we shivered with cold and terror as we hid under the crates. Along the way, the Gendarmes stopped the truck and poked around the crates, but luckily didn't find us. Perhaps it was because of the heavy rain and hail and their reluctance to stay out in such inclement weather. The convent consisted of an old age home, a boarding school for wealthy girls, and an orphanage. Those of us in the orphanage worked in the potato fields (not the strawberry fields, because they knew that we would eat the berries). We were taught to darn and repair clothes for ourselves and for the elderly. Our education was limited to two hours a day. Our diet was reasonably adequate, including our daily spoon of cod-liver-oil. The discipline was very strict and poor Betty was often locked in a closet in the classroom. She could not seem to sit still and be quiet. The Reverend Mother kept enticing us to convert to Catholicism, telling us that we could be adopted by a Baroness or Countess and placed in the boarding school. I cannot say that we were not tempted, because we knew that the food and the accommodations were so much better. Although two of the Jewish girls did convert, my sister Flora promised Mama we would remain Jews and used the excuse that my father needed to give his permission and that he was unreachable in America. I still remember the one girl, Renée, who converted, passing me and teasing: "Guess what we had for lunch today? Hot cocoa and cookies for dessert." My yearning was so great, that somehow, cocoa came to represent all the things that I could never have. Maybe that is why I am addicted to cocoa, and never a day goes by that I do not have several cups.

Six weeks before the end of the war, when there were no more members of our immediate and extended family alive, Mama sent a note via *Pere* Bruno to be delivered to the Reverend Mother, Marie Chrysostome. The note said that if Mama did not survive, please be aware that the children have a living father, David Mendelovits, in America and he should be contacted. The Reverend Mother took pity and courageously invited Mama to stay at the convent using another identity. We were told that Mama would be coming to live at the convent and that when the time was right, we would meet with her. In the meanwhile, if we passed her in the hall, we were not to give any sign of recognition. No one was to know that she was our mother.

One night there was a tap on our shoulders. It was the Reverend Mother telling us to put on our slippers and follow her. Still seared in my mind and until the day I die, is the sight of Mama, alive. The joy when she hugged and kissed us! The war ended six weeks later and we four were now safely together. Hidden in 3 convents and now my passion for hot cocoa can be satisfied any time I want it.

Postscript: Charlotte's eldest sister, Flora Singer (of precious memory) was very active in Holocaust education. Flora taught French and German in Montgomery County high schools and always integrated lessons of mutual understanding and tolerance in her classes. Flora was 11 when her family was forced to go into hiding in 1942. Flora, like Charlotte and their littlest sister, Betty, spent two years in convents until Belgium was liberated. In 1995, Flora and two other Montgomery County educators devised a course that dealt with teaching the Holocaust. The course is still used today. She also spoke to teachers and students about her experiences during the Holocaust. In 2007, the Holocaust Memoirs Project published her memoir, *Flora: I Was But a Child*. The Potomac Chamber of Commerce named her Potomac citizen of the year. Sadly, Flora died in 2009, leaving her husband Jack, 2 children and 3 grandchildren. In August 2012, the Flora M. Singer Elementary School was named in her honor, a tribute to her legacy.

*Young Flora and Adult Flora*

# FLEEING THE NAZIS

*ETHEL ETUNIA BAUER KATZ*
*Przemsl, Poland, 1922*

## FEAR ENGRAVED ON MY SOUL

Although I was liberated on July 22, 1944, I was not free from fear. At night, horrible images would attack me. I remained terrified of my war memories. Trying to escape them, I would force my mind to clamp down and grab on to some neutral topic to think about, anything to distract me. But when sleep came, however, there was no control to curb my brain from churning out macabre dreams. I would awaken panting with a stifled scream. These were nightmares. Now for reality: My family—my father Asher Bauer, my sister, Bronia, my two brothers, Rumek and Molus and I were "buried alive" in bunkers, cellars and any cavity into which we could fit. With deprivation, hunger and murderers at our heels, fear was destroying us before the Nazis did.

In August 1943 we were hiding in a dilapidated two-room thatch-roofed mud hut. It was filled with straw from floor to ceiling; we hid in the attic. We dug a hole in the earthen floor with tools we found in the hallway and covered it with straw, hoping never to have to use it. But we did. One day we suddenly heard shouting. A screaming youngster, about eight years old, was running around our hut, banging on the walls and windows, and wrestling with the door. From the lookout window, through a peephole in the straw, we saw a group of Gestapo on the road in front of our door. Our hearts sank with fright. Convinced that the boy was leading the Gestapo to our hut, we rushed to our bunker, crawling through the hole we had dug under the oven. I will never–I can never–forget those moments which we were sure were the last of our lives. Words cannot import our terror and our despair. My father was praying, whispering *Shemah Isroel*. With only moments to live, there was a rush to express love, to say a forgotten something, to live a lifetime in minutes. There were the last convulsive embraces, the tears of love, grief, agony. Then we heard a faint murmur of father whispering to our mother: "*Fridzu, danken Gott du host nisht derleibt . . .* (Thank God you have not survived to see this), "*I lead my children not to the wedding canopy, but to death.*"

We crouched in our trench, barely breathing, fluttering hearts beseeching God, wordless love and heartbreak speaking through the language of tears. My sister Bronia, caressed us, breathing with difficulty, clutching her chest with one hand while pulling us tightly to her with the other; uttering broken words to keep our hope alive. With father praying for all of us, we waited. Dying before death . . . Suddenly the Gestapo was gone. Later we found out that they had been searching for partisans. We were reprieved for a time. There was relief, but no joy. Bronia had suffered a seizure in the bunker. The constant fear and deprivation were taking a toll. (From *Our Tomorrows Never Came.* (Fordham University Press 2000)

## THE WORST WAS YET TO COME

The worst was yet to come. On March 8th, 1944, the Banderowcy (a band of Ukrainian nationalist hoodlums) surrounded the house and stormed the door. They entered our home and murdered my family. Two weeks later, on March 23rd, the Soviet Forces broke through. They were two weeks too late.

We had tried to escape. We ran to the straw-packed rooms on the other side of the house hoping to find a secure place to hide. We had gone barely a step when we realized it was too late. The door was yielding to our attackers; they were about to seize us. Driven by terror, we ran for the windows in the back room. "Jump!" Bronia commanded. In a wild frenzy, my brothers and I scrambled for the window, Bronia lifting and pushing us. But to where? Where should we run? We were like trapped crazed animals, cringing in terror. Behind us we could hear Hitler's accomplices charging through the door and crashing into the house–dogs barking, owls screeching in a wild rage. There was havoc in the air and panic in our hearts. Where? Where? Our hearts throbbed. Which way to run? My pulse was racing! I was stunned, terrified, numb. "Run!" father implored. "They are inside! Run!" commanded Bronia. "Run!" my brother Molus, gasped. And we ran–in wild, blind, maddened terror. I saw nothing. The world around me merged into a nightmarish blur.

A shot rang out. Dogs howled. The owls on the roof . . . Oh I will never forget those owls and their shrieking piercing cries screaming as if urging us to flee the carnage. I continued to run blindly. There was no wall, no crevice, not even a scraggly tree. All around, flat as a table stretched a vast plain of glittering white snow and an angry full moon glaring down on a white night crackling with fire. Driven by raw fear, I kept running. Then a blow to my head hurled me to the ground and for a short second I gasped for air. But the impact turned the world dark and I fell, sprawled unconscious on the snow. I awoke disoriented. My eyes would not focus. I remained inert. As I tried to regain some mental power I sensed someone standing over me. I opened my eyes just enough to see black boots, and closed them, remaining motionless while the murderer stood over me. Finally, thinking me dead or at least sufficiently disabled, he left to help in the capture of my escaping family. I did not know where we had been running–and I still do not know when or how we became separated. Once the thug left me, I got to my feet, dazed and disoriented. Crawling at first, I followed my instinct to run, but my legs refused to carry me. I was running in spirit only. Away . . . away from a nightmare.

The questions pounded my brain. To whom should I run? Where should I go? I cried. I talked to myself, carrying the magnitude of my loss like a band around my heart. "*Tatko, tatko drogi, Tatusiu, Broniu,* dearest, children. They must be killing you now! God, please save them; help us! *Mamusiu* in heaven, dearest soul, beg for us, please, please, God!" I continued to run and crawl, my mind in delirium. "To whom should I turn? Who would take me in? Where could I hide? Moments later, despair overwhelmed me. Why should I run? What for? My loved ones are slaughtered. There is horror all around. It is an evil world. All I can expect is only more suffering." I didn't want to live–but I didn't want to die. I pressed on, away from the manor house, fervently mouthing a plea to God. The answer was only God's silence. I felt so frightened, so forlorn . . . that dreadful night on the open, snow-covered plain. I shivered with cold. My bare feet were frozen stumps. I was practically naked, wearing only a thin cotton dress. There was a full moon and I knew that running figures would be clearly visible to any pursuers. I had to decide if I should go to the neighboring village but I knew that even our former peasant benefactors would turn me away on such a moonlit night. We had always selected dark nights and out-of-the way places to meet our peasants for the bread pick-ups. Suddenly, I saw moving shapes across the field. I felt as though I had frozen into a pillar of ice. My mind screamed: "They have found me! They are coming toward me!" I reeled and felt myself disintegrating. Gripped by fear, I burrowed into the snow. From deep within me, with uncontrollable sobbing, I implored the Almighty: "God please, I don't want to die. I don't want to see them, to see death gloat over me, not again. I don't want to see the horror again." I curled myself still deeper in the snow, wrapped my arms around my head, and pressed my eyes deep into my knees. I didn't want to see the coming ugliness, yet I could hear death's footsteps crunching in the snow, coming toward me, coming closer. I mumbled every prayer I had ever learned and remembered. Only God would know what I meant.

As the crunch on the snow neared, I pleaded for a miracle with new urgency—and each new wave of sobbing ripped my heart to pieces. And then the footsteps stopped. Death had arrived—and I dissolved in agony.

*"Co sie stalo? Co sie tam dzieje?"* A Polish voice asking "What happened? What happened here?" Had I really heard a soft, concerned voice in my world of howling fury and chaos? Had I actually heard a voice of decency in the midst of savagery? I couldn't believe it. I stopped sobbing and remained still, lying in the snow, curled up with my knees to my chest. After a few moments, realizing that the voices were not an immediate danger, I slowly straightened my body and looked up to see three men, obviously upset, reaching down toward me. These were Polish youths who were guarding their neighborhood from attacks by Ukrainian marauders. They knew my father, recognized me and half carried me to their colony. *"Moj Boze"* My God, my God" I exhaled from the depths of my soul and that was all the young men could understand from my babble: "My God, my God."

~ ~ ~ ~ ~ ~ ~ ~ ~ ~ ~ ~

# INTERNMENT CAMPS

Adapted from *Bad Times, Good People*
*Walter Wolff*

By the end of August 1939 my brother Bruno, my mother, and I had all in order for our departure from Germany: passports, boat tickets for Shanghai, one valise and ten marks per person. Three days later, on September 1, 1939, Hitler invaded Poland and World War II began. We had no trouble crossing the border into Italy but never made it to the ship. We decided to stay in Italy, believing our chances to survive the war would be greater there. As we were already in Genoa from where the ship would have departed, we looked for and found a small synagogue. We were taken to the rabbi's home. He and his wife made us welcome as their guests until other living accommodations could be found for us. Although grateful to the community for welcoming us, we soon realized that they could not provide us with food indefinitely, and despite the odd jobs that my brother and I found, we were destitute. Against my mother and brother's objections, I decided to sell my beloved violin. The following morning I took it out of its case and cradled it in my arms as though it was a Stradivarious. I played my favorite Mozart piece, *Eine Kleine Nachtmusik*, while tears streamed down my face. Never before or after would any melody sound so haunting, so beautiful, so heartwarming.

Gently, as though it was as fragile as glassware, I replaced the violin in its carry case, closing a sweet chapter of my life. In order to find any sort of respectable position with a decent salary, I would need to learn Italian quickly. Although I had a facility for language, having learned English, French, Hebrew and Latin in school by listening to recordings of famous speeches on a gramophone, but now—without teacher, records or gramophone, my solution was to go to the local cinema and watch the same Italian motion picture all day long. After a few weeks, my crash course paid off and I was soon speaking Italian without an accent and began to teach my mother and brothers, but at a slower pace.

By June 1940, *Il Duce*, Benito Mussolini, made his infamous speech from the balcony of the *Palazzo Venezia* in Rome, declaring his war on the Allies and proclaiming his alliance with Germany. This resulted in the arrest and internment of all foreigners in general, and Jew in particular. Almost immediately, the Italian *polizia* surrounded the Jewish Quarter. We heard whistles blowing and commotion in the street. Soon the dreaded knocking reached our door. My brother opened the door. The police stormed in and ordered each of us to pack a small bag and be ready to leave in 10 minutes. My mother began to cry. In Italian, I asked one of the policemen where he was taking us. To my astonishment, he answered politely, explaining that we were being taken to internment camps. He assured us that we would not be treated badly and would be interned there only temporarily. Then I asked if the three of us would be together, and sadly, he replied in the negative. The thought of being separated from my family in a foreign country was terrifying and I was overcome by waves of nausea. By the time the police took us away, my mother was still weeping and my brother's face was ashen. The police were still rounding up Jews when we stepped outside. They assigned us to different busses. The commotion and confusion caused a mass panic. Before I could say goodbye to my mother or Bruno, they were gone. We were put on different busses and taken away. My mother was taken to a place in the province of *Potenza*. My brother was interned in a camp called *Ferramonti* near the city *of Cosenza* in *Calabria*, and I was sent to an empty cloister with another 200 interned in a city called *Campagna* in the province of *Salerno*. The cloister, a medieval monastery building, had a large dining room. We were assigned bedrooms. Six of us shared a small, clean room with comfortable accommodations. We each had our own cot, pillow, sheets and blankets and an *armoire* for our personal items.

My brother's camp was completely different from mine. *Ferramonti* looked like an army camp, lined with rows of wooden barracks. He and the other internees slept in double-tiered bunk beds and took their meals in a separate barrack called the Mess Hall. The public toilets and showers were located in another building down the road. It had probably been used as an army base camp for the Italian military at one time. In some ways, *Ferramonti's* outward appearance could be compared to *Dachau* and *Buchenwald* but without the high-voltage wires, watchtowers, machine guns, and vicious dogs.

Unlike what we had experienced in Germany, the Italian people bore no ill will against foreigners, particularly the Jews who sought refuge in their country during Hitler's reign of terror, and even though they were forced to comply with Mussolini's orders.

# IN THE CAMPS

## *ARRIVAL AND LIFE IN AUSCHWITZ*
### *by Annie Bleiberg*

For the rest of the world, March 14, 1943 was a nice end-of-winter, early-spring sunny day. For the Jews of *Krakau* it was the opposite. It was the day of the liquidation of the *Krakau* Ghetto, the final journey to the Birkenau gas chambers.

I and 300 other young women and men who were held in the *Ordnungs Dienst* jail within the ghetto were the last to be loaded onto the open trucks and driven to Auschwitz. The Germans, very sure of their victory, were as bold and sadistic with us as could be. In their minds it was only a matter of time until all the Jews were caught and exterminated.

It was a short ride from *Krakau* to *Auschwitz*, just a little over an hour. One man jumped from the moving truck. He was shot in mid-air. Upon arrival we were unloaded onto a ramp and separated, men from women. One woman, somewhat older than the rest of us, was pulled out of our midst and sent to a group that was taken straight to the crematorium. We saw the flames shooting from the chimneys into the sky and smelled the stench of burning flesh. We stood there stony and motionless, and waited . . . and waited . . . unable to think of anything but death. Later, as we were marched into the camp, I noticed a few men digging ditches. I found myself wishing if only the Germans would put me to work, to do anything–just to live another day . . . or maybe two . . . . After waiting for two hours I was no longer feeling, just standing there numb. Since it was too late to "process" us that day, eventually they put us in barracks without food to spend the night on the bare floor. The next morning we were taken for an *entlausung* (a de-lousing.) and ordered to undress. We stood naked before the SS who were amusing themselves by mocking us. Their leers, talk and laughter hit us like bullets. A faint sensation of my blood being drained off drop by drop overtook me. I saw no more and felt no more. Once they cut our hair to the scalp we no longer recognized each other or ourselves. After that, they sent us to shower. To our surprise, it was a real shower, water and soap, not the expected Cyclon B poison of the gas chambers. Our new attire consisted of the Russian POWs' old pants and jackets that had an inch-wide line of dead lice in each seam. Having to put this on my body made my stomach turn. Even after 60 years I can still feel that twist in my stomach each time I think about it. We received no underwear. I was lucky—I got a real pair of shoes, men's shoes, two sizes too big, but they had shoelaces. Many of us got two left, or two right shoes; others got wooden clogs that would get stuck and lost in the muddy roads of the camp. That would mean real trouble. To complete the process, we got a number tattooed on our left arm—mine was 38330. In addition, those of us who came from jail got a triangle next to the number marking us as rebels and political prisoners. From that time on we had no name. We were numbers.

It felt soothing to hear a proverb from the nurse who administered the tattoo: *Es wird nicht so heiss gegessen wie gekocht!*—"things are not as scorching in the eating as in the cooking." Were things to be "not so bad" after all? Did she mean to calm us? To comfort us? Could she be one of those rare Germans with some human feelings? Maybe . . . and perhaps she did manage to give me a tiny bit of hope for a split second. I don't know. What I do know is that the first night in Auschwitz I made a decision—consciously or not—I decided to live, or die, as a Jew. In Krakau I had been beaten almost to death for trying to pass as an Aryan. Never again! One burden, just to be in Auschwitz, was more than enough. The next day we received "new clothes," the typical worn-out camp attire, a blue and gray striped skirt and jacket, and I was to begin my dreary existence in Auschwitz-Birkenau. At four in the morning the lights went on. The piercing sound of a whistle announced that it was time to get up. We scrambled as fast as we could, straightened up our blankets, got dressed, and ran to line up for breakfast, which consisted of a bowl of tea–nothing else. If you saved a piece of bread from the night before and nobody stole it, you were lucky. But such luck was not always with you. Usually you ate your entire portion for supper and were still hungry. Morning, evening, night, your empty stomach demanded food. As for that breakfast tea, it had a character all of its own: no taste, no aroma, no sweetener, just lukewarm brown water with a bitter aftertaste. Four of us who shared a shelf/bunk, drank it to warm our stomach, reserving one bowl between us for washing. We dabbed our caked eyelids and smeared some on our pale cheeks for a healthier look during selections. This was part of our survival technique. Five o'clock was the *Appel*–roll-call. We would stand there in straight rows of five, rain or shine, until the numbers tallied and all were accounted for. Sometimes it was hours until someone called out "blocks!"–a body inside a bunk. Dead or alive, the count had to be satisfied. Then, under the surveillance of the SS and dogs, we would be marched to the site of our work. My first work *Kommando* (detail) was to demolish the remaining walls of bombed out houses, to clean the debris, stack the bricks and haul them in wheelbarrows from site to site. Next, was the shoe *Kommando*. We sorted and paired the stacks of shoes that had been left behind at the crematoria undressing rooms moments before the mass murder. This job, though physically easier, was very tough . . . One day the *Kommando*-supervisor, an *S.S. frau*, offered to present me to the *Oberscharfuehrer*–head labor task-force inspector. Just to be called to appear before him was enough to make one faint. I gathered all my strength and followed her to him in a run. Standing before him I was unable to utter a word. He sized me up but asked nothing. I said nothing. He sent me away. In the evening I was informed that I was being transferred to the *Canada Kommando*, a work group in charge of sorting the clothing that people brought with them or were wearing on their last march to the gas chamber. This was the best one could hope for in Auschwitz-Birkenau. The best *Kommando* . . . the best chance for survival.

Although it was strictly forbidden, some among us managed to take what food was left in the pockets of the gas-chamber-bound or a few valuable articles they had sewn into their garments. These could be bartered in the kitchen for bread, a bit of thicker soup–sometimes with even a rare morsel of horsemeat in it–or cigarettes. This barter system occasionally found its way to the outside of the camp gates. The name for this activity was *organizieren*. Such "organizing" carried a built-in threat: *Lass dich nicht erwischen!* Just don't get caught! The penalty was five lashes each from two SS men, one on each side. Nobody survived. There were other forms of punishment, all ending in death. The lunch we were given consisted of nettle or other green-leaf soup or just water thickened with flour. Our work would resume until sundown and then the long march back to the camp. Many did not make it back. For the sake of the *Appel*, the roll call, we had to carry their corpses back to the camp. The SS saw to it that the dogs also did their share of harassing us. Sometimes we wondered who was more vicious, the dogs or the SS? The day would end with another roll-call, another line for the thin soup, a slice of bread and a pat of margarine–a food ration too little to live by and too much to die from. Numb with exhaustion, we lay down on the hard boards with a few straws for a mattress and retired for the night. Some never got up. The food, in addition to lacking all nutrients, caused many of us severe diarrhea and rash–a sure ticket to the gas chambers. When I arrived in *Auschwitz* in 1943, there were no roads, no running water and no sewage canals, only mud and open ditches. After a rainfall many an inmate would lose a shoe or get stuck in the quagmire unable to get up. Some would fall in or be kicked into a ditch by a passing SS man, to drown. Many inmates died in the process of building the roads and installing the water pipes. The Germans seemed to have long range plans for the camp.

In 1944 it was clear that Germany was losing the war. They were retreating westward. Hitler, wanting to erase all traces of his murderous deeds, ordered the bulldozing of the camps. They razed them all to the ground and planted forests, which stand there to this day. The inmates from the Eastern camps were transferred to the ones in the West. In October, I, along with 500 other inmates, was sent to *Mahrisch–Weisswasser*, a small labor camp, which in comparison to *Birkenau* seemed like a sanatorium. I was thus spared the infamous death march of 1945. The Soviet army liberated me at the end of the war. Only a handful of Jews survived.

*BORIS CHARTAN*
*Poland*

## AN INSTINCT FOR JUSTICE

Sometimes experiences you had when you were young influence the way you make your decisions all your life. Here is a story I will never forget. It is about my father and I think it has always been an influence on me. I was in a slave labor camp with my father. While we were in the camp, there was a typhus epidemic. Typhus is contagious from people, but lice also carry it so not only were the sick people quarantined but also their clothing even their shoes were taken from them and disinfected. The sick people were put in a separate place where they lay on the floor. There were no bunks there. Either they died or they came back to their regular barracks if they survived. There was one boy who after recovering came back to our barracks where my father and I slept in adjacent bunks. In the morning the boy joined the line to report for work. He was about 17 years old. Now, every morning, you were woken up for work, lined up by the *kapo* and counted. Our *kapo* was Jewish, but he was a *son-of-a-gun*. If he didn't like something, he didn't hesitate to use the big club he was always carrying. Well, there we were–all lined up, getting counted–I was in front of the boy and my father was behind him. When the boy, who was barefoot, came next to the *kapo*, he asked him for his shoes back. At this, the *kapo* clubbed him again and again with his club. My father came to the boy's defense, grabbed the club and swung it and clubbed the *kapo*. We went to work all day. We didn't know what would happen. Would my father be shot? Would we all be shot? That night, the guards came for my father. They took him to the *Kommandant* of the camp. They faced each other, one standing, one behind the desk.

(Speaking in German)

"Do you know what you did!" the *Kommandant* demanded. "This cannot be tolerated here! You will be punished, punished severely! You will receive 59 lashes with this whip!"

"Alright," my father demanded in German, "but I want you to do it."

My father lowered his pants and bent over. The *Kommandant* stood over him with the whip. He struck him once. He struck him twice. He struck him maybe one or two more times and then he stopped and told him to leave. A week later, the *Kommandant* came to my father and told him he wanted him to work in his home. Every day my father went to the *Kommandant's* home to clean, to haul out the garbage, to do whatever was needed. One day, the *Kommandant* came to my father and told him to run away because the slave labor camp was going to have an *aktion*. It would be disbanded. Then he said, in German to my father. "I hope you survive this war."

*JACK WERBER*

## SAVING CHILDREN:
## DIARY OF A BUCHENWALD SURVIVOR
## AND RESCUER *

I, Jack Werber born in Radom, Poland in 1914, was one of the early arrivals in Buchenwald, the first of my family to be shipped out of our town, Radom. Years later, in 1944, a transport arrived from Radom, bringing a man named Solohub. He brought me the news that my father, my wife Rachel, my little three-year old daughter Emma, as well as my entire family, were dead. I fell into a deep depression. My friends tried to console me but to no avail until in 1944, a group of 2000 prisoners arrived—fathers and sons, and some fatherless boys. The 700 boys from the transport ranged in age from 6 to 16, with most between 13 and 15. Seeing them instantly brought to mind what had happened to my own child. I decided to try to do something to help them avoid the fate of my beloved Emma. I remembered how an earlier transport of Gypsy children had been transferred to an unknown destination and we assumed they wound up dead. I knew that if nothing were done, these children would meet the same end. We had to act fast because the transport trains were only supposed to make brief stops in Buchenwald en route to other destinations. How was it possible to save any children at all?

Buchenwald was a work camp for political prisoners. The organizational structure as created by the Nazis required a minimal number of German officers. The responsibility for the day to day running of the camp was delegated to inmates, first to the criminals whom the Nazis trusted more, but ultimately to the political prisoners, a group that contained the Underground operatives. By the last few months of the war, as the threat of defeat loomed, German officers became more concerned about their personal safety than with what was going on in Buchenwald. They seldom entered the barracks.

With the consent of Emil Carlebach, a leader of the Underground, I called a meeting of the Jewish members. Rescuing the children became our group's prime project. We obtained extra food for the children, willingly or under pressure, from the German prisoners and Jewish prisoners who had German wives and who received packages from home. We also asked the office secretaries to change the birth dates of the children so they would be listed as older and therefore eligible to work. Officially, you had to be sixteen to remain in Buchenwald. We assured the Underground that the SS was losing control of the camp and we, the Jewish Underground members, would take full responsibility for the welfare of the children. I ended my appeal with the words: "Look, it's a risk, but maybe the children will survive by some miracle, so let's take a chance and try to save them."

Gustave Schiller was known to be "a real rough guy." Rumor had it that in prewar Germany he had been part of the criminal underworld, nevertheless, the children who survived remember Schiller, the deputy *blockaltester* of Block 66, with fondness. My own job as barrack secretary enabled me to care for the 150 or so children in block 23 on a daily basis. I did this for about ten months until the war ended. I saw each one of them as if he were my own.

Together, we organized food for the children, mostly from people who working outside the camp, had extra. The kitchen *kapo* belonged to the Underground and he also set aside food for the youngsters. Quite a few of the blocks had special bowls or baskets into which inmates put scraps of bread. Karl Siegmeyer, a German communist from Leipzig, Hans Reines, an assimilated Czech Jew and others helped although there were some inmates unwilling to share their food. By not reporting right away those who had died and by giving the Nazis higher counts of inmates, we were able to get extra loaves of bread. Clothing was harder to get since Buchenwald was a men's camp. There was no choice but for the younger children to wear the same clothes for weeks on end. Most importantly, I tried to give the children love and compassion. This was very crucial because the majority no longer had living parents. The very act of doing this gave my life meaning. The decision was made to scatter the children into different barracks. The majority went into the Small Camp, as inmates placed there were waiting to be shipped to other work sites or their death, but were not required to work and thus we did not have to find jobs for the children placed there. They were housed in Block 66, a wooden barrack that eventually became an all-children's block under the leadership of a Czech political prisoner. Elie Wiesel, Israel Lau–the future Chief Rabbi of Israel, and his brother, Naftali Lavi– who later became an Israeli diplomat, were also in this block. Some of the men who took care of them were non-Jewish political prisoners. The Jewish block leader, Gustave Schiller, made sure that the food was given out fairly and spent a great deal of time with the children who came to him with all their problems.

The rest of the children were placed in barracks 23, 22, and 8. These had adults as well as children. Smaller groups of children were scattered throughout various other blocks. The children were suspicious, however. They were afraid that being broken up into small groups was a trick to get them to participate in medical experiments. In other camps, whenever children under sixteen years of age were put into a separate group it meant that they were too young to work and would therefore be killed. Older children who could pass for sixteen were assigned to work commandos. These entries were fictitious and the children never actually worked.

We were sometimes able to arrange for the roll call in the Small Camp to be held indoors, which meant that the youngsters were not exposed to terrible cold and snow in the winter. The challenge for us was to keep them alive, mentally and spiritually. Because of the terrible things they had seen, the children were no longer childlike. Our group, therefore, decided to set up a school for them, but we had to convince the Underground not to oppose our efforts. We identified people whom we felt we could approach to teach the children. We explained to them that this was dangerous work and they could lose their lives if they were caught. Mordechai Strigler, later editor of the Yiddish *Forward,* gave the children hope by telling them stories of Jewish resistance and courage in the past, and promising them that one day they would have revenge against their tormentors. We took a violin from the storehouse of confiscated items and gave it to Brandt, a violinist who played Jewish songs for the children, while David Neumann who had a beautiful voice gave the children singing lessons. Meir Gottlieb was the drama instructor and also taught Jewish subjects such as: Yiddish songs and Hebrew language. Everything was from memory. This led to choir performances, plays and poetry readings. The children stood up, usually on top of several tables that we put together, and acted. Sometimes we invited the non-Jewish members of the Underground so they should see that we were really giving the children an education. Conducting these classes was exceedingly dangerous. On several occasions when the SS unexpectedly approached the barracks, we had to evacuate the younger children through the windows.

In Barrack 8, two opposite educational approaches were used at the same time. The Russian communists taught according to Communist Party dogma in their program for Russian children. But there were also Jewish kids from the Carpathian Mountains in Barrack 8 who were taught about the Jewish religion and Zionism by Israel Rob. As far as I know, the two groups did not mix. Incredible as it sounds, we actually had a "classroom" in Buchenwald, complete with blackboards (a piece of wood painted black) and used empty cement bags as writing paper. If the Germans approached, our own guards would yell "18" and the paper was destroyed and the pencils hidden. We also became amateur psychologists having to deal with children traumatized by war, deprived of parental affection and old beyond their years. Dreaming about future careers helped pass the time and took their minds off the nightmare they were living in camp. When the SS wanted to inspect the Small Camp, they were told that with people coming from all over there was the risk of an epidemic. Sometimes we got phony notes from the hospital stating that they were ill and had to stay indoors.

When the end of the war drew near, the SS were determined to remove the Jews from the camp. The Underground decided that the Jews should disobey a roll call that would have exposed them. The Nazis became enraged and demanded that the *lageralteste* identify the Jews. He did not. The Nazis responded by arresting the head *lageralteste* and threw him in a bunker the size of a phone book in the basement with no food. Despite this, the prisoners refused to give in. The Nazis finally gave up but killings of new Jewish transports still continued. We learned that the SS had a list of fifty-seven political prisoners that were to be killed before they gave up the camp. We hid them in a bunker secretly dug by the Underground. The Jewish cell of the Underground had prepared another bunker next to the children's block in the Small Camp that we stocked with bottles of water and food. We thought that if the children were to be evacuated, we would go with them on the transport, but if the SS were to seek only the Jewish leaders we would hide in the bunker.

The last few days were chaotic as more and more prisoners began to defy orders. The Nazis murdered twenty-four political prisoners. We were put in TB wards of the hospital because the Nazis were terrified of catching TB. When we heard a siren and an announcement that all SS officers were to leave the camp, the Underground went into action and removed a cache of hidden weapons that they had acquired through the years. Everyone was given an assignment. All told, many Nazis were killed and most had surrendered. We captured 220 SS men, and our own casualties were very light. We survived to give witness to the greatest act of barbarity in human history, but most important, we managed to save nearly 700 children who had miraculously survived in the heart of the Nazi death machine.

The book from which the above was taken is titled: SAVING CHILDREN: DIARY OF A BUCHENWALD SURVIVORAND RESCUER by Jack Werber and William B. Helmreich.

*EDDIE WEINSTEIN,*
*Born in Losice, Poland 1923*

**Eddie Weinstein's story, the most horrendous of all, was used for older classes and adults.**

# MY DAYS IN TREBLINKA

One evening the SS men divided us into labor details. I was sent to join a forty–man labor crew. Each of us received a broom. Working in pairs, we cleaned the railroad cars after their passengers had been removed.

Now we knew why the Germans had made us fix up the platform: to dupe their new victims into believing that they were about to be interned in a labor camp. All the rumors about international committees were no more than wishful thinking. The first new transport arrived the very next day. Twenty cars, each guarded by an SS man, stopped alongside the platform. The train brought people from Warsaw who still looked relatively healthy and certainly were in better condition than those in the transport from *Losice*. The weather had cooled off; the cars were less crowded. The Germans prodded the passengers to exit the cattle cars quickly. As they rushed to comply, the workers cleaned up after them. All the men, women and children were quickly pushed into a hut where they were ordered to disrobe; from there they were led directly to the gas chambers. The empty railroad cars were towed out of the station. As soon as all the newcomers had finished undressing the Germans prodded the workers to remove their clothing, parcels, and shoes as quickly as possible and carry them to a spot behind the long hut. A short time later a locomotive arrived, pulling another twenty cars. We repeated the process for the rest of the transport.

New transports stopped at the platform the next day, but now we were more sophisticated. The moment each train stopped we went into action and handed our brooms to some of the new arrivals. The brooms proved that they were workers, and we in turn, were protected from immediate gassing by the red patches on our clothing. The newcomers swept out the cars and we removed the trash from the train and dumped it into the burning pit. Afterwards, the newcomers mixed with the veteran workers and returned the brooms. At roll call our murderers could not distinguish between "legal" and "illegal" laborers. In their frustration the guards shot many people from both groups.

In retrospect, I do not think the Germans cared about our ruse one way or another. Certain that we would die in the end it was all the same to them who dragged out the bodies and who sorted the clothing. They spared those among the newcomers who said they were construction workers because at that time they were building new facilities to improve their slaughterhouse and make it more efficient. We also heard that they spare pretty women, whom they kept around for gang rape by German officers and Ukrainian guards and then murdered them. Only men were employed in the part of Treblinka where I worked. Once someone called my attention to a young woman dressed as a teenage boy who was sorting the clothes with us. I don't know how long she survived. As each transport arrived, the women were always the first who were ordered to take off their clothes. An SS officer we called *Lalka*–because of his doll-like features–strolled alongside them after they were naked and whipped those who, ashamed of their nudity, tried to cover their private parts. Sometimes he lashed one of them simply to inflict pain.

By now the transports were coming every day. One day was much like the next; the same incidents recurred again and again. Once, as I swept the interior of a car, an SS man suddenly struck me with his whip and ordered me to help a woman, who was unable to stand, climb out of the car. The idea was to show the rest of the victims how well the ill were being treated. Then he ordered one of the workers to take the woman to the field hospital for care. The newcomers really believed that the ailing woman would be taken to an infirmary. None of them realized that the "field hospital" was in fact just a giant pit, about thirty yards in diameter, which was always ablaze. They would place those who were sick or disabled on the ground at the edge of the pit facing in. The SS man in charge circulated among them and shot them in the back of the neck; then the workers cast them into the pit. Some of the victims were still breathing when they were tossed in with the other bodies. The pit was separated from the spacious field by a barrier of fresh pine branches, which were replaced from time to time to conceal the "infirmary" from the newcomers until the last moment.

Twenty minutes after I helped the woman climb out of the railroad car I was told that some infants were sitting by the pit, and no one else was there because the SS soldier had taken his lunch break. I gathered some trash and went over there. I saw the woman whom I had removed from the car sitting at the edge of the pit and staring in fright into the burning inferno containing half-cremated bodies of old people and children, mixed with smoldering trash. She tried to stand up but her legs would not hold her. She looked at the workers who stirred the embers—remnants of human beings—so they would burn better. Nearby were about a dozen infants, too young to have learned to walk. They were not crying—they did not understand what was happening. They looked about, probably hoping to find their mother or father. Later on, I heard that right after he returned from his lunch-break the SS man shot them all and ordered the workers to throw their tiny bodies into the flames. Of all my memories at that accursed place the vision of those babies is the worst. I see their faces whenever I remember Treblinka. After I escaped, the owner of a fish hatchery hid me for 17 months.

### RICHARD WEILHEIMER
*Born in Ludwigsburg, Germany, 1932*

Richard Weilheimer was born in Ludwigshafen, Germany in 1931, to a prominent Jewish family whose ancestors had lived there for many years. His brother Ernst was born 4 years later. After Kristallnacht, the family was deported in 1941 to Gurs, a concentration/holding camp for Auschwitz. With the help of the Quakers, Richard's father approved the transfer of his sons to an orphanage. Never complaining about his own circumstances, the father corresponded with his sons and kept up their spirits and above all, reminded them to preserve their dignity. In 1942, again with the help of the Quakers, just before the Nazi invasion of the un-occupied part of France, Richard, age 10 and Ernst 5, were smuggled on to the last boat leaving Marseille. In the USA, they were picked up by a relative. Their mother had died from cancer in Gurs and his father was deported and gassed. Richard and his lovely wife, Sheila, were charming, talented, wonderful people. Richard was especially sensitive about remembering and recognizing the non-Jewish individuals and organizations that were active in saving lives while risking their own. He gave memorable talks in Philadelphia, thanking the Quakers for their rescue efforts and he was instrumental in bringing the 90-year-old Danish Quaker, Ms. Alice Resch Synnestuedet, who rescued him, his brother, and others for a visit to the USA where she was given thanks and recognition for her efforts during the war. In the final years of his life, Richard wrote and published a book about his experiences, which he titled: *Be Happy, Be Free, Dance*! It is a survivor's message to his children and grandchildren on how to confront, act and enjoy life no matter the circumstances.

David Gewirtzman, his close friend, who wrote this tribute to him, has also left us. The two of them graced the earth during the time, we had them. (Marcia Posner, ed.)

~ ~ ~ ~ ~ ~ ~ ~ ~ ~

2014 finds us entering our second decade. Our mission remains the same, however our presentations are evolving. We are re-evaluating old knowledge, looking through another lens as to how best to teach the lessons learned during the Holocaust. New sensibilities and sensitivities will help us overcome the darkness of deeds and share the triump of the spirit. We are inspired by Abraham Lincoln's words: "To sin by silence when they should protest, makes cowards of men. We refused to be silent.

## LETTERS FROM MY FATHER

### *GURS, FRANCE*
### *RICHARD WEILHEIMER*

My seventh birthday party never took place. There was no celebration. My mother, younger brother, Ernst, age five and I had just abandoned the attic hiding place where we took refuge for the week after the November 9, 1938 pogroms of *Kristallnacht,* the "night of the broken glass." I can't remember if Hitler's hoodlums who invaded our home allowed my father to kiss us good-by before they arrested him and sent him on his journey to Dachau, the first concentration camp the Nazis built. But I vividly recall the destruction of our home and remaining possessions, and the flames spewing from our synagogue, the very house of worship where my grandfather was the Cantor. It was the first violent mass action by Nazis against the Jews. For us it was the beginning of the Holocaust. And then there was that day of terror, October 22, 1940. The Gestapo allowed us one hour to squeeze clothing and our entire celebration of life, the accumulation of memorabilia into a single suitcase for each of us. Whatever had to be left behind was never to be seen by us again. The only thing I know to have been packed was a photo album. It miraculously survived. It was the family legacy my father wanted his sons to have.

We were the first transport of Jews deported from Germany in Hitler's goal of making that country *Judenfrei,* free of Jews and the only human cargo to be shipped to the west. Camp de Gurs in Vichy France was a dismal stopover, an intermediate solution. We did not then know that we were in a holding pattern to await the construction of factories for mass murder. The American Friends Service Committee, Quakers, negotiated the release of some children. Ernst and I were among those released to a French Orphanage. While there, it was possible to correspond on a limited basis with our parents left behind. The Vichy administration found this helpful in promoting the ruse of resettlement. The stark misery of the adult world behind the barbed wire fences was particularly incongruous to the near normal, innocent life they wished for their children. The letters from our parents were generally filled with cheerful messages and micro-concerns of everyday life. We children in turn did not grasp nor understand the realities of the situation. They encouraged us to live well even as they were doomed to die. Many of our parents' letters never reached us. Some were censored with indelible ink. I later discarded others that I had carried with me. After all, wouldn't we see our father soon? Hadn't he promised to follow us to America? From those remaining, all written in German and now in the archives of the United States Holocaust Memorial Museum, the following excerpts are gleaned:

## Max Weilheimer, (MW)–Gurs, Waiting Room to Auschwitz

We are very pleased with your letter of 3/16. We see from it that you are healthy and well settled. Always behave, be obedient and learn well. Most of all, remain healthy and in good spirits. I would be pleased if you would write by yourself *Richardle* and not let other boys write for you. Let us know everything in detail, as we are very interested in what you and *Ernstele* do. Several days ago I sent you a parcel with articles of clothing for *Ernstele* and for both of you zwieback and chocolate. Hopefully it will get to you and you will enjoy it. I was glad to hear that all the sweets tasted good. We received them from our relatives and as soon as we get more, we will send you another package. It seems that you like it very much there and you are allowed to play and go on hikes often. Dear *Richardle* watch out carefully for *Ernstele*. Are you allowed to take the white dog on hikes with you? Passover is coming soon; will you get *matzohs*? It is good to be with so many children. Do you have nice beds and do you sleep together? Do you, dear *Richardle*, have lessons or do you only play? Do you both already speak some French? Do you have friends yet? Do eat much so that you will grow tall. How is the weather? Are you often outdoors? Dear *Richardle*, when you have your writing day, please answer my questions. *Ernstele*, are you still the chief of your section? We were glad to hear that *Ernstele* and you are well. It also makes me happy that *Ernstele* plays in the yard with his car that was given to him here. Always write in detail about both of you so that we are informed.

Do you hike often? Is everything well with you? Did *Ernstele* gain weight and you, dear *Richardle*, did you grow? You drew so nicely; I kept the pictures safely. Make us happy often and draw us pictures. Perhaps you can sketch your playroom or bedroom so that we can get a better idea where you live. Please answer our various questions, which we asked in our last letter. What do you get to eat? Do you always get enough?

What do you actually do in school? Do you play and paint also? Do you hike often? Do you live in nice surroundings? Are there woods and hills?

I had to laugh over your report of Ernstele playing with the streetcar on the school desk. He loved doing this at home also. Are you learning well and how do you spend your time? When do you go to bed and what more can you tell us? Have fun at your playtime and go outdoors often. When you eat chocolate don't bite into it as your teeth might break. I am sending you a parcel again today: 1 green shirt, 1 pair of underpants 2 pairs of socks and sweets. What did you write about in your school essay and did you have to write it in German or French? Uncle Muni is feeling good, and he is still here in Barrack 15.

My dear *Ernstele*, you really don't have to be afraid of the thunderstorms. We have many thunderstorms here too and are not afraid. The good Lord protects us all so that nothing happens. We are pleased that you have enough good food to eat. You must eat heartily so that you remain strong and grow. It is wonderful that the books please you and that you read them often. The one about the rabbits is so very nice. So my dear boys, stay well and ambitious so that you will grow up to be fine men. Play outdoors often, as it is healthy and gives you a good appetite. Did you have pictures taken? We would enjoy one very much. Do you already speak French well? Let us know how you spend your day.

Many thanks for your letter but I ask of you dear *Richardle*, the next time write it all by yourself even if you make mistakes. Enjoy playing; be happy and merry. Eat whatever you get so you will have enough. I feel better. I located a pair of training pants for *Ernstele* and will send it at the next opportunity. What do you do all day long? You write that you wait for mail. Hopefully my last letter was received by you in the meantime.

We wanted to write to you before but only had a chance today. I will give you news on a regular basis in the future. As per you request, *Richardle*, I will number all my letters. I find this system very good as you will then be able to determine if you are receiving all of them. This also indicates an example of order, I am today, sending you an envelope so that you will be able to write to us again. I hear that you are now allowed to write every fifteen days. My beloved *Richardle*, *Mutti* and I were joyous when we received your nice letter. Keep writing often as it always gives us great pleasure. My beloved *Ernstele*, I am happy that you are healthy again and discharged from the infirmary. It's great that *Ernstele* gained weight and now you must gain also. I sent you a little package and included shoelaces and polish. Did you read a lot in both your books? Is the rabbit picture book nice?

## RW

I did not know that our mother had undergone surgery for breast cancer prior to our deportation from Ludwigshafen. The word "cancer" was taboo; no one spoke of it and it was in remission prior to deportation. I don't know if the recurrence was coincidental or a result of the stress and anxiety of our forced departure and depraved new life, but just two months after our arrival in *Gurs,* mother was bedridden for what we children thought was rheumatism. Almost every letter from our parents contained a brief report on mother's condition. Most were optimistic but some mentioned her pain. The only doctors at *Gurs* were fellow inmates who had neither medication nor painkillers; drugs would not be wasted on Jews. Mother's health deteriorated steadily and her pain became unbearable, still letters from *Camp de Gurs* conveyed eternal optimism.

## MW

It was very thoughtful of you to inquire about Mutti. Thank God she feels better but she is still sick and in the infirmary. But hopefully she will soon be able to get out of bed.

## My Dear Children!

I was very happy to receive your letter dear *Richardle.* Thank you for your report. It always pleases me that *Ernstele* is also well and I pray to God daily that He keeps you healthy. Hopefully it will not be too long until *Mutti,* you two and I will again be together and we can catch up on everything. *Mutti* always has much pain and still lies in the infirmary but I hope that she will soon get better. I feel good, meaning I'm well. So referring to your letter, my dear *Richardle*, I am always pleased when you ask how *Mutti* is doing because that indicates your concern.

Do you pray daily and how are you doing with the French language?

I delivered your regards to the people on Barrack 11 and they all thank you much and want me to send you greetings as well. The *Elikanns* are no longer with us, they were sent to *Recebedou*. Dear *Richardle*, you asked if I still had my position. Yes I still have it and much more. I took over the leadership of the Religious services since Mr. Oppenheimer was sent away from here. I am also on the committee to obtain *matzohs* and other things for the Passover kitchen. I am no longer in charge of the children's food preparation since there aren't any children here anymore. Dear *Richardle*, it was very thoughtful of you to congratulate both of us for our birthdays. I had mine yesterday, and *Mutti* will have hers on 4/24. I thank you for remembering. I visited with *Mutti* and we spent some pleasant hours together. Hopefully we will all be well and together on our next birthdays. Dear *Mutti* made up a very nice birthday poem for me and had arranged for something for me to eat.

Mr. Stahl, the teacher, is still here but he is sick and lies in the infirmary so I could not yet give him your regards but will do so in the next days. In any case it is very nice of you to think about him. Teacher Durlacher is no longer here. A few days ago he was sent to *Le Milles*. That camp is located near *Toulouse*. Your letter for Mr. Wallenstein was returned here. Mr. Wallenstein was recently sent to camp *Recebedou*. I could not give your regards to Leo's father since he was sent to camp *Recebedou*. Many from here have already been sent away; we in Barrack 11 now number only 18 people. Uncle Ludwig and Aunt Tilde and Mr. Stefel went to *Recebedou* as well. So my dear children, stay well, God protect you.

Dear, good and wonderful *Mutti* sadly died as the Director has notified you.

Today, I received the word that you were informed. I thank the Director very much for that as well as Mrs. Zwilling, who we are informed also takes good care of you. Give hearty regards from me to both. The dear God and the holy spirit of dear *Mutti* who will always watch over us also thanks them. Heartfelt thanks for the wonderful letter from the Director and the children—your dear friends, and for your nice letter dear *Richardle.* All correspondence affected me deeply and the condolences and expressions of sympathy did me good. I can't thank each individual so please let them all read this letter. Thank God I have much work here. *Mutti's* pains were always increasing, and as dear God meant well with her, after she had been bedridden for 7 months, he relieved her of her terrible suffering. You surely will remember our good, beautiful, wonderful *Mutti* and I have many pictures and notations in your photo albums, which we will look at often in the future together. Our dear *Mutti* died during the night of Thursday July 18, 1941.

Our dear *Mutti* was only 39 years old in April. To remember our dear good *Mutti,* we wrote everything down and sent it to the aunts in America for the time when you are older and understand everything. I will let you read everything then. Now we must stay strong, pull together and go on with life. Whatever we do, especially you, always consider if we are doing it in the spirit of our dear *Mutti* and how she would have done it, so we act correctly. Keep her in good memory and honor always as our golden *Mutti* has earned it. I have again registered you for a children's transport to our relatives in America and I hope that you will soon get there. *Oma* and *Opa* and I too will be there so that we will again be together. We will take our dear *Mutti* with us in memory and photos.

RW

Mother died at the premature age of thirty-nine. Her death was incomprehensible to me. I could not recall having someone close to me, someone I so loved, die.

## MW

My dear children! I received your letter *No.24* of March 26 today, and I am rushing to reply to you at once. This time I was especially happy with your lines since I assume that you will soon sail for the USA. You will surely be happy about this, and well taken care of and attentively looked after. It is a relief for me to know that you will once again have your own home with our dear relatives. All the loved ones have written that they will gladly take you in, care for you, rear you, look after you and provide for your education and future. You will be welcomed and I therefore gave my approval for the trip. It is still undetermined when the journey will take place, although I would be happy if you could begin your trip soon. May God bless you and look after you. I also give my fatherly blessings for the trip and my wishes for a good crossing and a happy future. Give regards and kisses to all the relatives.

## RW

Some events defy explanation. My father obtained a short-term safe conduct pass out of Gurs. Perhaps the authorities calculated that he would return, as many of his relatives were still in the camp. He was able to witness our departure, which I believe was the last vessel containing refugees to leave France.

## MW

You sailed out to sea yesterday, Thursday June 25 about 4 P.M. They would not allow us near the steamship. I would so much have loved to see you and speak with you once again. I went in the afternoon to the jetty on the harbor and saw the *Imerethie II* anchored there. But I could only come to the gate, some 200 meters away from the ship. At 4 o'clock, I saw the gangplank retracted and anchor pulled, and shortly after, a small tugboat towed your ship out. People stood at the pier waving and shouting their good-byes. Tragically I could not be with them and soon the boat was out of sight.

My thoughts were with you. So my dear, good children, I again wish you all the best and above all, good health. Travel with God. May He protect and keep you well. May He provide you with a joyous future filled with good luck and may he allow you to grow into healthy, Jewish youngsters who can stand tall among men in this difficult world. You are so good, loved and upstanding and you will endear yourselves and be welcome. I send regards from all the people here who know you, and they wish you everything good. I will be glad when you are among our loved ones and once again have your own good home. I hope to join you; that is what our dear *Mutti* wanted. We will never forget her. She would have loved to travel with us but God wanted it different. I am sending these lines at once via airmail so that you will have greetings from me upon your arrival. I pray to God daily for you and your voyage, which will hopefully be good. Take care of yourselves, especially in the heat, and you, my dear Richard, always look after dear Ernst. All will become right with God's help. You don't have to be so serious, my dear Richard. Stay happy, cheerful and good, as our dear *Mutti* was also. I don't want to make a lot of words now; you already know everything. Travel with good luck. *Oma* and the other loved ones will await you and care for you. I hope soon to be with you again and to stay with you.

RW

In a letter, thanking the Quakers for their role in our departure, my father stated:

I was at the gates of the deck when the boat put out to sea, but my boys could not know that, nor see me. My heart nearly broke then.

~ ~ ~ ~ ~ ~ ~ ~ ~ ~ ~ ~ ~ ~ ~

The last letter anyone in America received from Papi was sent to my Aunt and Uncle. He began it in Camp de Gurs on September 22, 1942 and concluded it the following day.

## MW

Wednesday, the 23rd, 1942

My Dear Ones! At this moment, I am packing. I'm being sent away. Live well, stay healthy; hopefully we will see each other again soon. Please take care of my children. Hopefully we will see each other again in good health. Greet and kiss my dear children many thousand times and all of you be heartily greeted and kissed, especially dear Mother. In haste from your loving, Max.

From: Weilheimer, Richard. *Be Happy, Be Free, Dance: A Grandfather's Book for His Grandchildren.* (available from HMTC)

Max Weilheimer perished in Auschwitz. Our wonderful, talented friend, Richard Weilheimer passed away several years ago.

Before Richard died, he had located Alice, the wonderful Quaker lady who had rescued so many children who would have otherwise been sent to Auschwitz; and brought her to the United States where she met with many of the other saved children, now grandparents. A photo of Alice and Richard follow on the next page.

The roster of Holocaust survivors would have been even shorter
had it not been for the heroic "Righteous Among Nations" who
risked their liberty and often their lives to do the moral and
humane thing. Too often we talk only of victims, perpetrators
and bystanders.

Five years ago, fifty-five years after being rescued from Nazi and
Vichy captors, a series of coincidence caused me to rediscover
my rescuer.   In December, 1998, together with other survivors,
we brought Alice Resch Synnestvedt, a volunteer with the Quakers
during the Holocaust, to the United States for celebration and a
wide range of honors.

This summer, several of us child-survivors met in Copenhagen,
the city Alice long ago called home.  We came from Israel, France,
Germany, Switzerland and the United States for another reunion
with this ninety-four year old feisty woman of of valor.  This page
is gratefully  dedicated in her honor and in memory of my parents.

**Lilly Weilheimer**
**Gurs - 1941**

**Max Weilheimer**
**Sobibor - 1943**

**Richard and Sheila Weilheimer**

*Richard and Alice, the lady who saved him.*

*Partners in life!*

~ ~ ~ ~ ~ ~ ~ ~ ~ ~ ~ ~ ~ ~ ~ ~

# A RETURN TO THE TOWN OF MY YOUTH

*WALTER MEIRHOF*
*Erfurt, Germany*

After seeing my father beaten and taken away by storm troopers on *Kristallnacht* in spite of efforts by the gentile family living upstairs to stop them, I thought that I would never return. But in 1996, 57 years after leaving the city of my birth, Erfurt, Germany, I finally left with my wife on a trip back to Germany. I had misgivings, but my curiosity about finding things I would remember got the best of me. It turned out to be an amazing experience, and very positive. The many Germans I spoke to, none older than about 55, were all very friendly and thrilled upon hearing that I wanted to revisit my city. In attending services on Friday night at the synagogue, rebuilt on the same site as the one destroyed, I met two sisters, the only two from the original congregation still living there although I did not remember them. They had been in a concentration camp, survived and returned to the same city. It turned out that the younger of the two and I had gone to Hebrew School together. In August of the same year, I received an invitation from the *Oberbürgermeister*, the Mayor, to return to my city together with 20 others who were born there. It was an amazing experience. It included a visit to Buchenwald, the concentration camp my father was taken to and from which he survived. I will never know for sure how he got out and ended up in our city hospital (I am convinced that a Nazi prison guard who secretly sympathized, got him out) where my mother and I saw him and I could barely recognize him. Although I realized that there were some anti-Semitic skinheads around Germany as all over the world, I could not blame the current generation of people, even if their parents or grandparents could have been some of the terrible Nazis. I felt true and sincere friendship in meeting and talking to many people. The aftermath of these two trips–four former elementary school classmates (1932-1936), none of them Jewish and I did not remember them–had tried over many years to find out what happened to me after I was told by my middle school teacher one day "to go home and never come back." In different ways they found out that I was alive and where I lived. I have corresponded with all of them ever since and met one in Stockholm, Sweden this past summer. It was in late 1996 that I found out about the Holocaust Memorial and Educational Center. After taking a training course I became a survivor docent. I realized how important it was to talk to the young generation about my personal experience and to impress upon them that this should never happen again.

# CHAPTER 15

## "NOT ONLY TO REMEMBER:" TRAGEDY'S LESSONS

*JACQUELINE MUREKATETE*

L ONG BEFORE WE concerned ourselves with issues in other countries, Dr. Adrienne O'Brien, Chair of the Communications Department at the N.Y. Institute of Technology and a member of our Advisory Board, recommended that since we teach "tolerance" workshops as well as the Holocaust, we should adjust the name of our

Center. Howard Maier discussed her comments at the next meeting of the Communications Committee with Marvin Waldman, Co-Chair of the committee. He immediately recognized the importance of Adrienne's comments and suggested that we change our name to incorporate the word "TOLERANCE," which we have done.

David Gewirtzman, too, would often say: "The Holocaust did not start with Auschwitz and the other death camps; it started with the degrading and negative stereotyping of minorities, especially the Jews. He would remind us of the importance of respecting the differences among us and felt strongly, that teaching the "lessons" of the Holocaust was as important as teaching its history. The opportunity to act upon this belief occurred with David and Jacqueline's first encounter.

She, a 7th grade student of a Queens New York high school, burst into tears upon hearing his talk. When the usual students' thank you letters arrived, David's wife Lillian singled out Jacqueline's letter from the rest and read it to him. It appears below:

Mr. David Gewirtzman

c/o Holocaust Memorial Center

Dear Mr. Gewirtzman,

I want to start by thanking you so much for taking time in your schedule to come to my class and share your experience with my class and I. Your kindness and effort is very much appreciated. When I hear of such things as the Holocaust, I always ask myself why? How? How can intelligent human beings treat their fellow human beings in such and evil and inhuman way?

A lot of times I have been very disappointed with human beings as a whole. Why can't we love one another and get along the way human beings are supposed to [well in my imaginary world, anyway].

A few times I have asked myself if there are two races in this world, human beings and human-like beings. This might sound funny but I can't seem to understand why can some human beings commit such evil as the Holocaust and others would never even imagine such a thing. When I think of myself, I think of a person who would never treat a fellow human being in such a way as the victims of the Holocaust were treated. So to me it's like, if I can't imagine doing such things, then how can some of my fellow human beings do it?

I, myself, have in someway gone through such an experience as you had. In 1994, there was genocide in my country, Rwanda, [a small country in the south east of Africa]. We have two ethnic groups living there, and my ethnic group was the victim of the genocide. I, myself, ended up losing my family, my parents, and all my brothers and sisters, not to mention numerous relatives. I was the only one left in my family.

At one time, I too, like you, had a feeling of guilt for being alive. Why was I left? I asked myself. I never really got an answer to that, but now I am thankful that I am left. Maybe I can make a difference in this world if I try, and maybe I can do my part in making sure that no other human being goes through the same experience as I did.

Again, I want to thank you so much for coming to my class. I will always be grateful to have had the opportunity to meet you. I know for sure that in the future when I look at my High School experience, your visit will be one of the highlights, if not the greatest experience that I had.

The most important lesson I learned from you was that as human beings, we face an ugly disease, HATE, and the only weapon we have against it is EDUCATION. I will try my best to use this weapon in fighting this terrible disease.

Again I want to thank you very very much for coming to my school, my class and sharing your Holocaust experience with us. My heart goes out to you and to other fellow human beings who had to go through such a horrible experience.

I wish you and your family nothing but the best now and in the future.

Sincerely yours,
Jacqueline Mureketate

Jacqueline, an ethnic Tutsi, had been adopted by her uncle from the United States. Years before, he too, had escaped from a similar situation in Rwanda. He had flown to Rwanda, found little Jacqueline in the orphanage, adopted her and brought her to safety.

She wrote "that she had learned from him (David) that despite the horrors vented upon his family and other helpless Jews by the Nazis while most stood by or cooperated with the offenders, he did not preach revenge." David's mandate to the students was that they should never join in oppression, nor should they desert the innocent people who were its targets. Instead of bitterness, his message to the class was to be mindful of the hurts and needs of others and to be a defender, not a bystander if someone has become the target of injustice. Jacqueline was immensely impressed by his response. It did not preach hate, but help.

"I finally found someone who understood what I went through because he went through the same thing," Jacqueline wrote several years later. She vowed to do similarly. It changed her life. She began to be David's speaking partner, speaking all over the world. David and Lillian took her into their embrace–David providing the wise, fatherly guidance that set her on the path she takes today and Lillian, a mother's care and affection. They love her, mentored her throughout her education and

 attended her wedding. Meanwhile, Jacqueline has achieved her B.S. in Politics from New York University in 2007, and her J.D. (the Juris Doctor, a professional doctorate and first professional graduate degree in law) in 2012 from Benjamin N. Cardozo School of Law.* At the present time, she is seeking to have her autobiography published. Jacqueline Murekatete, is a much beloved member of our community and is symbolic of the expansion of our mission.

The Center's exhibits have also become more cognizant of genocides in other times and places. They include the "Armenian Genocide" (1915), identified primarily as the genocide that reassured Hitler of the world's probable tolerance for his planned acts of genocide, also genocides in: Sarajevo-Bosnia-Herzegovina, Cambodia, China, Guatemala, Kosovo, the Ukraine, Rwanda and other sites in Africa.

~ ~ ~ ~ ~ ~ ~ ~ ~ ~ ~ ~ ~

We have also become more concerned with the community than previously. In addition to teaching about the Holocaust and the bullying suffered by Jews in Fascist communities, we began to discuss prejudice and bullying in our own communities and conducting programs and workshops to deal with it. We have emphasized the teaching of tolerance to students and adults and to police cadets, adding the police program, *Law Enforcement and Society: Lessons of the Holocaust*, making the Center extremely relevant today. * More about Jacqueline in Appendix

# EPILOGUE

## Honey Kern, Teacher; Annie Bleiberg, Survivor

THE HOLOCAUST MEMORIAL and Tolerance Center, has played a huge part in my work, my studies, and my life. Back in 1995, when I first volunteered to help Chairman Boris Chartan, the Center had a different name: The Holocaust Memorial and Educational Center of Nassau County. I remember seeing an excellent exhibit there in 1995: "Arbeit Macht Frei–An Exhibit of Holocaust Sculptures" by Harold Lewis.

I am not a Holocaust survivor, nor is anyone in my family. Luckily for me and the generations that followed, they came to the USA running from the pogroms in Russia. Still, I am committed to Holocaust education for my family, my students, and myself. When I was an ill young girl left at home with a TV near my bed, there were few channels then, but one was showing actual black and white footage of the liberation of the concentration camps by the Allies. I remember that when my mother came home from work, I cried and asked her what the "Holocaust was, and who were those people in the film." That was the beginning of my education.

Matt Chartan, Boris Chartan's son, and I were colleagues at Cold Spring Harbor High School. I had just finished organizing the opening exhibit in our new high school's art gallery. It was named: "The Holocaust." We worked with a grant from New York State that involved students, the Heckscher Museum in Huntington, parents, survivors and the art department. It included many artifacts from the Center and other sources. The exhibit was a great success. My students went on to interview both Boris (a Survivor) and Matt Chartan (Second Generation) for their Internet magazine: *An End to Intolerance, 1995,* pps:15-18. Hard copies can probably still be found in the Center's Louis Posner Memorial Library and online. Through the years, the Holocaust Memorial and Tolerance Center has given me so many opportunities to continue my work in Holocaust education. I have met wonderful survivors, among them, David Gewirtzman and Jacqueline Murekatete, "Survivor Soulmates" who visited my school and spoke to students with the help of the HMTC and then Education Director, Regina White. As a designated United States Holocaust Memorial Teaching Fellow, the Center selected me and two other Center volunteers to go to Washington, D.C. to train for the *Law Enforcement and Society Program.* This was a great honor since the program was allocated to only 3 Centers. It was wonderful to work with my colleagues and the police cadets.

Most of all, I have had the joy of working with visiting students and adults in the Tolerance Programs, the Annual Arts Competition, and the Educational Advisory Committee. It's hard to believe, but I've met thousands of students at the HMTC over the last 18 years. I've seen their eyes when they go through the permanent exhibit, their faces when they listen to survivors' testimony. They ask good questions and are well-behaved. Most are delighted when I tell them that they can call me by my real first name (Honey) because in Australia, students call their teachers by their first names.

So, for me, the Holocaust education experience at the HMTC has been an ongoing one. Of course, the staff, especially the main office, helps to keep us happy and well fed (coffee and snacks). The unique topic we deal with requires us to be kind to each other and work from our hearts. This is another lesson I have learned.

~ ~ ~ ~ ~ ~ ~ ~ ~ ~

## Annie Bleiberg, Survivor

When I asked Auschwitz survivor Annie Bleiberg, if she was happy with how the Center had developed, how it had moved from being solely about the Holocaust to one including "Tolerance," she thought a minute and then she said: "Yes, Marcia, I am. We have to bring our history to the present day so it will live on. It will have no meaning otherwise to the present generation."

# ACKNOWLEDGEMENTS:

I OFFER MY DEEPEST appreciation and gratitude to colleagues who enriched this book with their stories and experiences. Many, many thanks, as well, to my editors and helpmates, among them: Lila Alexander, Ilise Bernstein, Gloria Jackel, Beverly Nassau and Sheila Rind.

# SURVIVORS AND LIBERATORS

**Stephen Berger**

S TEVE WAS BORN and raised in *Debrecin*, Hungary, where he attended elementary school and the Jewish Gymnasium. After the German occupation of Hungary he was forced into the city ghetto and was later sent to *Strasshof* concentration camp and then to a slave labor camp in Austria. After the liberation by Allied Forces, Steve briefly returned to Hungary where he discovered the Germans and their Hungarian collaborators had murdered 26 members of his family. At that point, he joined the Zionist movement, left Hungary, and helped European Jews to emigrate to Palestine. Steve also contributed to Israel's War for Independence.

# Annie Bleiberg

Annie was born in *Oleszye*, Poland. Soon after the Germans occupied Poland in 1939, they established ghettos and forced Jews, including Annie and her family, into them. When the ghetto was liquidated, the Jewish inhabitants were crammed into a train and sent to *Belzec*, an annihilation camp in the Lublin District in the General *Gouvernement*. Annie's father had secreted tools with him. He widened the bars of the train's small high window, then he and Annie escaped from the moving train jumping through its window, although her mother and sister did not. Annie began a life in hiding, was later able to obtain false I.D. papers and joined the Resistance. She and others were betrayed, however, by a classmate and ultimately was sent to *Auschwitz-Birkenau*. After the war, Annie married, came to the United States and settled in the Bronx, where she was active in a variety of Jewish organizations. Annie relocated in Woodbury, Long Island to be closer to her daughter's family and to the HTMC where she had begun to speak.

# Eve Boden

Eve was born in 1935. In 1940, following the German invasion of France, she and her parents were deported to France where they were imprisoned in the *Gurs* transit camp. Eve remained in *Gurs* with her parents until March 1941 when she was separated from her them and sent to a Catholic orphanage in the *Vichy* region, which was not occupied by Germany. On her birthday in 1942, at the age of 7, Eve was sent to the United States where she lived with an uncle for one month. After that, she stayed in a series of foster homes sponsored by the UJA. Today, Eve is a therapist and resides on Long Island.

# Boris Chartan

Boris Chartan was born in *Podkamien*, Poland. When the Nazis occupied the region of Poland in which he lived in 1941, Boris was sent to the *Sasow* labor camp, where he remained until the end of 1942. At that time, he escaped from the camp into the forest. A Polish family saved him and helped to reunite him with his family. After the war, Boris and his parents lived in a Displaced Persons Camp until leaving for the United States. Ultimately, Boris became the Nassau County Commissioner of General Services, eventually resigning from this position in order to be better able to administer to the *Holocaust Memorial and Educational Center of Nassau County* that he had established with the help of County Executive Thomas Gulotta in 1992. Boris served as its President for a decade.

# Herbert Cooper

Vienna, Austria was home to Herb Cooper during his childhood. His life changed forever in 1938 when the Nazis annexed Austria. In that same year, in the aftermath of the November Pogrom ( 9-10 November, also known as *Kristallnacht*), Jews were prohibited to attend non-Jewish schools and eventually even Jewish schools were closed. While the majority of Herb's extended family perished in the Holocaust, his immediate family escaped to the United States in 1939. In America, Herb studied to become an engineer and contributed to the success of the US space program.

# Julius Eisenstein

Born in *Tomaszow*, Poland, Julius was one of five children. Julius, his brother, and his future wife survived a number of camps, including

Auschwitz-Birkenau. The remainder of his family however, his father and mother and his three sisters, were murdered in Treblinka, a death camp not far from Warsaw. When the war ended, American troops liberated the last camp in which Julius had been incarcerated. A photographer captured the moment and 40 years later Julius was reunited with the US soldier who appeared in the photo with him.

## Janet Ettelman

Janet was a native of the small industrial city of *Mannheim*, Germany. She witnessed the November Pogrom in 1938 after which her parents immediately intensified their efforts to escape Germany. She and her father managed to leave on the last boat out of Italy. They barely escaped death as the Germans torpedoed that ship on its return to Europe. Janet's mother and brother fled later, her mother as a chaperone for "The Thousand Children" upon which she convinced the authorities to take her son as well. In the US, Janet pursued a career in education; she taught English and Social Studies.

## Lillian Gewirtzman

Lillian was born in *Grabowiec*, located in a region of Poland occupied by the Soviets until 1941. When the Russians, then an Axis partner, invaded Eastern Poland, they deported her and her family to Siberia. The family fled farther into the USSR in front of the subsequent German invasion, escaping the worst horrors of the Holocaust. They spent various amounts of time in Siberia, Ukraine, and Azerbaijan. Between 1946 and 1951, Lillian lived in a Displaced Persons Camp in *Ulm*, Germany. Hard to believe, but Lillian traveled by public bus from the camp to a German High School, speaking little or no German at that time. Her experience in the camp prompted her to curate the Center's Displaced Persons Exhibit, which is available for display and which has been shown throughout the US and internationally. Lillian and David met after arriving in the US, where they owned several pharmacies in succession.

## Charlotte Gillman

*Antwerp*, Belgium was the birthplace and home of Charlotte Gilman until the end of World War II. During the war, she and her two sisters were hidden in a series of Catholic convents. The vast majority of Charlotte's family, over 200 people, were interned briefly at *Malines/Mechelin* (the major transit camp in Belgium) and deported to Auschwitz-Birkenau, where they were murdered. Charlotte, her sisters, and their mother (who had been hiding in various places nearby) reunited with Charlotte's father in the United States after 8 ½ years of separation. Charlotte has kept in touch with some of her rescuers over the years since the war.

## Gloria Glantz

Gloria Glantz was born in *Wegrow* Poland, in 1939. She had a very loving, large family which included many uncles aunts, cousins, 2 older brothers, and grandparents. To save her life, her parents enlisted the help of a simple, righteous Christian family. Gloria's journey to America was a very circuitous and unusual one. In her lifetime Gloria has lived in 4 countries and on two continents. In her professional life as a teacher, she has made it a mission to see that the *Shoah* is not forgotten. She is the winner of a fellowship from the *American Gathering of Jewish Holocaust Survivors*, *American Federation of Teachers*, and the *Jewish Labor Committee* to study the Holocaust and Resistance. She is also the 2002 recipient of *The Spirit of Anne Frank Outstanding Educator Award.*

## Margaret Goldberger

Margaret was born in Berlin. She became part of the *Kindertransport* after *Kristallnacht,* when England agreed to take in 10,000 Jewish children under age 17. She lived in England until 1946, when she immigrated to the US. She serves on the Executive Board of the *Kindertransport* Association and is an active speaker on the Holocaust.

## Lottie Hess

Lottie was born in *Unsleben*, Germany in 1925. Lottie's family and her family's business, a granary, had been a part of the town and its economy for generations. The Nazis' anti-Jewish laws affected her family immediately. Her father's business suffered; she was ostracized by former friends; and men she knew, were sent to *Dachau*. Her family made plans to leave. First her father came to the US in 1937 on an affidavit provided by his uncle. He then brought the rest of the family in July 1938. While her family escaped, others in the town did not. Many were deported to *Ibizcica* (near Lublin, Poland) and were never heard from again.

## Werner Hess

Werner was born and raised in *Frankfurt/Main*, Germany. When Hitler came to power, he experienced a sudden loss of belonging. His best friend, a gentile, could no longer play or even talk to him. He was thrown off of his soccer team for being Jewish. In 1936, realizing he would not be able to attend college and that he wanted to leave Germany, Werner dropped out of school and began studying a trade. During the November Pogrom (*Kristallnach*t), Werner's parents' fish store was destroyed. The following day, the Nazis came for his father, who was dying from cancer.

They wanted to take Werner instead. He reported to the collection point the next day, but was never sent away. In January 1939, Werner escaped to England and reached the US in 1940. He was drafted a few years later, served in the Pacific until 1946 when he was discharged. He married that same year.

## Herman Horowitz

Herman is the son of Russian immigrants to the United States. He grew up on a farm and was forced to leave high school before graduation because of the hardships of the Depression. Shortly after the Japanese attacked Pearl Harbor and the US entered the war, Herman joined the Army. He participated in the Normandy invasion in June 1944 and fought across Europe as part of General Patton's Seventh Armored Division. He took part in the "Battle of the Bulge," after which his unit liberated *Ohrdruf* and *Bergen-Belsen* concentration camps. Back in the US after the war, Herman joined his father in law's appliance business, where he remained for 45 years.

## Ethel Katz

Ethel was born and grew up in *Buczacz*, Poland, which is now part of Ukraine. Her family was large and close-knit. The German Army entered the town in 1941 followed closely by mobile killing squads who murdered her twin brother and other young Jewish men in a forest near the town. The rest of her family escaped immediate destruction by hiding in barns and fields for several years, reliant upon their non-Jewish neighbors for food. Later, Ethel's family members were murdered in their hiding place. Ethel narrowly escaped and survived the last few months of the war on her own. The Soviet Army liberated her town in 1944. After the war, Ethel emigrated to the United States, where she married and raised a family. She has written a memoir of her experiences during the Holocaust, *Our Tomorrows Never Came*.

## Susan Lipsey

Susan's father and uncle owned and operated a lumber company in the town of *Baranowicze*, Poland, where Susan was born. The Russians occupied the region of Poland in which she lived in 1939. They took over the family's business and home at the same time. The Soviets threatened to deport Susan and her family to Siberia, but they managed to reach *Vilna* (Lithuania). In that city, a Japanese diplomat named Sugihara issued visas to thousands of Jews, including Susan's family, which enabled them to leave Europe and escape the Nazi threat. Susan's family went to Japan and then to Shanghai, where they lived in the ghetto until the end of the war, after which they immigrated to the United States.

## Asher Matathias

Asher's parents were residents of *Volos*, Greece when the Germans began to target the Jews of that city in 1943. Non-Jewish Greek friends of the family were instrumental in their survival. They convinced Asher's parents that the Nazi threat was serious and that they should leave. The family fled to the hills, where his mother gave birth to Asher. They survived in a cave for two years relying on the assistance and generosity of non-Jewish friends, who brought food and provided protection. Nazis frequently patrolled the area and on one occasion they found Asher and his mother. Fortunately, the soldier in charge had a baby at home in Germany and let them be. Following the war, Asher and his family returned to Volos and rebuilt a life there, but after a series of earthquakes in the early 1950s, they decided to relocate to the United States. In this country, Asher has pursued a career in education, married, and raised a family.

## Ruth Meador

Ruth was born in *Kassel*, Germany. Following the November Pogrom (*Kristallnacht*), her parents succeeded in placing her on a *Kindertransport* train to Holland. She was seven years old. In Amsterdam, Ruth lived with approximately 80 other children in the town hall for over a year. The Germans occupied Holland in 1940 at which point a woman named Trude Weijmuller Meir, a non-Jew, arranged for all 80 children to be sent to England. Ruth remained in England for the duration of the war and eventually came to the United States.

## Erika Novick

Erika was born in *Karlsruhe*, Germany. Her father, a physician, was warned by a Christian patient that the Nazis were coming for him. The family was able to escape to *Nice* and then to England. While she and her sister attended boarding school, her mother taught and her father worked as a gardener.

## Lily Perry

Lily Perry was born in Vienna, Austria in 1928. Lily's mother and father had lived in Austria for some time, but both of their families originated from Poland. When she was 10 years old, Hitler annexed Austria to Germany, and with that event the course of her family's life changed forever. Before the annexation, Lily's family had gentile friends and neighbors; they were part of the Austrian community. Lily loved dogs and enjoyed school. Her father owned a store. With the annexation, Jewish neighbors were humiliated, arrested and sent to concentration camps. Eventually, her father lost his store. The family sought to escape Austria. They planned to go to Shanghai, but were able to gain admittance to the United States arriving there in 1938. But many relatives were unable to escape and perished during the Holocaust. Lily's husband was also a survivor. He endured the *Dachau* camp. They met after the war in the United States, where they built a new family and a new life.

## Werner Reich

Werner and his family were residents of Berlin when the Nazis came to power in 1933. His father, an engineer, lost his job soon thereafter prompting the family to move to Yugoslavia. This, however, was only a brief reprieve as Nazi influence soon reached that country. Werner's mother placed him in hiding with several families, but he was eventually found by the Gestapo and sent to jail and then into the camp system where he went from *Theresienstadt* to *Auschwitz-Birkenau* and finally to *Mauthausen*, where he was liberated in 1945. After the war, he returned briefly to Yugoslavia and then went to England in 1947 where he was trained as a pipefitter. He emigrated to the US in 1955 and eventually became an engineer.

## Arlette Sanders

A native of Paris, France, Arlette fled France with her parents and siblings, escaping through Spain and Portugal. They lived in Lisbon for a year and finally were able to leave Europe in 1941. Arlette became an educator, and served as Assistant Superintendent of Secondary Instruction in the Great Neck Schools.

## Karl Schapiro

When Karl and his parents were thrown out of Germany, they became refugees for 2 years, eventually settling in the Town of Kalusz in Eastern Poland. In 1941, the Germans occupied Kalusz. All Jews were forced into a ghetto. Karl's childhood came to a stop. He lived as a hidden child first in the ghetto, then in a forced labor camp and finally, for 1.5 years in a hole dug under a barn. When Karl and his parents were liberated, they returned to Kalusz to look for survivors. Of the town's 5,500 Jews (which included 1200 children) only about 20 had survived, with Karl being the only child. The family left the town, never to return. They immigrated to the USA where Karl started his first normal education at the age of 14. Graduating from Cooper Union and from Columbia, he pursued a career in engineering management, married, and raised a family. Now Karl devotes his time to teaching about tolerance, enjoying his grandchildren and doing volunteer work in Israel.

## Helga Shepard

Helga's parents were Polish, but she was born in Germany. Following the violence and terror of the November Pogrom (*Kristallnacht*), her parents sent her on a Kindertransport to England via the Netherlands. While most children found a safe haven in England, Helga did not. She was placed in a family that used her as a servant and treated her very poorly. She also lived through the German bombing of London. Nevertheless, she survived the war, was reunited with her parents, and came to the United States in 1953.

## Judy Traub

A native of Lamosc, Poland, Judy and her family were exiled to Siberia as political prisoners following the German invasion. They lived in Siberia, Central Asia and Germany before immigrating to the US in 1951. Judy was a school librarian and Hebrew school teacher.

## Anita Weisbord

Anita was born in Vienna, Austria. Germany annexed Austria in March 1938 and Austrian Jews immediately became subject to German anti-Jewish measures. The situation for Jews intensified in the wake of the November Pogrom (*Kristallnacht*). That event touched Anita's family directly. Her father was arrested and sent to *Dachau* concentration camp. Soon thereafter, Anita's mother sent her on a *Kindertransport* to England. She remained there for the duration of the war and eventually reunited with her family. After the war, she came to the United States, where she has lived ever since.

## Millie Werber

Millie, a native of Poland, called the city of Radom home. When the Germans invaded, she was sent as slave labor to an ammunition factory. The skills she acquired there helped her survive *Auschwitz-Birkenau* and the Lippstadt labor camp. Since the end of the war, Millie has resided in the United States. Among her proudest achievements was that as President of the Ladies Auxiliary of the Radom Mutual Cultural Center, Millie helped build medical clinics in Israel.

# APPENDIX I

## JACQUELINE MUREKETATE

S INCE GIVING HER first presentation in 2001 with David, Jacqueline has spoken in more than 300 forums including: high schools, universities, community centers, NGO (Non-Governmental Organization) events, UN agencies and faith-based communities across the United States as well as in Germany, Israel, Ireland, Bosnia and Belgium. She also addressed the United Nations Assembly on the 10th year anniversary of the 1994 genocide in Rwanda and regularly participates in high-level human rights and genocide prevention forums and conferences.

The press has brought her voice to an even greater audience through features in the *New York Times, Washington Post, Huffington Post, Jerusalem Post, UN Chronicle, UN Africa Renewal Magazine, Newsday,* many other popular trade magazines. Jacqueline has been invited to speak on *NPR, Voice of America, CNN, PBS, NBC, CBS,* ABC, *MTV* and other media outlets worldwide. She has also been featured in the Polo Ralph Lauren

G.I.V.E. campaign and Kenneth Cole's Awareness: Inspiring Stories About How to Make a Difference.

In 2007, Jacqueline founded *Jacqueline's Human Rights Corner*, a genocide prevention program under the umbrella of MCW (*Miracle Corners of the World*). She organizes genocide prevention education programs for young people and adults. She raised money to build and support a community center in Rwanda, many of them genocide orphans, that opened in 2011. Aside from appearing widely in the press through features in the *New York Times, Washington Post, Huffington Post, Jerusalem Post, UN Chronicle* and many other publications, she has received a number of outstanding awards for her genocide prevention efforts. Among them are: the Anti-Defamation League's *Ina Kay Award* in 2002; the 2004 *Global Peace and Tolerance Award* from *Friends of the United Nations*; the 2008 *Moral Courage Award* from the *American Jewish Committee*; the 2008 *Ellis Island Medal of Honor Award* (which put her name in the *Congressional Record*, the 2010 *Do Something Award* from the *National Ethnic Coalition*; the 2011 Imbuto Foundation's *Celebrating Young Rwandan Achievers Award* from the First Lady of Rwanda and the 2012 *New York University Distinguished Young Alumna* award.

# APPENDIX 2

## LETTERS

### Letter to Annie Bleiberg from the U.S. Navy

**DEPARTMENT OF THE NAVY**
STATE UNIVERSITY OF NEW YORK MARITIME COLLEGE
NAVAL RESERVE OFFICERS TRAINING CORPS
6 PENNYFIELD AVENUE
FORT SCHUYLER, BRONX, N.Y. 10465-4198

April 6, 2010

Dear Ms. Bleiberg,

Annie - Thank you very much for taking the time to speak with my class of Marines and Naval ROTC Midshipmen during our visit to the Holocaust Memorial and Tolerance Center in Glen Cove on March 24. It was a memorable and moving afternoon.

Your zest for living and charisma are the best possible testimony to the horrors you experienced. All of us see you as an example that life should be lived to the fullest no matter what may come. You are living our Marine Corps' motto "Semper Fidelis": always faithful.

Please know that you impacted us all. We are better for having heard your story. And, the students that will shortly be entrusted with leading our country's fine young Marines and Sailors and upholding our country's values will be better officers for having met you.

If there is anything I can ever do for you, please do not hesitate to contact me. I hope that future classes will have the opportunity to meet with you as well. And, I look forward to seeing you again.

I wish you all the best, continued happiness and health –

Sincerely and respectfully,

Gregory A. Gwynn
Lieutenant Colonel
U. S. Marine Corps

## Letters to Herman (Hy) Horowitz

*Hy Horowitz, a Liberator, contributed several letters sent to him by students who had heard him speak in their school.*

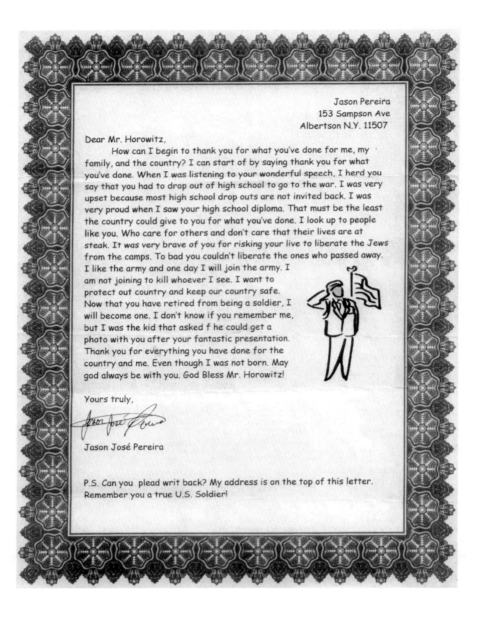

Jason Pereira
153 Sampson Ave
Albertson N.Y. 11507

Dear Mr. Horowitz,

How can I begin to thank you for what you've done for me, my family, and the country? I can start of by saying thank you for what you've done. When I was listening to your wonderful speech, I herd you say that you had to drop out of high school to go to the war. I was very upset because most high school drop outs are not invited back. I was very proud when I saw your high school diploma. That must be the least the country could give to you for what you've done. I look up to people like you. Who care for others and don't care that their lives are at steak. It was very brave of you for risking your live to liberate the Jews from the camps. To bad you couldn't liberate the ones who passed away. I like the army and one day I will join the army. I am not joining to kill whoever I see. I want to protect out country and keep our country safe. Now that you have retired from being a soldier, I will become one. I don't know if you remember me, but I was the kid that asked f he could get a photo with you after your fantastic presentation. Thank you for everything you have done for the country and me. Even though I was not born. May god always be with you. God Bless Mr. Horowitz!

Yours truly,

Jason José Pereira

P.S. Can you plead writ back? My address is on the top of this letter. Remember you a true U.S. Soldier!

"It is really a true honor to get to meet someone like yourself and to hear the stories from personal experiences; to be able to see a true liberator like yourself up close . . . It must take a lot of bravery and strength to do what you did and then to have to keep those horrible images and experiences in your head in order to pass them on to the next generation. I know how important it is for us to know about such dark times in order to try to prevent such inhuman behaviors from repeating the past, so that we can see a brighter future. Your stories touched me and I hope that my letter was enough of a thank you. I wish there was another way for me to show you how much I appreciate you coming to our school.

Sincerely, Laure

Dear Mr. Horowitz,

Thank you for coming to the Holocaust Memorial and Tolerance Center and speaking with us about your experience as a liberator. I am a Jew, myself. All of my grandmother's family died during the Holocaust; so hearing your stories made me very upset, yet interested as well. There are many things that I learned from your stories, such as that many people actually cried tears of joy, kissed and embraced you for coming to rescue them. They must have been really desperate during this time. I also wanted to personally thank you one-on-one. Thank you for helping Jews all over the world be made safe from those evil Nazis. Without you, it would have been very possible for our religion to be gone

## and . . .

## Letters to Werner Reich

Dear Werner,

*I thought the best way to express how effective your talk was would be to share some of my students' responses to your visit:*

"The part of [his] story that sticks with me is when he brought up the Hitler/Nazi sign and said "when you see this sign don't think it's against Jews; think it's against humanity." The reason that stuck with me is because I had never thought about that until now, and I agree."

"What I remember is the one diplomat who gave out visas to 6000 Jews. He saved many lives. Silence is not an option."

"Today I heard about some of the roles people took: the Nazi Oppressors, the Bystanders (the good people who did nothing). I noticed that there was lots of mention of Bystanders; it really is important to do something."

*Those were just a few of many comments. Thank you ever so much. Hoping this is the beginning of fruitful friendship.*

*Antoinette*

Dear Mr. Reich,

"I just wanted to let you know that your speaking at the school was really inspirational. Everything really hit me a bit harder than it did in middle school and I was really very much embarrassed to find that in so many situations I have been one of the "good people who do nothing" because all too many times, I've just walked away or done nothing simply because I was afraid of feeling awkward or being embarrassed somehow. Ever since you spoke, I've been working to change that. On the Day of Silence, which is a day speaking out against bullying due to sexuality; I participated by wearing duct tape. Normally, I would have never done this because a) it is inconvenient b) what if somebody thinks I am not straight because I am wearing the tape? However, I did it anyway. Also, just today, I saw a girl crying. I didn't know her but I gave a big hug and she said it made her feel better. I know these are really just small things, but I hope that they will make a difference. And also, these things didn't feel small for me, because I have never done anything like them before. Thank you so much for speaking, because you have helped me realize that in order to work for a better future, I will have to speak out and rise above my fears. You really inspired me and I hope you know that."

(No name)

# APPENDIX 3

## HMTC Awards and Honors

*A Look Back...*

| 1992 | 1994 | 1996 | 2000 | 2002 |
|------|------|------|------|------|
| **The Grand Opening** | **The Museum** | **The Louis Posner Memorial Library** | **The Bruce Morrell Education Award** | **The Children's Memorial Garden** |
| The Holocaust Memorial and Education Center of Nassau County's grand opening ribbon cutting ceremony. | The museum is created and public programs extend the reach of the Center's resources across Long Island. | The Louis Posner Memorial Library welcomes visitors and begins a collection of resources for students and adults, from Kindergarten through post graduale researchers. | The Annual Bruce Morrell Education Award is established to recognize a Survivor or Educator who has raised the bar on teaching about the Holocaust and its lessons. | The Children's Memorial Garden is dedicated as a living memorial to the million and a half Jewish children murdered during the Holocaust and other children who perished during World War II. |
| *Photo: (L to R) Monsignor Donald Beckmann, HMTC Founder and Chairman Emeritus Boris Chartan, Hon. Thomas Gulotta, Rabbi Myron Fenster, Hon. Thomas Suozzi* | *Photo: The Holocaust Museum* | *Photo: Louis Posner Memorial Library's first collection* | *Photo, (L to R) HMTC Senior Director of Education and Community Affairs, Beth Lilach presents the 2011 Bruce Morrell Education Award to S. Isaac Mekel, Director of Development, American Society for Yad Vashem* | *Photo: The Children's Memorial Garden* |

## 2005

## 2006

## 2008

## 2010

## 2012

| **Tolerance & Anti-Bullying Program** | **Law Enforcement & Society Program** | **The Workplace Diversity Program** | **The Grand Reopening** | **The 20 Year Lease Signing** |
|---|---|---|---|---|
| The Tolerance & Anti-bullying workshops to equip students with the tools and resources to address contemporary issues of prejudice and intolerance begin. | The "Law Enforcement and Society: Lessons of the Holocaust" program becomes a mandated program for all Nassau County Police Department recruits. | The Workplace Diversity Program is created for employers like North Shore/LIJ Health System to teach individuals how to engender respect and diversity in their workplace. | The $3.5 million renovation for a new 2500sq. ft, state-of-the art, multi-media Holocaust exhibit showcasing artifacts, archival footage and testimony from local Survivors is complete, including the Louis Posner Memorial Library. | Nassau County extends the Holocaust Memorial and Tolerance Center's lease committing the former Pratt Estate as home to the museum and ongoing educational programs until 2035. |

*Photo:*
*Survivor Annie Bleiberg provides testimony to middle school students*

*Photo:*
*Police cadets participate in "Law Enforcement and Society: Lessons of the Holocaust"*

*Photo:*
*Employees participate in the Workplace Diversity Program*

*Photo:*
*(L to R) HMTC Board Director Peter Klein, Hon. Kathleen Rice, HMTC Vice Chairman Stanley Sanders, Fmr. Nassau County Police Commissioner Lawrence Mulvey, HMTC Board Director David Gewirtzman, HMTC Board Director Gloria Glantz, HMTC Chairman Howard Maier, Hon. Carl Marcellino, HMTC Vice Chairman Steven Markowitz, Hon. Ralph Suozzi, Hon. Charles Lavine*

*Photo:*
*(L to R) HMTC Vice Chairman Steven Markowitz, HMTC Chairman Howard Maier, Nassau County Executive Edward Mangano, HMTC Founder and Chairman Emeritus, Boris Chartan, HMTC Board of Directors, members of the County Executive's Jewish Advisory Council, representatives of the Nassau County Government*

# Past Honorees

**1993**
Honorable Thomas S. Gulotta
Jerry Lazarus
Naomi & Jerry Lippman
Sam Mandelker
Most Rev. Bishop John R. McGann

**1994**
Boris M. Chartan
Roselee & Bruce Morrell

**1995**
Dr. Frank Field
Seymour Reich

**1996**
Most Rev. Msgr. Donald M. Beckmann
Irving Roth

**1997**
Jean & Jacob Stein
Eileen & Neil Tannor

**1998**
Malcolm Hoenlein

**1999**
Isaac Blachor
Howard S. Maier

**2000**
Dr. Marcia W. Posner
Phyllis & Stanley Sanders

**2001**
Susan & Lawrence Kadish

*Community Service Award*
Mark Broxmeyer

**2002**
Cookie & Murray Slimowitz
Edward & Jolanta Zamecki

**2003**
Ellen & Howard Brous

**2004**
"The Year of the Survivors"

*Humanitarian Award*
David Gewirtzman & Jacqueline Murekatete

**2005**
Boris M. Chartan

**2006**
Michael J. Dowling

**2007**
Honorable Thomas P. DiNapoli

**2008**
Jacob Stein
The Mindel Family

**2009**
Morris Lener
Barbara & Alan Rosenzweig
Honorable Howard S. Weitzman

**2010**
Honorable Thomas S. Gulotta
Peter Klein
Lawrence W. Mulvey

**2011**
Lena Elias Russo
Sheri & Bernard Vishnick

*Public Service Award*
Honorable Carolyn McCarthy

## BRUCE MORRELL EDUCATION AWARD

**2000**
Richard Weilheimer

**2001**
David Gewirtzman

**2002**
Gloria Jackel

**2003**
Wilma Diamond

**2004**
Abbie Laskey
Donna Rosenblum

**2005**
Werner Reich

**2006**
Herman Horowitz

**2007**
Dr. Regina T. White

**2008**
Honorable Carl Marcellino

**2009**
Gloria Glantz

**2010**
Meryl Menashe

**2011**
S. Isaac Mekel

## 2012
Flora & Frank Lalezarian
Erika Witover

## 2013
Honorable Jon Cooper
Jack Foley

# BRUCE MORRELL EDUCATION AWARD

**2000**
Richard Weilheimer

**2001**
David Gewirtzman

**2002**
Gloria Jackel

**2003**
Wilma Diamond

**2004**
Abbie Laskey
Donna Rosenblum

**2005**
Werner Reich

**2006**
Herman Horowitz

**2007**
Dr. Regina T. White

**2008**
Honorable Carl Marcellino

**2009**
Gloria Glantz

**2010**
Meryl Menashe

**2011**
S. Isaac Mekel

**2012**
Beth Lilach

**2013**
Lori Gately

# GLOSSARY

*Appel*–role call

*Auschwitz-Birkenau*–a death camp

*Beignets–a jelly filled cream puff*

*Belzec*–a death camp

*Birkenau*–concentration camp

*Blockaltester–German soldier appointed to be the head of a camp blocks–a body within a bunk*

*Buchenwald–a slave labor camp*

*Canada Kommando–*, a work group in charge of sorting the clothing that people brought with them, or were wearing on their last march to the gas chamber

*Crakow Ghetto–a section of the city of Crakow used to intern Jews*

*Crematorium–where bodies were incarcerated in the camps*

*Dachau-Concentration Camp*

*Enlausing–delousing*

*Es wird nicht so heiss gegessen wie gekocht!–*Things are not as scorching in the eating as in the cooking.

*Flossenburg Concentration Camp*

*Gendarme–A French policeman*

*Goldene Medina–*"Golden Land," (referring to the United States)

*Judenrein–*Free of Jews

*Kaddish–Prayer for the Dead*

*Kapo–a guard in a camp, who is also a prisoner*

*Kartoshki–*potato

*Khalla–*auntie (in the Turkic language of Azerbaijan)

*Kindertransport*–The transporting by train and boat of Jewish children after Kristallnacht primarily to England, also to Switzerland, and some to Belgium

*Kino*–movie theater

*Krakau*–Ghetto, also spelled Crakow and Crakau

*Kristallnacht*–Night of Broken Glass (or the Progrom)

*Kvell* or *Shep Nachas*–gaining a prideful pleasure

*Kommandant*–the head of a concentration camp

*Kommando*–a work detail

*Krakau–also spelled Cracow, a city in Poland, also a ghetto*

*Lageralteste–an offical in the baracks*

*Lass dich nicht erwischen!*–just don't get caught

*Mahrisch–Weisswasser*–a small labor camp

*Mauthousen*–Concentration Camp

*milchama*–the war

*Mutti–Mother, German*

*Nachas*–pride from

Nansen Passport–Limited to special conditions

*Oberburgermeister*–mayor

*Oberscharfueher*–head labor task-force inspector.

*Ohrdruf*–Slave Labor Camp

*Oma–Grandmother, German*

*Ordnungs Dienst*–a jail

*Organizieren–a barter system*

*Papi–Grandfather, German*

*Shalom*–peace, a greeting in Hebrew

*Shtetl*–village

*Shoah*–Holocaust

*S.S. frau*–Nazi woman

*Velodrom*e–huge indoor stadium used for bike races

*Wannsee Conference*–where the "Final Solution" was formulated

*wasser*–water (Yiddish)

# BIBLIOGRAPHY

Titles Mentioned in This Book

Albright, Madeline. *Madame Secretary: A Memoir.*

Bettina, Barbara. *It Happened in Italy.*

Bowman, Steven. *Jewish Resistance in Wartime Greece.*

Burghardt, Dr. Linda. *Night Falls on Vienna: Escape and Survival at the Dawn of the Holocaust.*

Chang, Iris. *The Rape of Nanking.*

Eisner, Peter. *The Pope's Last Crusade: How an American Jesuit Helped Pope Pius XI's Campaign to Stop Hitler.* (HarperCollins 2013)

Ford, Jamie. *Hotel on the Corner of Bitter and Sweet.*

Friedman, Pavel. *The Butterfly.* (poem)

Greene, Joshua. *Justice at Dachau: The Trials of an American Prosecutor.* (Random House)

Gruber, Dr. Ruth. *Haven: The Dramatic Story of 1000 World War II Refugees and How They Came to America.* Based on case histories she recorded as she interviewed the refugees. (Putnam)

Gurevitch, Inge. *Infectious Diseases in Critical Care Nursing: Prevention and Precaution* (Aspen Series in Critical Care Nursing, 1989)

Jurman, Alicia Appleman. *Alicia, My Story.*

Katz, Etunia Bauer. *Our Tomorrows Never Came.* Fordham U. Press.

Kavanaugh, Sarah. *ORT: WWII and the Rehabilitation of Holocaust Survivors.* Forward by David Cesarani. (Valentine Mitchell, 2008). Available through Valentine Mitchell–www.vmbooks.com

Klein, Peter and Angelica Berrie. *A Passion for Giving: Tools and Inspiration for Creating a Charitable Foundation.* (Wiley. 2011)

Lau, Israel Meir. (Chief Rabbi) *Out of the Depths: The Story of a Child of Buchenwald Who Returned Home at Last.* Foreword by Shimon Peres and Elie Wiesel. Sterling, 2011.

Leff, Laurel. *Buried by the Times: The Holocaust and America's Most Important Newspaper.* Cambridge University Press.

Manes, Philipp. *As If It Were Life: A World War II Diary from the Theresiendstadt Ghetto.*

Mayer, Jack H. *Life in a Jar: The Irena Sendler Project.*

Mokhtari, Fariborz. *In the Lion's Shadow: The Iranian Schindler and His Homeland in Iran.*

Moss, Alexandra. *The Weeds Sing.*

Oglivie, Sarah and Scott Miller. *Refuge Denied: The Saint Louis Passengers and the Holocaust.*

Otterman, Dr. Bernard. *Black Grass and Other Stories.* (including the "Golem of Auschwitz")

Rolde, Neil. *Breckinridge Long: American Eichmann ??? An Enquiry Into the Character of the Man Who Denied Visas to the News.* Polar Bear Books.

Roth, Irving and Edward Roth. *Bondi's Brother.* Shoah Educational Enterprise

Roth, John K. and Michael Berenbaum, eds. *Holocaust: Relgious and Philosophical Implications.* Paragon, 1989.

Schroeder, Peter W. and Schroeder-Hildebrand, Dagmar. *Six Million Paper Clips: The Making of a Children's Holocaust Memorial.*, 2004

Shavit, David. *Hunger for the Printed Word: Books and Libraries in the Jewish Ghettos in Nazi Occupied Europe.*

Singer, Flora. *Flora: I Was But a Child.* Yad Vashem: Holocaust Survivors Memoirs Project, 2007

Taitz, Emily. Holocaust Survivors: A Biographical Dictionary, Vols. 1 & 2. Greenwood Press.

Taylor, Peter Lane with Christos Nicola. *The Secret of the Priest's Grotto: A Holocaust Survival Story.* Illus. with colored photographs. (All Ages)

Weilheimer, Richard. *Be Happy, Be Free, Dance: A Grandfather's Book for His Grandchildren.* (available from HMTC)

Werber, Jack with William Helmreich. *Saving Children: Diary of a Buchenwald Survivor and Rescuer.* Transaction Publishers.

# INDEX

Cover designed and expedited by:

RTS Print Services
1150 Shames Drive,
Westbury NY 11590

Technical Consultant
Steven Goethner
SoftKare
394 Penfi eld Road
Fairfi eld, CT 06824

Edwards Brothers Malloy
Thorofare, NJ  USA
October 28, 2014